Keeping
my Sisters'
Secrets

Keeping *my* Sisters' Secrets

BEEZY MARSH

PAN BOOKS

First published 2017 by Pan Books
an imprint of Pan Macmillan
20 New Wharf Road, London N1 9RR
Associated companies throughout the world
www.panmacmillan.com

ISBN 978-1-5098-4265-0

1 3 5 7 9 8 6 4 2

A CIP catalogue record for this book is available from the British Library.

Typeset by Ellipsis, Glasgow
Printed and bound by CPI Group (UK) Ltd, Croydon, CR0 4YY

To the memory of Londoners
who lost their lives in the Second World War.

Prologue

1931

The grimy streets of Lambeth, nestled beside the river Thames, had changed little since the days of Charles Dickens, when the poorest working classes lived cheek-by-jowl with thieves and drunkards. Women living there took in piece-work such as laundry or fur-pulling to help make ends meet, just as their mothers and grandmothers had done before them. Their husbands worked long hours, either in the factories as labourers, as costermongers or down at the docks. And that was if they were lucky enough to have their men in work. Families were large – five or six children, or more – and diseases including scarlet fever and diphtheria were fatal and much-feared. The threat of poverty was ever present but the temptation for husbands to drown their sorrows in one of the many local pubs could lead to the whole family being thrown out into the street when the rent- and tallyman came knocking for their dues.

These little rows of two-up, two-downs were tight-knit communities where scores were sometimes settled with fists. The police would only venture down there in pairs and rarely after nightfall when the dim glow of gaslight did little to illuminate pea-souper fogs. Yet for those growing up in this corner of Lambeth, the cobbled streets, the stench of the river, the shouts of the factory workers, the nosy neighbours and the rumble of the trains over at Waterloo meant one thing – home.

This is the story of three sisters growing up in one such street, Howley Terrace, in the years between the wars. It is the story of their hopes and dreams and struggles for a better life when the odds were stacked against them.

This is the story of the Lambeth girls, Peggy, Kathleen and Eva, who learned to keep each other's secrets in a bond of sisterhood, which even dire poverty, violence and war could not break.

1

Eva, May 1931

She didn't really mind getting up so early.

Eva could hear her father downstairs in the scullery, clattering about making himself a pot of tea before work. It was barely light outside but if he didn't leave the house soon, she'd miss all the best buns at the bakery over in Covent Garden.

Eva waited until she heard him pulling on his boots and the front door slam shut before she forced her feet out of her warm nest in the flannelette sheets and onto the bare boards of the bedroom floor. Kathleen, her sister, lay next to her, soundly asleep. Her hair was tied in rags, which spread out on the pillow like little snakes. Mum didn't bother putting Eva's hair in rags. 'Dead straight, like your father's,' she told her. 'There's little or no point trying to make it curly.' Kathleen, on the other hand, had near-perfect ringlets even without the help of mother and her nightly rag-ties. Eva toyed with the idea of yanking one of those raggy little tails but thought better of it. She didn't want to wake the whole street with Kathleen's squealing.

Instead, Eva grasped her own thick, long black hair and tied it with a grubby ribbon before pulling on her pinafore and making her way out onto the landing. Mum, already dressed in her housecoat and slippers, was standing there, holding out a pillowcase for her.

'Mind he doesn't see you,' she whispered.

Eva took the pillowcase and nodded solemnly. If Dad knew what she was up to, it would earn her a belting, not that she cared. She'd felt the buckle end of his belt on more than one occasion. The welts went down after a while and all that remained was an empty feeling inside, which was worse than hunger. At least bread made her feel a bit better. Day-old bread from Godden and Hanken bakery was a mainstay of their diet and a cheap way for Mum to fill their rumbling bellies when the housekeeping was running short – which was most of the time, these days. But Eva's father wouldn't tolerate her queuing up for handouts with the children from the Thieves' Kitchen of the Seven Dials, like some common urchin.

Eva was eight, nearly nine in fact, so she was too young to go out to work but she would have done if she could, just to help Mum. She was the youngest after Frank but was more daring than any of her brothers and sisters. Kathleen would soon be eleven and she should really have made the trip but liked her sleep too much to bother, same as her twin, Jim. Peggy was thirteen and would be leaving school in a year or so but she was a goody-two-shoes, Dad's favourite, and wouldn't dare do anything to risk his anger.

The early mornings were making Eva tired and she was prone to catching forty winks in the afternoons during lessons. Her teacher at St Patrick's had said as much when she met her mother on the Walworth Road last week: 'Eva really does need to get to bed earlier, Mrs Fraser!'

Eva hurried down their tiny street, each house with the same two storeys of grimy bricks as the last, before turning left onto Waterloo Bridge. She knew the route by heart: up Bow Street, into Long Acre and over to Great Newport Street.

Flower sellers in long skirts and straw hats, their woollen shawls pulled tightly around their shoulders, were already at their pitches and the drunks from the night before were still lying in the gutter as Eva ran the last hundred yards to the bakery door. She was the last one there. A row of ragged children, some with dirty faces and no shoes, jostled in front of her, brandishing their pennies.

Eva drew herself up to her full height and flicked imaginary dust off her pinafore as she looked down her nose at them. Yes, she was poor but she was clean; Mum always made sure of that, even though Eva hated having her face wiped with a dishcloth before she left the house. The tin bath took pride of place in the scullery once a week and she got her turn in it. She scratched her head. Nits again, probably, but Mum would sort that out with a metal comb later. Eva winced at the thought of her hair being pulled and scraped. She sighed as she waited her turn, the penny in her hand growing sweaty. What if there was nothing left for her to take home?

Dad had a good job as a wood sawyer down at the cricket bat factory but with five of them to feed on wages of two pounds a week, there just wasn't enough to go around. It was all their mother could do to keep shoes on their feet. Frankie's were full of holes, mainly because he was the youngest and got all the hand-me-downs. And that was before Mum got to paying out the 'insurances'. Eva didn't fully understand what they were but it was to do with the hospital and teeth and the like. Mum said, 'Don't worry your head about it, chicken,' but Eva did worry. Especially when she saw her mother twisting her thin gold wedding band round and round her finger and her eyes red-rimmed from crying when all the money had run out by Wednesday.

The insurances had seemed to go up after Frankie got run over by a lorry a couple of years back. Eva swallowed hard at the memory of it. She was supposed to be minding him while Mum went out to clean at one of the little hotels up by Waterloo Station to earn a few pennies more. She had another job in the mornings cleaning over at the Imperial Chemical Industries building but that didn't pay enough.

It had all happened so fast. They were playing in the streets with the other kids from Howley Terrace, larking about. Someone had a dog which had caught a rat and they poked at the dead body a bit with some sticks and watched it ooze blood. 'Massive teeth,' said one boy. 'Like yer grandad!' said Frankie, poking him in the ribs and making everyone hoot with laughter.

Frankie got bored of it all in the end. Kathleen turned her nose up and went to go skipping with Doreen from a few doors down. Peggy had her head stuck in a book, as usual, and was sitting on the front step, reading. Eva was only chatting to her pal, Gladys, for an instant about the new clothes her Nanny Day had knitted for her peg dolly, which made her look so pretty. Then she heard Frankie shout: 'Got any cards, mister?' just as one of the lorries from the wastepaper factory at the top of the road came trundling past.

'Frankie! Wait!' Eva called, but he didn't hear and ran forwards, hands outstretched, as the driver chucked a few cigarette cards out onto the cobbles. Frankie bent down to pick them up without noticing a second lorry following close behind. Eva screamed. Then she ran. It was too late. Frankie disappeared under the wheels and there was the most horrible sound. The driver did his best to stop but couldn't and Eva watched in horror as Frankie's broken body emerged at the other end of the truck.

Women came running from the terraced houses and it suddenly seemed the whole street was there, watching Frankie's little body, his head crushed and bleeding, oozing onto the greasy cobblestones, his eyes closed, his face white as a sheet.

The driver got out of the cab, shaking: 'Oh my God!' He turned to the crowd and pleaded with them as the mood changed from shock to anger. 'Me brakes don't work that quick, see?'

Eva knelt down beside Frank to help, but the grown-ups were already loading him onto the tailgate of the lorry and it was off to St Thomas's Hospital. Peggy ran to get Mum from her cleaning at the hotel and Kathleen and Jim ran a mile to Stuart Surridge's factory to get Dad. Eva clung to Frankie on the back of that lorry, sobbing, as Mrs Avens from a few doors down tried to shush her and tell her to let go of him but she wouldn't. The doctors had to prise her off Frankie when they got to the hospital. They rushed him off on a stretcher, away through the double doors, his head swathed in bandages.

Then Nanny Day came to the hospital with Mum crying. Dad, looking ashen, his hands thrust into his coat pockets, rushed past Eva. Nanny Day, still wearing her best white apron over her long skirts, took Eva from Mrs Avens's arms and held her hand. 'Now, don't be fretting about it or blaming yourself,' she told Eva, her bright blue eyes shining with tears. 'The good Lord will protect our Frankie, just you wait and see.' She crossed herself. 'Come on, Eva, let's get you back indoors.'

Nanny Day walked the half-mile back along Belvedere Road, past the Lion Brewery and the factories, clasping Eva's hand the whole time. Eva had been terrified of that lion statue when she was smaller, and Nanny Day still joked about it jumping down and gobbling her up, when she was naughty. It was a huge beast, looming high above the brewery gate, its body blackened by soot but its face still peering majestically into the distance. Now she was a bit older, whenever she walked past Eva pondered how long it must have taken someone to carve him. She still joined in the fun when Nanny Day had a joke with them about going on a lion hunt.

There were no jokes today. When they got to Howley Terrace, the neighbours were sitting out on their steps, waiting. Some had even brought chairs out and, from the look on their faces as Eva and Nanny Day walked by, the accident was the chief topic of conversation. A couple of them started to approach but Nanny Day cut right through, like a ship in full sail, and took Eva through the front door.

Eva picked up her dolly and her nightdress and Nanny Day took some tea from the caddy and put it in a brown paper bag, which Mum kept neatly folded in the single drawer of the kitchen table. She was running a bit short at home and extra supplies of Nanny's strong brown tea with a splash of evaporated milk would be needed to keep everyone's spirits up. The street fell silent as they emerged from number 6 Howley Terrace. Eva pulled the door shut. They didn't lock it – there was nothing worth stealing, and in any case, people kept an eye out for each other in their neighbourhood. Rather too much, in her father's opinion: 'A right nosy lot.'

The murmurs about how Frankie was doing and whether he would pull through died away as they walked back down Howley Terrace, into Tenison Street and across Waterloo Road and into Cornwall Road, to Nanny Day's house. The blood was still rushing in Eva's ears at the thought of the accident but coming to her grandparents' house calmed her at last. All the children had been born here, at 100 Cornwall Road, and Eva loved coming to stay because she got to have bread and dripping whenever she liked, even if Grandad did tell her to sling her hook when she pestered him for another piece, toasted on the open fire.

Today was different. After a mug of cocoa she was tucked up in Nanny Day's bed with Kathleen and Peggy already there and sleeping soundly. Jim had already nodded off in the rocking chair in the front room. Eva fell almost instantly into a deep sleep. 'Shock,' she heard Nanny Day whisper to Grandad, just as she was drifting off. He was standing on the landing outside, wondering if he was going to have to kip on the sofa again because his leg was bloody killing him and he would have preferred a proper bed for the night, even though he loved those little urchins dearly.

The girls didn't see their parents for nearly a week and the routine of getting up, going to school and coming home and avoiding Grandad – 'Gertcha!' – was interspersed with visits from the parish priest. Eva took to hiding under the kitchen table to eavesdrop as it was the only way to find out how her beloved little brother was getting on. Nanny Day would always cover the table with her best white linen tablecloth on days when the priest was due. It hung almost to the floor and Eva concealed herself underneath the table, quiet as a mouse, and marvelled at the father's highly polished shoes, which must surely have come from heaven itself, they were so clean and shiny.

At first, Eva thought she was being punished by her parents' absence but little by little, through the grown-up talk she overheard at the kitchen table, as she sat hugging her knees and hardly daring to breathe, she found out it was because Frankie was so sick. His head had swelled to twice its size and they had to pack it in ice and then he got an infection called meningitis which made everything hurt badly.

After a fortnight she was allowed to go on a visit. Only for a few minutes and there was no question of everyone going because the hospital was very strict about over-exciting him. The smell of disinfectant hit her first. The floor was lino, polished so much you could almost see your face in it. There was a table in the middle of the ward with flowers in a vase and children all pale, propped up in bed like little soldiers, for visiting time. All except Frankie, who was allowed to lie back on one pillow, on account of his head injury. 'Hello, Eve,' he murmured, and Eva squeezed his hand. He was like Frankie, only a lot thinner, with a bigger head and a bandage on it.

The nurses wore crisp white uniforms and smelt of starch and only one of them smiled. Every time she went there Eva knew in her heart that it was all her fault. She swore then to protect Frankie and do everything she could to make him well. Getting the bread every day to help Mum was part of it. He did get better but he was never quite the same again.

She felt something poking her in the ribs, bringing her back to reality. It was a little girl with scruffier plaits than her own, and big rip in her pinafore. 'It's your turn next,' she said, looking up at Eva with beady eyes. 'Get a move on, will yer?'

Eva tutted at her but shuffled forwards to take her place at the head of the queue, glad that the wait was over. Her stomach rumbled loudly.

The baker, a big fella, still had a crate full of day-old buns and loaves to get rid of. She handed over her penny and opened her pillowcase, praying he would fill it right up for her. She was one of his regular early-morning customers and he gave her a wink as he slipped a jam tart in there, for her to munch on the way home. Eva winked back at him, grateful as ever for his kindness.

Eva emerged triumphantly from the shop with her pillowcase stuffed to the gunnels. She heard the clock strike half past the hour as she sat down on some steps to devour the jam tart. Costermongers were wheeling their barrows out in Covent Garden, and the shouts which marked the start of the working day filled the air.

She'd be home in plenty of time to give the others their breakfast and she'd make sure Frankie got one of the best buns. Eva crossed back over Waterloo Bridge, heading for home, swinging her pillowcase as she went. A row of railway arches lay under the bridge, opposite the yards of her street, and the hotels above them would sometimes chuck their rubbish on the people living down below. The rats were already making themselves busy finding something to eat. Eva watched them for a second, instinctively clasping her pillowcase a little tighter as she watched the longtails rootling about in a heap of vegetable peelings and old chicken bones. Everything in their street, on four legs or two, was always on the hunt for food.

Getting the bread was one thing, but Eva knew there must be other ways to help Mum and her family – and she was determined to find them.

2

Peggy, August 1931

From her vantage point on the front doorstep, Peggy had made a secret study of the way the women moved up and down the street. Clasping the book in her hand seemed to make her invisible in Howley Terrace, apart from the jeers of 'bookworm' from her younger sisters and some of their silly little street friends. She read endlessly: books borrowed from the public library and her most treasured, on loan from her teacher, Mrs Price, who recognized her pupil's love of learning but knew that the family budget would not extend to buying literature.

Women seemed to think that Peggy was so absorbed in her reading that she could no longer see them or hear what they were talking about. Children of her age were still treated like children and weren't supposed to hear grown-up talk, so Peggy would bury her head and prick up her ears as the street went about its business. On Howley Terrace everything was so crammed together that it was almost impossible to have a private conversation, in any case. Any raised voices in the street would draw a crowd and arguments inside had to be conducted in a stage whisper or the neighbours would have their ear to the wall.

The younger housewives, in their early twenties, who had just one or two kids, were already careworn. Mostly they had mothers or sisters living around the corner who would help them out a bit, and they seemed to be the ones with the time and inclination for a gossip. The young housewives would stand around on their doorsteps in the late afternoon, drinking tea, before their husbands came home. They always wore a clean pinny as they chatted, to show the world that the day's work was done. Dad always gave such women short shrift: 'Idling again, are we, Mary?'

The older ones – her mum's age, really – with five or more little ones round them, seemed weighed down, trudging endlessly back and forth from the communal laundry to the shops and back, fetching and carrying. Not for them the doorstep chatter; they simply had too much to do. Some worked part-time at the London Wastepaper Factory at the top of the road and would emerge at the end of the day covered in dust, the sacking still tied around their legs to keep the rats away. The more children they had, the more swollen their legs and feet, the more bent their backs and the more haggard their faces.

Peggy shuddered. Was this what life had in store for her? She'd just started her monthlies and had thought she was dying when she woke up in a bloody sheet one morning. Mum had to explain all that and the facts of life.

Sometimes the women stopped and chatted for a few minutes and Peggy could overhear snatches of their conversation about aching teeth, backs and worse. 'Women's things' that had happened 'since I had my last'. When one woman suggested going to the doctor, the other would sigh and say, 'I'm still paying him off a shilling a week for the last time,' or, 'It'll get better soon, I'm sure.' The really weak and poor got coupons for extra milk from the Welfare Officer to build them up but they never drank it. They'd rather give it to their children instead and go to bed hungry.

Come to think of it, her mother wasn't plagued by bad feet or swollen legs or rotten teeth. She put that down to her Irish blood, from Nanny Day. Nanny was a force of nature, standing nearly five feet ten, and hailed from County Kildare. She worked as a cook at the Union Jack Club on Waterloo Road, and woe betide anyone who complained about her skills in the kitchen. She made Peggy laugh by gathering the children to her skirts and warning them, in the broadest accent imaginable: 'Never trust the Irish, my lovelies.' Nanny Day looked after Peggy and her brothers and sisters when Mum needed a rest, as well as caring for Grandad, whose leg had been badly shot in the Boer War and had never recovered. His mind seemed to have been affected too because some days he would be fine and others he just talked gibberish or would throw things around the kitchen until Nanny Day slapped him.

In any case, Mum wasn't one to stand round idly chatting. She'd say her 'good mornings', smile, trade a few pleasantries and then say she'd have to 'push on', which was true because she had not one, but three cleaning jobs to keep the family afloat. Now Peggy was getting older, her mother liked to take her into her confidence a little about the ways of the street. Peggy enjoyed that and tried to absorb as much of her mum's wisdom as possible. It set her apart from her sisters too.

'Don't ever gossip for gossip's sake, Peggy,' Mum told her, 'or they'll be talking about you behind your back next. You don't want people knowing your business so you don't need to know anyone else's, unless there is something you can do to help them and you really need to know what is going on.'

Her mother was right, of course. It just seemed that some people in their street made it their business to find out what everyone else was up to. Take Mrs Davies at number 16. Dad called her the News of the World because she was not only likely to poke her nose in but she'd broadcast it all too. She'd stand on that doorstep from dawn till dusk, keeping a beady eye out for passers-by. The coalman and the milkman, who liked a chat, tried to avoid her. Others in the street were not so lucky: 'Not at school today?' or 'Clock off early?' She made it her business to find out. Peggy just put her head down and hurried on but once she hadn't been feeling well with a cold and came home early from school. To her shame, Mrs Davies came running down the street and announced it to her mother, before Peggy could tell her.

But there was a different sort of gossip. It was still done in a quiet way, but it was all right. Like the woman who had – well, Peggy knew she shouldn't say the word because her mother didn't like it – but it was cancer. People said, 'She's very poorly' instead. Mum and the other women in Howley Terrace would take turns minding her three kids or cooking meals and some had even tried to organize a rota to cover her shifts at the jam factory but the foreman found out and let her go.

Things were hard because the woman wasn't going to get better. She couldn't keep house and she couldn't do the laundry any more at the baths in Mason Street on wash days – Mondays. Somehow, Mum managed to do that for her too. Peggy had offered to help but Mum wouldn't hear of it because of the dirty talk that went on in that laundry room. Peggy had once overhead the raucous whoops of laughter as women ran their husband's underclothes through the mangle while she waited outside the door for her mother to finish their linen. She didn't want Mum to think she had been eavesdropping. That wasn't something she would ever do.

The other thing she had overheard while she was sitting reading on the doorstep the other day was Mrs Davies talking about the husband of the woman who wasn't going to get better, in hushed tones. Glances were exchanged as Mrs Davies said she'd heard his boots tapping their way up the cobblestones after midnight and one of the other women folded her arms and said she had heard from a lady in Tenison Street that his boots had been coming from that direction. Peggy guessed that he'd been visiting someone in Tenison Street very late indeed.

'Ain't right,' said Mrs Davies. 'With his missus being sick an' all.'

'Ain't right of *her* round the corner having him over,' the other women said. 'We ought to get something up for her to make her think twice, the dirty cow.'

Not that Peggy had been listening to the whole conversation, because she hadn't. That would be wrong. She finished her chapter and closed her book. Dad would be on his way home soon. The street in the heat of a late August afternoon was full of the shrieks of young kids scampering up and down the cobbles, chasing each other, kicking up the dust from the gutters. They made their fun out of a bit of rope, a plank of wood, anything really. Peggy was the same when she was younger. She didn't feel like joining in any more. She was too grown up, probably.

She sighed. The smell of the river, just a couple of hundred yards away, caught her in the back of her throat. She had always hated that smell. It was awful, a proper stink, and on hot days it just hung in the air all day. Some people got away from Lambeth in the summer, packing themselves off to Kent, hopping. Whole streets would go – women and children and grannies, all packed off together to pick the hops and live in big huts. Peggy had heard about it and it sounded like a dream come true, with fresh air and countryside and even fresh eggs from the farmer. But Mum couldn't leave her cleaning jobs and Dad was needed at the factory, so there was no chance of her coming back from a month away in the fields of Kent with the sun in her hair. She was stuck in Lambeth with the river Thames stinking to high heaven instead. She saw her dad then, trudging down the street, head down, doing his best to ignore everyone. Peggy rushed up to greet him.

In an instant, his face lit up: 'Hello, Peg, what you reading there?'

'Dickens,' she said. '*Hard Times.*' Well, she was reading it but she hadn't got very far with it this afternoon.

'We're having hard times of our own, Peggy.' He laughed. Dad handed over a ha'penny and Peggy tucked her book under her arm. There was no need for him to ask, it was their little teatime ritual. She headed off to the shop in Belvedere Road to pick up the *Evening News*, his favourite paper. But when she got there, she found a crowd of men standing around outside, smoking, their hands in their pockets, eyes downcast. One of them was reading aloud to the others: 'It says here he has gone, resigned from the Labour Party.' A man from Tenison Street, who worked on the docks, shouted: 'Bloody coward! After telling us all to take a wage cut for the good of the country.' Another man piped up: 'And they've been cutting the help from the likes of me. I've been laid off a month now, with three mouths to feed.' There were murmurs of agreement.

Peggy pushed past, with a polite ''Scuse me', and made her way into the shop. She read the headline 'Day and Night of Great Excitement – HIS MAJESTY CONFERS WITH PARTY LEADERS'. There was a picture on the front page of a man with a moustache, and another one of policemen holding back a big crowd in Downing Street. Peggy knew from reading the paper with her father in the past that the man was the Prime Minister, Ramsay Macdonald. She needed to get home. She ran down Belvedere Road and into the little turning to Howley Terrace, nearly knocking over that nosy parker Mrs Davies, who was gossiping on the corner. Mum was already serving up stewed pieces and vegetables for Dad by the time Peggy got through the door and into the scullery.

'Look,' Peggy said, holding the paper up high. 'Macdonald's left the Labour Party and the men in the street say he is a coward!'

'Slow down, Peg,' said Dad, through a mouthful of stew. 'Let me see.' He read for what seemed like an eternity, before looking up at her again. Sometimes he took ages to explain what all the politics of it meant but Peggy was prepared to wait.

Peggy thought her father was the wisest man in the street, if not the whole district, because he had travelled and seen the world in the Merchant Navy. And he wasn't even born in this country like most people's dads. He was a Canadian, a part of the British Empire, and had come over here during the Great War to help out by bringing a convoy of food. He had met her mother while she was working as a cleaner at the Union Jack Club and they fell in love and married and so he never went back. Well, he did try once, at the end of the war when Peggy was just a baby but Nanny Day had had such a bad dream about them going that she wouldn't hear of it and begged and begged them to stay. It was a good thing they did because the ship they were supposed to be sailing on sank to the bottom of the ocean. At least, that is what Nanny Day told her, although she wasn't supposed to tell anyone about it, because it was a sort of family secret.

Peggy couldn't work out why but her father didn't talk much about Canada, other than to say his mother was from a tribe of Indians living by the Fraser River. She wasn't supposed to talk about that either, in case people made fun of her or her brothers and sisters. And when he was growing up he lived with fur traders and in a fort and on some lakes, but life was hard and so he ran away to join the Navy. He even lied about his age to get in because he was just ten at the time, the same age as Eva, really, which was a funny thought. She imagined Eva having to scrub the decks and climb the rigging. That made her laugh out loud.

'It's no laughing matter, Peg,' said Dad sternly.

'Sorry,' she said. She couldn't very well explain why she was laughing at a time like this. 'What does it all mean?' Peggy always asked him to explain what the papers meant because there always seemed to be more to it than the headlines exclaimed.

'The King wants him to make a government with the Conservatives but that isn't what people voted for and they won't help the likes of us,' he said. 'It means life is going to get tougher but we will have to cope somehow.'

Her mum spun around, her ladle still in her pot of stew, a look of irritation etched on her features. 'Oh, stop filling her head with all that nonsense, James. It's not like she's going to rule the country!' The only reason Mum tolerated his newspapers was because she could make good use of them when he had read them, cutting them into neat squares to hang on a peg in the lavvy in the back yard.

She put her hands on her hips, as if she meant business: 'Now, James, I wanted to talk to you about having some extra housekeeping because Frankie needs a new pair of boots and I'm running a bit short . . .'

The silence seemed to last forever. Then he looked up at her, the tenderness in his eyes gone.

'What do you mean, Margaret, running short?'

'It's just things are getting expensive: the coal, the food, all the clothing and then there's the rent and the insurances . . .' Mum started to fidget with the corners of her apron.

'Expensive,' he murmured, staring at his food.

'Well, am I to go to the parish, then, to ask for some boots?' She put her hands on her hips again, raising her voice to him. 'The shame of wearing them, James! They have the labels on so they can't be pawned and all the neighbours will know! Is that what you want for your children?'

'Goddamn you, Margaret!' He slammed his hand on the table so hard that the gravy splattered off the blue and white crockery. 'I expect you to manage, woman. I am working myself to the bone to provide for this family but it isn't enough, is it?'

In an instant, he got to his feet, raised his hand and delivered a ringing slap to the side of her face. Mum cried out. Peggy looked at the table. She shouldn't be here. She was frozen, unable to move.

'Get upstairs, Peg,' said Dad, under his breath.

As she left the room, she found Eva, Frankie and Kathleen gathered, wide-eyed, in the tiny hallway and ushered them all in front of her up the stairs. They were as quiet as mice and they could hear their mother sobbing in the yard.

Later that night, when the sun finally went down, she heard her mother pulling the bed out in the front room, where her parents always slept. She listened intently. There were a few more sobs, then silence. Peg lay gazing out at the sky through the thin curtains which her mother had sewed in an attempt to brighten the little bedroom. She thought of her mother's fingers sewing that material, every stitch, to make life better for them all. Through the darkness, Peggy heard a faint tap-tapping coming from the scullery.

In the morning, when she went downstairs, her father had already left for work but Frankie's boots were mended, as good as new, on the kitchen table.

3

Kathleen, February 1932

'The British Empire,' intoned Miss Price, 'is one of the wonders of the world, a great achievement of which we must all be proud.'

Chalk dust flew off the blackboard as she wrote, in her neat copperplate handwriting: 'Australia, Canada, Africa, the West Indies, Burma and India . . .'

Georgie Harwood put up his hand.

It was as if she had eyes in the back of her head, because she said, without turning around: 'Yes, George, what is it this time?'

'Miss, India wants independence, don't it, miss?'

'Well, yes, George, perhaps it does but the Empire is a very good thing and we don't want to let it go now, do we?'

'My dad says—'

'That is quite enough, George,' said Miss Price curtly. 'This is St Patrick's Catholic School not a meeting of the local *trade union*.' She emphasized those two words, to signal her distaste.

'But, it is true, Miss!' he protested.

'That is quite enough!'

She slammed her hand down on the desk, breaking her chalk in two in the process. The class gasped.

'Come here,' she said. Her eyes were like little grey stones behind her glasses. Kathleen thought she was really quite a horrid teacher, though she had her favourites, and her sister Peggy was one of them.

George got out of his seat and walked slowly, very slowly, to the front of the class.

'Hand out,' said Miss Price, pulling a wooden ruler from her desk drawer. He obeyed, mutely. She brought the ruler down three times on the palm of his fat little hand, each time saying, 'Do not interrupt!'

As he turned back to face the class, Kathleen could see that he was fighting back tears. Feeling sorry for poor George, who was really quite handsome with his blue eyes and blond hair, she smiled at him. He blushed.

Silly Georgie Harwood. He was always butting in. It was all his father's fault. He was a shop steward working on the docks and had got a lot to say for himself. George spent most his life repeating it to anyone who would listen.

Daddy seemed to like Mr Harwood and said he was a good fellow, but Mum said the family thought they were a cut above because they lived on the other side of the Waterloo Road, in Roupell Street, known as 'White Curtain Street'. That meant they thought they were a bit better than folks from Howley Terrace, really. They did jobs in offices and things like that. One of them even had a car, which Kathleen's brothers, Jim and Frankie, thought was the most terrific thing ever.

None of it seemed to do George any good at school

because he was always getting whacked with that ruler for talking. Why couldn't he just be quiet and let Miss Price get on with the lesson? She was a right old bossyboots and Kathleen had learned it was better to keep your mouth shut. She suppressed a cough because it would only annoy Miss Price further. Her throat had been hurting her for weeks now and although Mum did treat it with honey and lemon juice at first, that had run out and there was no way they could afford more. She swallowed, feeling as if someone was scratching the inside of her throat with their fingernails.

At least while the teacher was busy writing on the blackboard Kathleen was able to spend some time gazing out at the playground below and dreaming of her future up in the theatres of the West End. The tall buildings on the other side of the water were silhouetted against the darkening sky of a winter's afternoon but she knew that over there, up in the West End, was where her future lay. She would get a starring role, yes, she would. She'd been getting Eva and Frankie to do cartwheels and tumble turns while she worked on her role as the main attraction, the Sheikh of Araby. The question was, would she be able to borrow Mum's best tea towel and show Gladys from down the road her new act, without getting into trouble?

'Stop daydreaming, Kathleen!' shouted Miss Price, bringing her back to reality and the main exports of the British Empire. 'Pay attention or you won't be playing piano in assembly tomorrow!'

Kathleen sat bolt upright. She lived to play that piano, once a week. It was a big old thing, standing in the corner of the hall, and it made her feel special because *she* was the only one of the children who was allowed to touch it. It had 'John Broadwood and Sons' written on it in gold lettering above the keyboard and it was really quite old. The ivories were worn and cracked but she didn't mind about that. She even forgave it for going a semitone out of key in the hot weather.

Kathleen copied in her exercise book, in her best handwriting: 'Oil in the East and sugar in the West Indies, gold from Africa, rubber from Malaya and copper from Burma.'

As she finished, she couldn't help noticing that George Harwood was staring at her.

When Kathleen got home, a cart was pulled up outside, with a horse snuffling in its nosebag of oats, while the tallyman drank a cup of tea in the scullery. His hair was slicked back, revealing gaunt cheekbones, and his yellowing teeth were visible as he sipped. Kathleen couldn't help staring at him. He pulled his wares from his special suitcase which seemed to have hidden pockets stuffed with surprises. Mum bought some clothes pegs and was admiring two crisp white tea towels.

'But I can't afford them, so don't tempt me,' she said, pouring him another cup.

'Oh, come now, Mrs Fraser,' he said, his little brown eyes dancing with delight. 'You know I can put it all in my little book and hubby need never find out.'

He tapped his nose with the side of a slender nicotine-stained finger. Mum smiled. The tallyman seemed to be the only visitor to their home who could bring a smile to her face. Kathleen noticed that it made her look years younger. He pulled a stubby little pencil from the breast pocket of his waistcoat, which was buttoned up tight and straining slightly, and licked it before writing down everything she had bought in his little red notebook. And, more importantly, what she owed. The tea towels, meanwhile, had found their way, as if by magic, into the drawer of the kitchen table.

To Kathleen their whole life seemed to be attached by invisible strings to these male visitors with their little books whom she had known since she was a baby: the insurance man, the rent man, the tallyman. All of them came and went when her father was not present and she never talked about the men in front of him. It wasn't that Mum had told her not to; it just didn't seem right or as if he needed to know, in fact. It was an unspoken thing: that her mother could trust her not to say anything.

Eva came hurtling through the door into the kitchen, with Frankie in hot pursuit.

'You two,' said Kathleen, 'have got work to do with me!' She ushered them out into the yard and after ten minutes' rehearsal they came back into the kitchen, where Mum was spreading some margarine on slices of bread for their tea.

Kathleen put her hand to her throat again. It was still painful but she wasn't going to let it ruin her big moment. She didn't feel much like eating either. While her mother's back was turned, she whipped one of the precious new tea towels from the kitchen drawer and fastened it around her head.

'Ta-da!' she chimed, announcing the start of her show.

'Oh, my good Lord! Whatever next?' Mum cried, in fake surprise. Of course she'd known from the start that Kathleen was up to something, but she played along because she knew how much it meant to her to perform.

Kathleen began to sing, shimmying across the scullery: 'Well, I'm the Sheikh of Araby and your love belongs to me . . .'

Frankie dashed in and turned a cartwheel, narrowly avoiding the kitchen table and Eva chose this moment to follow him and jump down into the splits. With the tea towel slipping down over her eyes, Kathleen continued: 'At night, when you're asleep, into your tent, I'll creep . . .'

But she didn't get any further because she tripped over the giggling mass of legs and arms on the scullery floor.

Mum applauded wildly. 'Oh, that was lovely! Wait till Nanny Day sees that. She'll have you sold off to the circus.'

'It would be better if we had music,' said Kathleen apologetically, taking a deep bow.

Margaret was still humming the tune to herself as she tucked the children up in bed that night. Kathleen complained that her legs and arms were hurting now. Margaret muttered to herself that she should have gone to the chemist and got her a tonic at least, but she said a prayer over her. As she made her way downstairs, the guilt of not getting Kathleen to the doctor weighed on her. It was just the cost of it all. Later on, she checked the girls and then fell into a fitful sleep but was woken in the small hours by Eva standing at her bedside.

'It's Kathleen. She's gone and wet the bed,' said Eva, hopping from one foot to the other. 'Everything is soaking.'

Kathleen was twelve and her bedwetting days were long gone. Margaret sat bolt upright. James was still sleeping soundly next to her. He was so dog-tired after a day in the factory that it would take an earthquake to wake him. She lit a candle and ran upstairs and found Kathleen thrashing about in a heap of bedclothes. She put a hand to her forehead. It was burning up. She ran back downstairs into the scullery and plunged one of her precious new tea towels into a bowl of cold water standing in the sink. Margaret brought it upstairs, laid it on her daughter's burning forehead and said three Hail Marys. Kathleen opened her eyes and croaked: 'It hurts everywhere.'

There was nothing for it. James would have to fetch the doctor. They had paid into the Friendly Society for basic medical care from the doctor when they needed it but this would cost extra, being a night-time visit. James, still in a sleep stupor, pulled on his clothes and his boots and went off into the night, returning half an hour later with the doctor, carrying his big, black leather bag. The doctor was a tall man, so tall that he had to stoop to avoid banging his head on the lintel over the doorway to the little bedroom. He pulled out a stethoscope and listened to Kathleen's chest before taking her temperature, which he said was very high indeed.

'It's the fever, Mrs Fraser, rheumatic fever most likely,' he said. 'We will get her moved off to hospital at first light. Just try to keep her cool for the next few hours.'

*

Eva had no idea what the rheumatic fever was but she no longer cared that she'd been woken up by Kathleen and regretted that she had ever found her annoying or tweaked her plaits as she slept because she was so pretty and it wasn't fair. Eva only cared about her sister and whether she would ever get better. And when she did, she would be the best sister to Kathleen. In fact, she made her mind up there and then: she would get her a piano so she could sing all her favourite songs and have music and be in a show up in the West End.

4

Eva, March 1932

First it was her little brother Frankie, now it was her big sister Kathleen. Eva didn't ever want to get ill. She knew her sister was so sick that she probably didn't mind being away from home for weeks but Eva hated the idea of not being with her family. And then there were the rules. She hated the rules even more. No sitting on the bed, no touching the patient, no bringing in food (she ignored that rule and sneaked jam sarnies in for Kathleen), only two visitors per bed and don't even think about turning up a minute early or that old dragon of a ward sister will chew your ears off.

Kathleen lay back on her pillow, the dark circles under her eyes making her look much older, her beautiful curls all greasy because she was too ill to have a bath yet. When she smiled, she was still Kathleen but when she coughed it scared the life out of Eva because her whole body seemed to shake. Sister appeared at the end of the bed and rang the bell to signal the end of visiting time.

'Well, Kathleen,' said Mum, kissing her on the forehead, 'you just keep your spirits up, chicken, and we will have you home very soon.'

'Can Frankie come to visit, and Jim?' she asked.

Eva nodded. Frankie and Jim were off with Old Uncle Dennis, Nanny Day's brother, watching the Arsenal play, but she would make sure one of them came in her place next weekend. The Royal Hospital for Children and Women was only a stone's throw from their house but, with its grand, red-brick front entrance and echoing wards, it was a world away from their little terraced home. What if Kathleen got used to having a bed all to herself and never wanted to leave? Eva stifled a sob.

'Chin up, Eve,' said Kathleen. 'I might be allowed onto the balcony soon for some fresh air and I bet I will see you and Frankie playing out in the street!'

That balcony, with its columns, overlooking Waterloo Road, was like something out of a fairy tale. Eva felt a pang of jealousy and then reminded herself that Kathleen was only trying to find something to look forward to. Eva had overheard Mum telling Dad that Kathleen might always have a weak heart because of the rheumatic fever and it could take months to get over it.

Nanny Day was threatening to come up to the hospital with her special bone broth to make Kathleen better, just as she had with Uncle when he came back from the Great War with tuberculosis. The nurses at St Thomas's Hospital would wheel all the soldiers out for fresh air in their beds by the river Thames because that was how you got better from TB. So Nanny Day would come along and bring a big bowl of her bone broth and ladle that into Uncle Dennis as he lay there, coughing. The nurses knew better than to try to stop her. She'd give them a look, as if to say,

'What are you going to do, then?' and they would retreat, with a rustle of starched uniforms. Now Nanny Day was talking about coming up to nurse Kathleen herself and Eva wished she could be there to see the look on the ward sister's face when she did!

Later that afternoon, as Nanny Day helped to press some shirts in the scullery, she made her intentions clear. Mum took in a bit of laundry from the hotels to help make a few shillings more when she could and Nanny Day was always willing to lend a hand.

'It's been too long, Maggie, two weeks now and no improvement. They are not feeding her right. She needs my broth,' she said

'Please, Ma, I don't want to upset the doctors,' said Mum.

'Nonsense,' said Nanny Day, pulling some coins out of her purse and handing them to Eva. 'Go up to the Cut and see what bones the butcher can spare you and if he hasn't got much, give him those to change his mind.' She grabbed an onion and a potato from the side and began chopping with such vigour that Eva was pleased to beat a hasty retreat up to the shops.

Eva walked along Lower Marsh, past the barrows at the side of the road. A brewer's dray horse plodded past. Someone had parked a motor car and it was attracting attention from the kids from Ethelm Street. 'Eat'em Street' was what Eva and Frankie called it. It was so rough that the police would only walk down it in pairs.

Eva crossed over Waterloo Road and into the Cut – a bustling thoroughfare running from Waterloo Road to

Blackfriars Road, a cut through from one street to another. It was an exciting place to be. She preferred it to their little world in Howley Terrace, although they did have the muffin man and the tallyman, who might throw them a penny when the kids chased him, shouting 'throw out yer mouldies'. The Cut had proper shops and was full of life: the butcher, the grocer, the barber, the hardware store and Peacry's, the general dealer, which was her favourite because things hung on rails and hooks outside and it was like Aladdin's Cave in there. The banter that went on in those shops was something she loved to hear, although she didn't understand most of it. Everyone knew she was Nanny Day's granddaughter and all the shopkeepers had time for her nan and her mum.

The butcher was busy when she got there. People were buying their meat for Sunday – the one day when families like hers tried to have a full roast with meat, two veg and gravy. Whatever beef they had left after would be minced up on Monday and used to make a pie or given to her father cold, to keep him going. Mum never seemed to eat much. She made sure that Dad and the kids were all fed first before she would help herself to the smallest piece of meat.

Eva came away with a packet of beef bones, wrapped in newspaper. The butcher didn't charge her because he knew Old Uncle Dennis well. They had served together in the trenches in France during the Great War. Eva noticed that the butcher's hands didn't shake like Uncle Dennis's did, though. He was steady as a rock as he wielded that meat cleaver.

She still had her pennies from Nanny Day, which she would give back to her. As she passed the grocer's shop, some juicy oranges caught her eye. Wouldn't it be good if she could get one for Kathleen? She turned the coins over and over in her pocket. Nanny Day couldn't really afford it. Anyway, she had told Eva to get bones, not fruit, and Eva didn't want to risk her wrath. But she did want her sister to get better.

She wandered around in front of the shop for a few moments, waiting for a customer. A woman from Tenison Street came along and got into quite a discussion with the shopkeeper about the price of his apples, which had come all the way from Kent and were probably the juiciest this side of the river, or that was what he said. While they were debating the price for a pound of his finest, she crept alongside the crate of oranges, snatched two and tucked them under her parcel of bones. Her heart stopped for a second when the shopkeeper glanced over. She smiled at him, turned and skipped off, pleased with herself.

When she got home, Mrs Avens from down the road had installed herself at the tiny table in the scullery. Eva put the parcel of beef bones down on the table but held the oranges behind her back while Mrs Avens prattled on.

'I only went to the Poor Law because my Johnny can't find work and I'm struggling to make ends meet,' she was saying. Mum nodded sympathetically. Nanny Day harrumphed loudly over the ironing board. She'd seen that Johnny up at the Feathers Tavern in the Waterloo Road more times than she'd care to mention. Mrs Avens ignored her and carried on.

'Well, that nasty little man, Mr Pemberton, do you know what he said to me?' she said. She didn't wait for a reply: 'He said "That's a nice sideboard, Mrs Avens, how come you can afford that, then?" Well, you know it was my mother's. She was given it by a grand old lady who lived over by Hyde Park, in her will. She served her thirty years, she did. And more than earned that bleeding sideboard, I can tell you.'

Eva knew only too well how Mrs Avens's mother had earned her mahogany sideboard. Her mum said she'd heard the story so often that she felt she had cleaned the parquet floors and polished the bannisters in that house over and over herself for the last ten years.

'And that ain't all,' Mrs Avens went on. 'He was looking at my table linen and everything. When he found out I had a war pension from my late Arthur, well, that was it. I wasn't going to qualify. And he asked me if I really wanted to work. Well, you know I do, but my legs aren't what they were. My Johnny has fairly worn himself out looking for a job.'

Mum nodded again. Johnny was possibly the biggest good-for-nothing in the whole of Lambeth. Nanny Day opened her mouth to speak but Mum shot her a look. Eva knew that look well and it meant hold your tongue. She could almost hear her mother's thoughts: this was her street, her neighbour, and Nanny Day would not have to live with the consequences of any falling out.

'Oh that is terrible, yes,' said Mum. 'But I must be pushing on now. You'll have finished your tea?'

She swept the little cup away from Mrs Avens's grasp

before she could ask for a top-up and headed for the front door to show her out. Nanny Day, meanwhile, inspected the parcel of bones which Eva had brought and patted her on the head.

'What have you got there, Eva?' said Mum, as Eva produced her two oranges, which looked so juicy and delicious.

'Grocer gave them to me when I told him Kathleen was sick,' she lied.

'Well, thank the Lord for his charity,' said Mum. 'We'll have one with our tea and I'll take one up to the hospital tomorrow.'

'With my soup,' said Nanny Day, sploshing the bones into a big pot of water on the stove.

Mum sighed and raised her eyes to heaven. She knew when she was beaten.

'Yes, Ma, with your soup.'

Eva went out to play with Frankie, who was having the best fun building a big mountain with the other kids, using old crates and bits of wood they found lying on the ground up near the London Wastepaper Factory. They put it all in a big pile in Tenison Street, while some of the women, led by that gossipy Mrs Davies, looked on and nodded their approval.

As dusk fell, Mrs Davies disappeared for five minutes and then marched back around with a large rag doll figure, with a mop for hair and a stuffed cushion for a head, dressed in an old overcoat. She had pinned a piece of paper to it. It read 'SLAG'. The rag figure was plonked on the top of the pile. Eva didn't know what that word meant but the big boys started running around and around that pile of wood and crates, shouting it, much to the amusement of Mrs Davies and the other women. One of the bigger boys came running along with a bottle of paraffin oil and poured it on the crates. Then someone struck a match. The whole thing went up with a 'whoosh' and the flames shot six feet into the air. People came out of their houses and stared at the bonfire. Some of the women stood with arms folded. The men huddled away at one end of the street and the children darted up and down, shrieking with laughter.

Frankie was making everyone laugh doing such a funny dance that Eva couldn't help joining in. Only one person didn't seem to be sharing the joke. Eva saw a woman's face at the window of one of the houses. She was crying as she pulled the curtains shut. Her kids weren't out in the street larking about like the others. Someone chucked an old pram on the fire, making it belch black smoke. Soon all the children were covered with smuts and soot.

Peggy appeared on the street corner and signalled for Eva and Frankie to come home, now.

'Spoilsport!' said Eva, as her big sister clasped her hand and dragged her around the corner. Frankie was at the door first, to be greeted by their mother, who had a face like thunder.

'Get inside, now!' she shouted. Eva nearly jumped out of her skin. Mum was rarely angry and Eva couldn't remember the last time she had raised her voice like that.

She took them into the back yard and made them stand there in the darkness while she brought a bucket to the tap and filled it to the brim with cold water. She stalked off into the scullery and returned with the dreaded dishcloth. She dunked it into the freezing water and began to scrub away at the soot on their faces. 'No child of mine will ever be involved in shaming someone like that, do you hear?' she cried.

Eva started to sob and Frankie was blubbing. They hadn't a clue what she was talking about. It was only a bit of fun, but they knew better than to answer their mother back when she was like this. They were just grateful she hadn't pulled the tin bath down from its peg on the wall in the back yard and dunked them in that for good measure. They were sent to bed without any tea.

It was only the next day, as Eva was talking with her friend Gladys that she got an idea of why the woman had been crying. Eva didn't know for sure what Gladys meant when she said that the woman had been 'having it' with a fella from Howley Terrace whose wife was very poorly, but she knew it had made the grown-ups very angry. She had done a moonlight flit last night – taken her few belongings and her children and fled to her mother's house in Bermondsey, so they said. No one breathed a word of it again and, strangely, Eva thought, no one said anything to the fella in Howley Terrace. He still whistled as he came and went, on his way to work at the jam factory, as if nothing had happened at all.

5

Peggy, October 1932

There was more of a crowd outside the corner shop these days. Peggy noticed that men milled about, chatting, early on a Monday morning. They were waiting for news of casual work, any work. Their clothes grew shabbier with every passing week, their faces more gaunt and their eyes downcast. She hurried past, clutching her father's best blue serge suit. Mother sent her off before school to pawn it on Mondays and she went back on Friday, which was pay-day, to buy it back before her father noticed it was missing. It was just another way of supplementing their meagre income.

Mum warned her not to dawdle or listen to any of the silly chit-chat that went on in the pawnbroker's. Peggy had tried not to, of course, but she couldn't help but overhear some of the smutty jokes that the women told to the young male assistant. As they unwrapped their bundles, they would josh around with him and tease him about his good looks, or what he had got up to at the weekend, in the hope of making him blush. 'Ooh, he's blushing, see!' they would cackle to each other. It was all done to befuddle him into giving them the price they wanted for their goods.

Usually it worked and he gave them their asking price without too much bother, just so he could be rid of them.

Peggy simply handed over the suit, mutely, looking at the floor because the assistant was quite handsome and that gave her a feeling like butterflies in her stomach. She mumbled her thanks as he gave her some coins and was turning to go when she bumped into her teacher, Miss Price. Peggy was dumbstruck. There was no shame in pawning things but she hadn't expected to see Miss Price in there. The teacher was holding a gold locket in her hand, which Peggy knew must be a treasured heirloom of some sort. Miss Price blushed beetroot.

'Good morning, Peggy,' she said. 'I didn't expect to find you here.'

'No, miss,' was all she could manage.

'Well, I would be most grateful if we could forget all about our little encounter.'

'Yes, miss.'

And Peggy ran off home. It was a bitterly cold day, her fingers were freezing, but she now noticed that her hands were shaking too. She realized that it had nothing to do with the icy wind which was whipping through her thin coat. It was as if one of the main pillars supporting her whole world had collapsed. Miss Price was her teacher, she lived in a nice house, she wasn't poor and she couldn't have money troubles, could she? She was clever and she worked hard, so she couldn't be hard up.

Miss Price had been the person Peggy wanted to be most like when she grew up, ever since she put Peggy forward to try for a scholarship so she could go to the grammar school. It had come to nothing because Dad had refused, saying they would need her to start earning when she was fifteen, and so she stayed put, along with the other girls from the neighbourhood, whose only dreams seemed to be to work in the Hartley's jam factory. The plan was for Peggy to get a good job, as a trainee clerk perhaps, in the Post Office.

'That will mean more to this family than staying on at school till sixteen,' her dad told Miss Price. 'And it will be a proper career, not factory work.' Peggy understood her father's thinking but she still put Miss Price on a pedestal for believing that she was clever enough to try for a scholarship in the first place.

When Dad got home from work that evening, Peggy brought him his paper as usual and then struck up a conversation with him about wage cuts. She remembered reading about that.

'Yes, Peg,' he said, chewing on a bit of bread. 'Ten per cent across the board for all those in public services.'

That would include teachers. So, perhaps Miss Price was struggling, after all.

He shook open his newspaper. The main story was Hunger Marches coming to London from the most deprived areas of the North, with people protesting against the Means Test. That was a phrase Peggy had overheard up at the corner shop, usually followed by a stream of profanities, including some words she didn't know the meaning of. From what she understood, it was the job of the Poor Law authorities to go and check out whether the people on unemployment benefits were claiming too much money, according a new set of rules which were much hated by everyone in the street.

'A hundred thousand people went to welcome the marchers at Hyde Park yesterday, Peg,' said Dad. 'And the police made them pay for it. And don't believe the nonsense the politicians spout about the marchers being sent by Moscow. It's not all about Communism; people are starving.'

'Shush, James,' Mum said, snatching the paper away from him. 'She's too young to hear about all that.'

Peggy was about to protest that she wasn't too young, at fourteen, but there was a loud knock on the door. She went to answer it and found the dishevelled man from over the road who spoke with a funny accent. She knew his name was Joe and he had come up from the West Country a few months ago. He was one of the lucky few who still had work down at the docks.

'It's my wife,' he said, wringing his hands. 'The baby's coming. Please get your mother. I need her help. We don't know what to do.'

Help was organized almost before he had finished his sentence. Mrs Avens, who had been standing on her doorstep, ran inside to get hot water and some towels; Mum rolled her sleeves up and walked briskly across the road with Joe and Peggy trailing in her wake.

Mrs Davies was doing a great job of trumpeting the impending arrival to anyone who would listen and had drawn quite a crowd at the other end of the street. Eva was sent to get Nanny Day, who was the neighbourhood's unofficial midwife. Peggy entered the house with her mother and was almost overcome by the stench. A pile of rabbit skins and tails lay in a basket in the corner of the front room and there was fluff all over the floor.

'Haven't had time to clean up,' said Joe, shrugging his shoulders by way of apology. 'The wife's been doing some fur-pulling to help us make ends meet.' Peggy had seen the work before, as so many women did it to earn a little something, but it was back-breaking and soul-destroying, rubbing the down off the skins of those little beasts with a blunt knife until your fingers bled and the fluff getting up your nose and in your mouth. And then the furriers only paid pennies. Peggy's mum had tried it when she was younger but said she preferred to have her hands red raw from cleaning than deal with the awful smell and the fluff of those rabbits.

A loud scream came from upstairs.

'What is your wife's name, Joe?'

'It's Mary,' he said, the colour draining from his face.

Mary was lying on an old mattress on the floor of the upstairs bedroom. There were no curtains at the windows, just an old sheet pinned up to give some privacy. There were no bedclothes either. She just lay on top of her husband's coat. A crate in the corner served as a chair for Joe, who sat, helplessly, wringing his hands as his wife's face contorted with the pain.

'Hello, Mary,' said Peggy's mum. 'I'm Margaret, from across the road.'

'Help me!' she said. 'I'm dying.'

Margaret knelt down beside her and stroked her hair,

which was matted with sweat. Peggy moved to take her hand. Mary didn't look much older than her, and Peggy sent up a silent, selfish prayer that she wouldn't end up giving birth in such penury.

'Oh, Mary, you silly girl, you aren't dying. You are going to have a beautiful baby,' Mum said.

Without waiting to be invited in, Mrs Avens charged upstairs and plonked a basin of hot water and some towels down on the floor.

'Oh, you poor dear,' she said, looking around the room, 'You have barely anything to your name.' Tact was never her strong point. Mum shot her a glance.

'I'm so ashamed,' wailed Mary. 'I have no linen!'

'Don't worry,' said Mum, 'We will all spare you something.' And she sent Mrs Avens off, with a flea in her ear, to collect something from all the other women in the street.

Nanny Day arrived to take charge of the situation, just as the baby's head was appearing.

'The pain!' screamed Mary. 'Make it stop!'

'Now,' said Nanny Day, as Peggy held on to the girl's hand. 'When I tell you to push, push down, hard.'

Peggy tried not to look, honest she did, but she couldn't help but notice that something small, bloody and slippery was emerging from between Mary's legs.

Joe turned his face away, unable to watch. He shouldn't be here. This was women's work, something he knew nothing about and, frankly, you could see he didn't want to know, in any case. A split second later, there was a loud cry and he turned around to see the face of his first child. It was scrunched up and covered in blood. Mary lay back, exhausted, smiling at last. Nanny Day held the baby up, still attached by the cord to his mother. 'It's a boy!' she cooed. 'A beautiful baby boy!'

Joe knelt down beside Mary and kissed her forehead.

Mum whispered in his ear, 'There is a bit more work to do, Joe. Maybe you should wait outside.'

He didn't need to be asked twice. He'd seen enough blood and guts for one day. Word had spread like wildfire and as he stepped outside for some fresh air, a loud cheer went up from the men and women, his neighbours. He was slapped on the back, offered a smoke and whisked away to the pub for a celebratory pint before he knew what was happening.

Mrs Avens returned with a pile of sheets, a pillow, some towels and muslin cloths, as well as a drawer for the baby to sleep in. 'That is from my best sideboard,' she told Mary, who was feeding the baby and stroking his little face. 'I will need it back eventually, but you take your time, love.'

Over the coming weeks, the whole street kept an eye out for Mary and the baby. Eva was a frequent visitor, taking a few buns from her early-morning expeditions up to the bakery in Covent Garden, and everyone was amazed by the generosity of the greengrocer up at the Cut, who – Eva said – regularly donated an apple or an orange for the new mother.

'Funny that, because he never spares me as much as an extra pip from one of his apples, even with my bad legs,' grumbled Mrs Avens.

Peggy noticed that the atmosphere around the corner

shop on pay-day, which was Friday, had become tense, with men airing their grievances about the Means Test and Mr Pemberton from the Poor Law Authority in particular. It was the Poor Law's job to work out whether people qualified for any financial help under the new rules laid down by the Government, using the Means Test. Put simply, most people found they couldn't get as much help as they used to, even if they were on the breadline already. Meanwhile, the Poor Law also encouraged men who were out of work to make good use of their time. The latest outrage centred on some work schemes for the unemployed on the local allotments, as well as boot-mending and rag-rug making. 'It's little more than slave labour because they ain't going to pay us a penny. It's just keeping us busy,' said one man, spitting on the ground to signal his disgust.

Another added, 'In Bermondsey, the Poor Law are trying to work out how to give people an extra shilling, not take it away. That Pemberton wants to be taught a lesson.' According to Peggy's father, the authorities in Bermondsey were a radical lot who refused to axe people's benefits and were trying to find ways of bending the rules to give the needy an extra bit of help.

The next evening, Peggy spotted a notice in the shop window about a forthcoming meeting in the pub down the road, with speakers from the National Unemployed Workers' Movement, to discuss the Means Test. She made a mental note to tell her father about it. As she walked home along Howley Terrace in the failing light of dusk and smog, she spotted Mary coming out of her little terraced house, with her baby in her arms. Drawing near, she saw that Mary was wearing a hessian sack as a dress. Peggy waved at her but Mary just put her head down and scurried off.

When Peggy asked her mum why Mary was dressed like that, she sighed. 'She's pawned her clothes to make ends meet and now she feels she can't go out in the daylight because of the shame of it. There's a lot of folks worse off than we are.'

James put his newspaper down and announced that he was going to the pub for a quick pint, which was not like him because he rarely drank. It wasn't that Margaret begrudged him anything but they could barely afford it. Besides, she didn't want him coming home full of beer because, well, they already had five kids and she didn't want any more. She knew only too well how easily a little accident could happen in drink and nine months later there would be the patter of tiny feet and another mouth to feed. Like so many women in the street, her endless round of mending late into the evening seemed to have put paid to any further children but once the man of the house was three sheets to the wind . . .

'Don't be too late,' she said, to his departing back.

When James returned from the pub, she had pulled the blankets right up to her neck and was feigning sleep. 'It's all right, Margaret,' he breathed in her ear as he clambered in beside her. 'I've only had a pint. We were talking business, me and some of the other fellas from Tenison Street. Pemberton is coming to see that young couple from the

West Country tomorrow and I'm going to be there to put their case.'

Some of the men jokingly called Joe 'the country bumpkin' because he was so naive and trusting. The whole street knew they didn't have two brass farthings to rub together but the worry was that the Poor Law would run rings around them both, even though they were a deserving case.

'Don't you go getting into any bother,' said Margaret, turning to face him. 'I know you are trying to help but we can't be fighting other people's battles. We're all trying to do what we can to support them.'

'They just need someone to speak up for them,' said James. 'There's a meeting tomorrow night about how they are doing things in Bermondsey with the Poor Law. It doesn't make sense that the likes of Pemberton are penny-pinching when there are ways to help those who really need it.'

Margaret sighed. There was no point arguing with him. Everyone in the street looked up to him and she knew he wouldn't get involved unless he really felt it was necessary. He put his arms around her waist and hugged her and she felt safe in his arms, lying together there in the dark.

Mrs Davies from number 16 was loitering on her doorstep when James came home early from the cricket bat factory the next day.

'Clocked off early?' she ventured. When he didn't reply, she shouted after him, barely disguising the note of triumph in her voice. 'Mr Pemberton is already in there.

You're probably too late because he turned up a full half-hour early!'

James scowled and quickened his pace.

When he got to Joe's door, it was already open and Mr Pemberton was about to leave. James could hear Mary sobbing in the scullery.

'Wait,' said James, blocking his path. 'I need to talk to you.'

'Nothing more to be said,' said Mr Pemberton, flicking imaginary dust off his bowler hat as he crossed the threshold. His little moustache twitched with pleasure as he spoke. 'The matter is settled.'

'I have come to speak for them,' said James, catching sight of Joe sitting at the foot of the stairs, with his head in his hands. 'They need someone to help put their case.'

'Rules are rules,' said Mr Pemberton, popping his hat onto his head and buttoning his coat right up to the collar with deft little fingers. 'The Poor Law cannot make exceptions.'

'But they can and they do in Bermondsey, and well you know it,' said James.

Mr Pemberton, who wasn't used to people arguing with his decisions, for fear of losing an extra penny from their benefits, raised an eyebrow.

'Ah, yes, Red Bermondsey, the borough of comrades,' he spat. 'Well, it's a pity our country friends here don't live in Bermondsey, isn't it? They live in Lambeth.'

James moved alarmingly close to Mr Pemberton. 'How, in the name of God, are these people not deserving?' he said, seizing him by the collar and knocking his hat to the floor in the process.

'Take your hands off me!' cried Mr Pemberton. 'Or it will be the worse for you! I have witnesses, see?' He pointed to the women and children standing open-mouthed in their doorways. James Fraser had his hands around the throat of the Poor Law! Mr Pemberton had barely finished his sentence before the women pulled their children inside, slamming their front doors and leaving the street deserted.

'I don't think so,' said James, moving his face closer to that of Mr Pemberton, which had now gone puce with rage.

'You will regret this, you will all regret this,' shouted Mr Pemberton, stooping to retrieve his hat from the gutter. 'I shall be informing the constables about the behaviour of this street!' And, with that, he plonked his bowler hat back on top of his balding head and stalked off, to do more good.

James Fraser's besting of the Poor Law was the chief topic of conversation that night in the Waterman's Arms. Quite a crowd had gathered there for the meeting about the Means Test and the Poor Law, which the landlord was delighted about because wage cuts meant he wasn't pulling as many pints as he would like these days. Peggy had waited for her father to go to the meeting and her mother to pop out to Nanny Day's to collect some ironing before sneaking downstairs and out of the house, to go and take a look for herself. She pressed a ha'penny – her most precious gift from Old Uncle Dennis – into Eva's palm before she left the bedroom, warning her: 'Don't you dare tell!'

A thick fog hung in the night air. As she scurried along the greasy cobbles to her destination, she felt it creep down her throat and into her lungs. She knew she would get into terrible trouble if she was found out but the desire to hear the union leaders talk was overwhelming. She couldn't actually go into the pub, of course, but she planned to sneak a peek at what was going on through the doors or press her ear to the frosted glass.

A ruddy-faced man stood on a chair and shouted at the crowd, to call the meeting to order. There were a few cheers as he identified himself as a union leader from Bermondsey. Men stopped chattering and listened intently as he outlined the outrageous cuts imposed on the poor by the hated Means Test: 'Twenty-five shillings cut to six shillings, sixteen shillings reduced to ten shillings and sixpence. The worst case I know of was up North, where they cut it from twenty-six shillings to nothing.'

'Someone should lynch that bastard Pemberton!' came a voice from the darkest recesses of the pub.

'Brothers,' said the union leader, 'that is not the way. We will negotiate. We will protest. But it will be lawful.'

Peggy didn't hear the responses to that because she was distracted by someone pulling at her sleeve. She turned and saw that little pipsqueak Georgie Harwood from Kathleen's class.

'Get off me!' she said, brushing his arm aside.

'What are they saying?' he said, craning his neck to peer above the frosted glass.

'Get down!' said Peggy, reddening with annoyance. 'You are going to spoil everything. I am serious about this.'

'So am I,' said George, pushing himself so far forward that he threatened to tumble through the pub door. 'My dad is in there, you know. He will be speaking next.'

Peggy didn't reply but afforded him a bit more elbow room. It was only fair, as his dad was a trade union man. They listened to the list of areas where the Poor Law authorities were bending the rules to try to help those in need, much to the annoyance of the Government. Their eavesdropping was brought to an abrupt end by a voice booming in their ears: 'Well, well, what do we have here, then?'

They spun around and came face-to-face with a burly policeman. 'This is no place for children,' he said. 'Run along home.'

'But my dad is in there,' said George, earning himself a clip around the ear.

'Listen, sonny, I don't care if the King himself is in there, I am telling you to hop it, so I suggest you do just that. Now, hop it!'

Peggy grabbed George by the hand and started to pull him away. As she did so, she noticed more policemen, walking briskly, in pairs, coming down Belvedere Road. George was still protesting as she dragged him around the corner into Tenison Street, where they stopped under the dim glow of the street gas-lamp and kept watch on the pub.

Ten policemen gathered outside and then rushed through the doors, with their truncheons raised. There were shouts and the sound of breaking glass. Men spilt out into the street, fists flying, as the policemen battered them. In seconds, the crowd had surrounded Peggy and George at the top of Tenison Street.

'There's kids here!' one of the men shouted to a policeman. 'Back off!'

He was silenced by a blow to the side of his head from a passing officer: 'Take that back to Moscow, you red scum!'

Instinctively, Peggy grabbed George by the hand and started to run down Tenison Street but she hadn't gone more than ten yards before she heard the clatter of horses' hooves. She froze as the huge shapes loomed out of the darkness towards her. Policemen came cantering up the road on horses as big as anything she had seen pulling the brewer's cart. They rode straight into the retreating crowd of men, who were being beaten back by a line of policemen from the other end of the street.

'We're trapped!' said George breathlessly, as he flung himself out of the way and landed against a front door. Peggy didn't have time to react. She screamed as the flank of a passing horse struck her shoulder and knocked her to the floor. She tasted blood in her mouth as she lay on the cobbles and could now only see a tangle of legs and hear the shouts, as men brawled with each other in the dim gaslight. As she started to cry, she felt a pair of arms around her, pulling her to the safety of the doorstep. It was George.

He hammered on the front door, shouting, 'Please, let us in!' and it swung open.

A woman pulled them both inside and then barred the door with a chair, before shooing them into the scullery.

'What in God's name were you two doing out there?' she cried. 'Your mother will be livid!'

Peggy started to sob.

'It's all right, love,' said the woman, realizing that Peggy was hurt. 'I will get that cut cleaned up for you and we will get you home when this is all over. Aren't you Margaret's girl?'

'Yes,' she said, as her eyes darted about the room, taking in the clothes drying on an airer above the range, the half-eaten loaf on the table and little dog curled up on the floor, snoozing. It was a home much like her own. She put her fingers to her mouth. Her lip had swelled so much she felt like a circus clown. George held her hand as she rinsed her mouth out with salty water. It stung like hell.

It was a good hour before the street lay silent. Peggy was bundled up in a shawl and George and the woman walked her home.

Margaret screamed when she opened the door and saw Peggy's face. She hadn't even noticed she was missing because Eva had carefully stuffed pillows down the bed next to her and kept her promise not to tell. That would earn her little sister a belting, Peggy knew. Her father sat, ashen-faced, at the kitchen table. He was too angry and too shocked to speak. He nursed a cut on his forehead and a bruise was already blackening on his cheek.

'Get to bed, Peggy. We will deal with this in the morning,' he said.

He could have punished her there and then and she

wouldn't have fought him. But her father hadn't laid a finger on her for over a year. It was as if he felt she was too old for that now. Instead, he would refuse to speak to her for a week or ban her from reading the paper, which she found worse than being strapped, to be honest.

Only one person seemed to be in good spirits as the night drew to a close. George Harwood whistled his way back to Roupell Street in the dark. In his hand he carried a blue ribbon which had fallen from Peggy's hair as he rescued her from the battle of Tenison Street. He felt its softness between his fingers and vowed never to give it back until she kissed him.

6

Kathleen, March 1933

'Well, if she can't have a new dress for her first Holy Communion, it will bring shame on the entire family!'

As she rubbed sleep out of her eyes, Kathleen heard her mother's raised voice coming from the front room downstairs. She'd hated being away from her family when she was in hospital but at times like this, she wished she was back there. The rows between her parents were something she hadn't missed at all and, as she listened in the half-light of the dawn, she realized, with a stab of guilt, that she was the cause of it.

Her mother had promised her a brand-new special dress for her first Communion. The thought of that had kept her going while she was sick. She'd put up with the doctors endlessly listening to her chest and the treatments; there was a really embarrassing one where she had to stand in just her knickers in a room with the other children, wearing funny goggles, while the nurses turned on a big machine which made them all feel warm, like sunshine, because she didn't have enough vitamin D and the doctors said she needed more.

'Goddamn you, woman! Is there to be no end to the cost

of it all?' Dad's voice boomed through the rickety floor-boards of their bedroom. There was the sound of a slap, followed by a thud, and then crying. A few seconds later, the front door slammed.

Kathleen held her breath, unable to move. She glanced over at Eva, who was lying awake beside her. She must have heard it too. Peggy was still sleeping soundly in a single bed on the other side of the room. She got a bed all to herself because she was the eldest – which rankled with Kathleen, to be honest – and Mum always joked that she could sleep through an earthquake. Peg had been awake until late reading books by candlelight because after the fracas in Tenison Street, she'd been banned from looking at the paper, in case it put more ideas in her head about going on marches or to protest meetings.

Eva's hand found its way into hers. After what seemed like an eternity, Kathleen said: 'Shall we go and see?'

They crept downstairs and found their mother sitting at the little table in the scullery, with her head in her hands. She looked up when she heard them enter the room, and wiped her eyes on her nightdress. A mark was reddening on her cheek. 'Get back to bed, you two! It's still very early,' she said.

The girls didn't speak but went to her and she hugged them, crying as she did so. Eventually, she spoke. 'It was an accident. I tripped and fell. No point making a fuss. It is a just a silly thing; me being clumsy. It annoyed him, he's tired from working, that's all.'

Kathleen nodded and put her hand on her mum's shoulder.

'I don't need a new dress for Communion,' she said. 'I can use Peggy's old one.'

'That is not the point,' said Mum, with a note of harshness. 'You shall have a new dress. I shall see to it. Now, go upstairs and get some sleep and stop listening in to grown-up conversations!'

Kathleen climbed the stairs with a heavy heart. She had been so looking forward to the whole day; taking part in the Italian procession in Clerkenwell after the Communion at St Peter's, along with some of the other girls in her class, including her friend Nancy. Her real name was Annunziata, but their teacher couldn't pronounce that, so she was just known as Nancy. She had the most beautiful, thick, shiny hair which hung in ringlets without even needing rags and was getting a new dress specially made for her. Kathleen wouldn't look as pretty as Nancy now but she knew that asking for a new dress would only cause more trouble. She hadn't given a second thought to where the money for it was going to come from, let alone for the veil and gloves that she was supposed to wear. They always seemed to get by, to find the money somehow when it was needed and she had never questioned that.

Eva had gone very quiet. She went to the corner of the bedroom and pulled up a loose floorboard. The first light of dawn was just visible through the thin curtains at the window behind her. Eva eyed Kathleen for a moment as she spoke. 'If you tell about my secret hiding place, you will go to Hell and the Devil will get you and demons will stick red-hot pokers in your eyes.'

'I won't tell, I promise,' said Kathleen, crossing her fingers under the bedclothes, just in case, because it was always handy to have something to tell on Eva for.

'Swear on the life of our Lord Jesus.'

'I swear,' said Kathleen.

'Swear on Mary, Holy Mother of God,' said Eva.

'I swear on the Blessed Virgin Mary,' said Kathleen, still keeping her fingers crossed.

Eva pulled out one of Grandad's rusty old tobacco tins from her secret hiding place and opened it. It had a few coins in it – a shilling here, a thrupenny bit, a sixpence and some ha'pennies – but there was something else, folded up. Some paper. Eva took it out and unfolded it, to reveal not one but two red-brown ten-shilling notes. She lay them on the bedspread with great ceremony. Kathleen gasped. That was more money than she had ever seen in her life!

'Where did you get it, Eve?'

'Found it in the street near the Cut, didn't I?' she said, playing with the ends of her hair. 'I was saving up everything I find, to help buy you a piano.'

'But, Eve, that's just so . . . kind,' said Kathleen, who was looking at her sister in a new light. 'Let's show Mum, shall we?'

The girls stampeded back down the staircase.

'Mum, look, I found a quid!' said Eva, thrusting the notes towards her mother, who was finishing up a cup of tea. She had taken off her wedding ring and it lay on the table in front of her.

Their mother looked at the money, wide-eyed, and then back at Eva.

'Where on earth did you get this?'

The question hung in the air. Eva looked straight at her mother, without even blinking, and said: 'I found it in the street and picked it up and brought it home. I was keeping it for a piano for Kathleen.'

Mum stared at the wedding ring on the table in front of her. Then she crossed herself and raised her eyes to heaven. 'Dear Lord, thank you for giving me such a lucky, lucky child!'

She took the notes and clasped them, with tears in her eyes. 'Eva, you are the luckiest girl to find this for me now, when we need it most. Kathleen shall have her dress for church and Jim can have a new shirt too. I was going to pawn my ring and ask Nanny if she could help but I won't need to any more.'

She covered Eva with kisses and Kathleen hugged her sister so tightly, she thought she might break her. No one said anything else about Eva's miraculous find, least of all Kathleen, who was just delighted that she wouldn't have to wear Peggy's hand-me-downs on her big day.

Mum added, 'We won't mention this good fortune to your father. He might not understand. Let it just be our little secret.'

She was in a good mood for the rest of the day and hummed as she went about her work in the scullery and scrubbed at the front step with renewed vigour, so that it was gleaming by the time their father came home from work.

It was a beautiful April morning when Kathleen skipped up to the dressmaker's in the Cut, holding her mother's hand. Today was her final fitting before the Italian procession and her first Communion; the seamstress had been working on her dress for a whole month. It was waiting for her in the shop, hanging up in the little changing room at the back – which was basically just a cupboard full of rolls of material, with a curtain over the front. She felt butterflies in her stomach. There it was. The dress was white silk with a round neck and lace panels overlaid on the front, and a lace trim at the bottom. The sleeves were short and slightly puffed.

'Let me see your hands,' said the seamstress, before she handed the dress over to Kathleen to try it on. 'We don't want any mucky marks on it, do we?'

Kathleen pulled off her pinafore and took the dress off its hanger. She held it against herself and peered at her reflection in the changing-room mirror. She slipped the dress over her head, admiring the glide of the silk against her skin. She felt like a princess. Glancing down at her feet, she realized she still had her grubby socks on, so she pulled them off and chucked them on the floor. On the big day, she would be wearing a perfect little white pair of socks, with a lace trim to match her dress, her mother had said so.

The seamstress poked her head around the curtain, 'Shall I button you up?'

That made Kathleen feel really grown up. She turned around while the seamstress did up a row of little buttons which ran from the waist of the dress to the nape of her neck. The seamstress bent down and with a rustle, she produced a pair of white satin shoes from a nest of tissue paper in a cardboard box in the corner.

'I think they should fit you,' she said, with a smile. Kathleen slipped her feet into them, like Cinderella. The seamstress popped out of the changing room for a couple of seconds and returned with a lace veil and a headdress of silk flowers in white. Kathleen gasped. It was prettier and longer than the one her sister Peggy had worn for her Communion. She'd be spitting feathers when she saw it! With expert fingers, the seamstress arranged the veil on her head and topped it off with the headdress. It pinched a bit, but Kathleen didn't mind.

'Now, shall we show your mum?'

The curtain was pulled back and Mum stood there, with tears in her eyes. 'You look just beautiful,' she said. 'Nanny will be so proud of you. You really are just like a princess!'

Kathleen twirled about in front of the mirror and even gave a curtsey to an imaginary Prince Charming. The seamstress was already over at the till, writing up the bill. She glanced up at Mum. 'I put all that extra lace detail on the dress, just as you asked,' she said. 'It was a lot of work but I think you'll agree, she is going to outshine everybody.'

Mum nodded and opened her purse. She carefully took out the folded ten-shilling notes, smoothed them and placed them on the counter. 'It's all there,' she said.

'But you haven't paid for the shoes yet,' said the seamstress, tucking her pencil behind her ear.

'Of course, we'll have those too,' said Mum, forcing a tight little smile. 'But can you let me have them on tick?'

'No problem,' said the seamstress. 'I will just put it in my book. Pay me back a shilling a week, all right?'

Kathleen watched as her mother swallowed hard and opened her purse. She pulled out her last shilling. 'Of course,' she said.

Kathleen looked down at her shoes. They were so pretty but her mum had given her last penny and then some, just so she would have a day to remember in the church. Should she say that she didn't need them after all? Kathleen glanced up at her reflection. She did look just like a princess and the shoes completed the outfit, didn't they? So much of their life was bought on the never-never, it was just the way things were.

Her mother came over and took one last look at her.

'Kathleen, you are just such a little beauty,' she whispered.

Kathleen knew then that it would be wrong to go without. It was her job to look pretty, to make everyone in the family proud and keep up appearances before everyone, even God.

The seamstress bustled over, smiling, and helped her out of the dress, which was put back on its hanger until tomorrow. Kathleen would go to the shop and get dressed there, rather than risk the outfit being ruined at home. As they were leaving the shop, she spotted her friend Nancy and her mum making their way to the dressmaker's. Kathleen gave her a little wave. 'Just wait till tomorrow!' she said, under her breath.

Kathleen stood at the altar of St Peter's Church, in front of the priest, bowed her head and pressed her palms together, as if she were praying. A line of girls and boys, including her brother Jim, snaked its way down the aisle behind her, right to the back of the church. The smell of incense filled the air and made her feel quite giddy.

The Mass had lasted forever, so long, in fact, that her stomach had started to rumble. She'd spent ages studying all the beautiful pictures on the walls, the arches and the marble columns. All the gold everywhere made it look like a palace. Every pew was filled with people who had come to see their children take their first Holy Communion. She had been chosen to go up first to receive the sacrament, much to Nancy's disgust. At the priest's signal, she stepped forwards and held her hands together, palm up, in front of her, as she had been told to do. He placed a little round wafer into her hand and she popped it into her mouth. She paused for a second, waiting to see if she felt different now she was really Catholic but she didn't have much time to contemplate before she heard Nancy whisper in her ear: 'Move on, you've had your turn!'

Kathleen would have said something back but it wouldn't have been very Christian to do so, so she ignored her, just like the Lord Jesus would have wanted her to. Kathleen turned and smiled at her mum, Peggy and Nanny Day, who were there in the second row of pews, beaming back at her. Only her father was missing, as he couldn't get time off from the factory. There hadn't been enough room for Frankie and Eva to fit in as well, so they were outside with Old Uncle Dennis, mingling in a huge throng of people waiting for the procession for the Feast of Our Lady of Mount Carmel to start.

After the last of the children had taken the sacrament,

the priest made his way to the front door of the church, where he released three doves, to the cheers of the crowd. There were so many people lining the steps and along the road on both sides that there was barely room to move.

The girls, still wearing their veils, gathered in a little gaggle in the vaulted porch, waiting to see who would be given the honour of walking behind the priest. Kathleen looked up and was admiring the blue ceiling studded with gold stars when she felt a hand on her shoulder. The priest had picked her! She felt like the star of her very own show. There were a few murmurs of protest from some of the Italian mothers, not least of all Nancy's, but they were soon silenced by the glares of Nanny Day and her mother, who said loudly: 'She's as much right as anybody. She's Catholic, ain't she?'

Kathleen grinned from ear to ear as they set off up the narrow street, which was festooned with garlands of flowers running from one house to another, changing it from a grimy London street to a kind of paradise. Mothers held their babies up at open windows and cheered as she walked past. This corner of Clerkenwell lay less than a mile from Lambeth, across the water, and it was every bit as poor as her community but it was home to the Italian immigrants, who had made it their own, with their bars and shops. Some people were scared to go there, saying it was a den of thieves, but it held no fear for her or her family because they were all at school with the Italian kids and counted them as friends.

She spotted Frankie on Uncle Dennis's shoulders and returned his wave. The priest walked in front, swinging incense, and she walked immediately behind him, carrying a little posy of flowers. Behind her came the statue of Our Lady of Mount Carmel, carried aloft by six men. It was garlanded with roses in pink, yellow and cream, as well as some white lilies around the base. The combination of the scent of the flowers with the incense and the crowds made Kathleen feel she was walking on air.

Behind the statue came the children, some carrying banners from their churches, and behind them were other statues of saints. They made their way up Back Hill and on to some big roads, where mounted police had stopped the traffic to allow them through. The cheering and waving and clapping seemed to go on forever, as everyone came out of their houses to see the spectacle. Eventually, they made their way back to the church where Mum and Nanny Day hugged her as she reunited with the rest of her brothers and sisters. 'This is the best bit,' said Jim. 'Let's go and eat.'

They walked through Little Italy, down the warren of backstreets, where the most delicious smells of cooking were wafting through the air. Italian grannies, dressed all in black, had set out little stalls selling cakes, and sausages were sizzling in frying pans over open fires at the side of the road. Women were stirring big barrels of a thick porridge. Kathleen understood a few words of Italian from the girls at school but the women spoke so quickly that it took three goes to understand that they were offering her something called 'polenta'. She was just about to try her luck at a little coconut shy when the red-faced bosomy figure of their neighbour Mrs Avens hove into view, pushing her way through the crowd.

'It's James,' she said, grabbing their mother by the arm. 'You need to come straight away. There's been an accident at work.'

The party atmosphere ended as quickly as if someone had burst a balloon. They caught the bus back across the river and ran the last hundred yards to home. To her horror, Kathleen realized that her little satin shoes were now stained black with dirt from the road. When they got to the house, their father lay in bed in the front room – which was something the kids had never seen before. He was always up early before they woke and was the last to get to bed at night. His right hand was bandaged and all the colour had drained from his face.

'I'm sorry,' was all he could say, when he saw them all. Tears were rolling down his cheeks.

Mum rushed to him. 'My God, what's happened?'

'My finger. It was the band saw at work. I lost my finger . . .'

Kathleen ran to hug her father and he held her in his embrace. Looking down, she saw that blood had seeped through his bandages, staining her perfect white fairy-tale dress with flecks of crimson.

7

Eva, May 1933

A gloom settled over the house in the week following her dad's accident. He sat for hours, brooding, at the table in the scullery while her mother did her best to keep the family going, working all the hours that God sent and then probably a few more on top of that.

The bloodied stump where he had cut his finger off became infected and he cursed as Nanny Day put iodine on it or prepared little baths of hot salty water to try to make it better. After a fortnight off, her father went up to the factory and came back in even worse spirits.

'I can't have my old job back,' he told Mum. 'There's no work for me there now as I am. They needed my skills as a carpenter and I can't manage at that with my finger gone.'

Eva watched as her mother sank to her knees on the scullery floor and began to sob into her apron. 'We'll be out on the streets!'

'I won't let that happen,' said Dad, putting his arm around her.

Eva shut the front door quietly and walked to the corner shop on Belvedere Road. Her mind was made up. She'd done it once before to try to get Kathleen that piano but now her family really needed her.

The little bell rang as she pushed open the door.

The shopkeeper was half-deaf anyway, so he probably wouldn't hear her but she shouted out, 'Hello?'

His greying thatch of hair appeared from around the back of the shop. 'What can I get you?'

'Mum needs some candles,' said Eva. 'We're running out again.'

'I'll have to go downstairs to the basement for them,' said the shopkeeper. Eva was counting on that. As soon as she heard his footsteps creaking down the back stairs, she darted around to the till and yanked it open. There was no lock to stop her. Another ten-bob note would do, for now.

She grabbed the money, slammed the till shut, praying that the little 'ting' it made wouldn't be heard in the basement, and was back around the other side of the counter in a flash. 'I've changed me mind!' she yelled, making for the door and smacking straight into Mrs Davies, who was coming through it to get her daily update on the comings and goings in the neighbourhood.

'Why are you in such a rush?' she said, grabbing Eva by the arm.

'None of your business!' said Eva, breaking free and running off down the street. She tucked the money safely into the pocket of her pinafore and skipped around to Nanny Day's. Eva knew she couldn't just hand the cash over in front of her father, who would be bound to grill her about where she'd found it. She'd wait for a quiet moment later on and slip it into her mum's grateful hand.

Old Uncle Dennis was busy whittling away at bits of wood, making a toy cot for her and Kathleen when she got round there. Every few seconds or so, he would cough, the rattling cough which seemed as much a part of his personality as his smile.

'How's your dad?' said Nanny Day, pouring Eva a cup of tea.

Eva loved it that Nanny treated her a bit more like a grown-up.

'He's not going to work at the factory no more,' said Eva quietly. She understood, even at her age, that this was disastrous news.

'Oh, Jesus, Mary and Joseph,' said Nanny Day, sitting down and crossing herself. 'Tell your mother I will come around later. We'll have to see what can be done.'

Eva was just about to badger Grandad for some of the bread he was toasting over the fire when there was a loud knock at the door.

Eva heard Old Uncle Dennis say, 'What on earth do you want with our Eva? She's only a kid.'

Nanny Day stood up, looked at her, grabbed her by the arm and motioned for her to get under her long skirts, which reached right to the floor. Eva crouched down into a little ball, hugging her knees, scrunched in between Nanny Day's shiny little boots.

'Well, Eamon,' said Nanny Day. 'This is a surprise. What brings you to my door?'

'I'm looking for your Eva,' came the reply. 'I need to have a word with her about a very serious matter.'

'Fine words for a policeman,' said Nanny Day, with a

laugh. 'Are you PC O'Mahony now or can I still call you Eamon? She's a young girl, not a criminal. How's your mother keeping?'

'Oh, she's fine. Back troubling her but she's all right,' said the policeman.

'It's just I've not seen her in church lately,' said Nanny Day, before he could say anything more. 'And she always used to be such a regular attender. The priest mentioned it to me himself.'

'Well, it can be difficult for her to get about . . .'

'Much like our good Lord Jesus, struggling with the cross up to Calvary, I imagine.'

He sighed. 'I do need to see Eva to have a word. There's some money going missing from shops around here and a few people have noticed she's often about when it does. The kids in the street said she was here.'

'Well now, Eamon, I can't imagine for a minute that my Eva would be stealing anything, so you be careful about making those accusations. Particularly because I remember a certain little boy breaking windows in the school not so long ago and he was never caught, was he, Eamon?'

'I see your point,' he said. 'But I won't be able to turn a blind eye to it for much longer if it keeps happening.'

'You've had your say. Dennis will see you out,' said Nanny Day curtly. PC O'Mahony knew when he was beaten and left without saying another word.

Once the front door had banged shut, Eva emerged from her hiding place. Nanny Day sat back down in her favourite rocking chair and looked at Eva.

'Well?' she said. 'What have you got to say for yourself?'

Eva looked at the floor and then back at Nanny Day. 'I ain't done nothing wrong,' she said. 'I swear on the life of our Lord Jesus. It's people making up stories about me.'

Nanny rocked back and forth for a moment and then she said, 'Eva, people like us don't have much and if we start coming by good fortune, questions will be asked, so you'd better have some pretty good answers ready. Let he who is without sin cast the first stone, as our good Lord said. I know there's many round here shouldn't be casting any stones, but the point is they will. Now, you'd better pray Eamon O'Mahony hasn't been knocking on your door or your father will have your guts for garters. Go on home now and tell your mother I will be around later.'

When Eva got back home, she was sent straight upstairs, as Mum was entertaining another altogether unexpected visitor: Mr Pemberton from the Poor Law. Kathleen and Peggy were huddled in the boys' bedroom at the back, with their ears to the floorboards, straining to hear what was being said.

'Well, you never can tell, Mrs Fraser, when bad luck will strike, and I was very sorry to hear about your husband's accident, despite his behaviour towards me.'

'It has come as a terrible blow to us all,' came their mother's reply. 'I know what happened between you and James should never have happened but, believe me, it was in heat of the moment and he didn't mean you any harm. He was just trying to help that poor girl Mary from down the road. And now he has been laid off from the factory, we will be needing to make a claim for temporary relief.'

'I'm a reasonable man, Mrs Fraser,' said Mr Pemberton. 'I know you are a good, hard-working family and you have never been to the Poor Law before, but I will need full details of all your income and any savings and you know under the Means Test we are now very strict. I can see you keep a good house and with five children; it can't be easy for you . . .'

'I'm very grateful, Mr Pemberton.'

'Does your husband know you have asked for assistance?'

Her mother's reply was almost a whisper, so quiet that Eva could barely hear it. 'No. At least, not yet.'

'I see,' said Mr Pemberton. 'Well, I can't take matters further until he agrees to it.'

The ten-shilling note was burning a hole in Eva's pocket. She knew enough about her father's pride to realize that there was no way he'd have Mr Pemberton under his roof, let alone accept assistance from the Poor Law. Her mother needed her help more than ever now. It didn't matter that the cozzers were on to her; they'd have to catch her at it, and Eva was more determined than ever that this should not be the case.

'I'm going out,' she told Kathleen, heading back down the stairs and quietly lifting the latch on the front door.

Eva had heard all about Liz English from some of the older boys in the street but she'd never actually met her. 'Lumps and Bumps' they called her, or 'Lumps' for short, because she was always falling down drunk or getting a clip around the ear from the law for making a nuisance of herself. But behind her boozy breath and blackened teeth lay a cunning mind when it came to getting rid of nicked stuff for a good price.

The Feathers pub up on the Waterloo Road was her usual haunt, at least until she got chucked out for pestering the punters for a drink too many. Darkness was falling as Eva made her way there. On cold nights, Lumps liked to warm her bottom in front of the fire, making quite a spectacle of herself, because she didn't wear any knickers and would just lift her long skirts and do one cheek at a time. Tonight, in the dusk of a warm May evening, she was lolling about outside, bartering with some kids from the other side of the Cut about a case they had nicked from Waterloo Station. Her bleary eyes fixed on Eva.

'What d'you want, then?' she said, running her fingers through her bird's-nest hair. 'Not seen you around here before, have I?'

'No,' said Eva. 'But I'm going to be one of your regulars from now on.'

Lumps screeched with laughter and slapped one of the lads on the back, quite hard.

'Are you, now? And what's your speciality? Hoisting? Dipping?'

'Tell me what you want and I'll get it for you,' said Eva. 'But it's got to be a good price for me or it ain't worth my while.'

Lumps seized her by the collar. 'You ain't one of them little spies sent by the cozzers, are you? 'Cos if you are, I'll break your scrawny neck. I ain't going back to Holloway.'

Eva wriggled free. 'No, of course I ain't. I'm new to it,

that's all – but look, here's what I lifted today and I can get more.'

She produced her ten-shilling note and then snatched it away into her pocket again, before Lumps could lay a blackened finger on it.

'Quite the thief, aren't we?' said Lumps and Bumps, smiling. 'But keep doing that and you will bring the law to my door. Shopkeepers notice when their till takings are down a few quid. Cigarettes are nice and easy, though. There's always a demand for them. We can sell them on cheap in the pubs. I will take half of what you get.'

'That don't sound very fair,' said Eva.

Lumps grabbed her again. She had a wild look in her eyes as she spoke and the stench of her breath was almost overpowering. 'You don't argue with me, see? You ain't in no position to bargain with Old Liz. You want to get into my game, you play by my rules.'

Eva was shaking inside but she didn't show it. 'All right, I'll play by your rules. But you will see, I'm not like the others. I'm the best thief there is this side of Waterloo.'

Lumps let her go with a laugh. 'The best thief!' She staggered back inside the pub.

Eva trudged home. What was she letting herself in for? Stealing a bit of money to help her mother was one thing, or nicking a bit of fruit now and again, but Liz English was a fence, a proper part of the thief's game. Her father would beat the living daylights out of her, just for talking to the likes of Lumps. She suddenly got the urge to cuddle up in bed with Kathleen and talk about their dolls and their new cot from Uncle Dennis. But when she got home, her parents were arguing again.

'Treat me like a cripple, would you?' shouted Dad. 'Go behind my back? I'll teach you!'

Eva covered her ears and ran upstairs. She peered out of the back bedroom window. Her dad was standing over her mum.

She was on her knees now in the back yard, her hands covering her head as the blows rained down on her. 'I'll give you the Poor Law!'

Eva knew then, she had no choice.

8

Peggy, August 1933

'For God's sake, Peggy, I'm desperate! How much longer are you going to be in there?' Kathleen hammered on the door of the outside lavvy, hoping to dislodge her sister Peggy from her throne, but to no avail.

'Not much longer,' said Peggy. 'Now, go away.' She was spending at least half an hour in the evenings in the loo, and sometimes in the mornings too. But her time in that grim, damp outside lavatory was well spent, she reckoned.

Nobody realized, but she was becoming quite an expert at piecing together the cut-up bits of newspaper that their mother put on a nail out there. It was a bit like solving a jigsaw puzzle. She liked to get in there early, before her brothers, because once they had been there was not much chance of getting enough of the story to make sense of it. In the past few weeks she'd gleaned quite a bit of information and read the latest stories on the Means Test. From what she had managed to gather, some of the Poor Law authorities which had shown kindness were now being forced to reduce benefits further and there were rumblings in the workplace about stopping anyone with Communist sympathies from holding a union position. Unemployment was rising and it was expected that there would be three million out of work by the end of the year.

She now saw first-hand the dreadful effect of that, as her dad joined the men milling about by the shop looking for work. He had found something to do, minding the carts for one of the fruit and veg stalls up in Covent Garden for a family who lived around the corner. But it was just a few days here and there and paid pennies, most of which he seemed to spend drowning his sorrows in the pub. He wasn't like the father she knew and respected any more. And the bruises and black eyes suffered by her mother seemed to be getting more frequent and harder for everyone to ignore, especially the neighbours.

It was as if a certain level of argy-bargy between married couples was to be expected but Dad was just about crossing the line now. She'd seen the looks he'd been getting from Mrs Davies and Mrs Avens, who used to smile and say 'Good morning' to him. Now they shot him filthy glances and tutted as they went off to the communal laundry.

Peggy was more than ready to leave school. She knew that her family needed her to start earning, and with that in mind, she'd applied for a job at the Post Office. She expected to hear back any day now and she was trying to walk taller and be more like the girls who headed off to work in the factories, rather than the schoolgirls playing in the street.

Yet the thought of not learning more from her teacher, Miss Price, weighed heavily on her, and there was something, or rather someone else, she would miss too, although she never spoke of it. In the months since the battle of Tenison Street, she'd found an ally in her quest for knowledge in the shape of George Harwood. He regularly met her outside the school gates and they would dally along the streets towards her home while he told her all about the latest news from the shop floor, as well as anything he had managed to memorize from his father's newspapers. George's dad spoke very highly of a bloke called Wal Hannington out of Camden Town who had even been jailed for a year for his Communist views. George thought that was heroic but Peggy wasn't so sure.

Kathleen had spotted them once, walking home deep in conversation, and had run past, yelling, 'Georgie loves Peggy!' which was so embarrassing and silly. George blushed beetroot and Peggy had pretended not to notice.

Sometimes they would wander along by the river to look at the barges but Peggy didn't really like going down there too much because of the brasses who plied their trade in the murky alleyways. On more than one occasion they'd chanced across a punter with his trousers round his ankles and been told to clear off, in no uncertain terms. That time it was Peggy's turn to blush. George was very gallant: 'Don't worry, Peg, I will protect you.'

'I don't need protecting!' she said, shrugging his hand off her arm. But secretly, somewhere inside, she quite liked having George around. He wasn't like the other boys of his age and certainly was nothing like her brothers. He was more serious and he had lovely clear blue eyes. He had been reading a lot of books lately about Communism.

'It ain't all bad,' he said. 'In fact, it makes sense for folks like us.'

George had lent her a book to read on the subject. She hid it under her cardigan and stuffed it down the gap between the bed and the wall in case Mum saw it, because that surely would make her go spare. Filling her head with silly ideas, was what she'd call it, and that didn't seem right when the family had real troubles of its own. Her mother was looking thinner than ever and spent so much time crying quietly that her eyes seemed to be permanently red-ringed and her face all blotchy.

Peggy watched as her mother persuaded the rent collector for one more week's grace. 'You will have to pay next week,' he said, putting a black mark next to their name in his rent book. 'You know I've been reasonable, Mrs Fraser, because you are good tenants, but you are working and I hear that Mr Fraser is doing some odd jobs up at Covent Garden, so you have got to find a way to put some money aside for the rent from now on.' That meant they were three weeks behind in total now. Peggy hadn't worked out how they were still surviving at all but she knew that Eva had something to do with it. She had caught her stuffing a few shillings into her mother's pinny and had seen the smile on Mum's face when Eva came through the door.

'I'm going to get work, Mum. I'll find out what is happening at the Post Office,' she said, laying her hand on her mother's shoulder.

Just then, Nanny Day bustled in. 'Well, I prayed for a

miracle and, Margaret, I think the good Lord has delivered it for us,' she said.

Mum looked up, disbelief etched on her fine features.

'Grandad was on his shift as night-watchman and heard that the boiler man has been given the heave-ho, so he put James forward and the foreman said he can have a try-out, starting next week!'

'Oh, thank God!' said Mum, clapping her hands together. 'Peggy, go up to the Post Office and see what is happening with your job and then get up to Covent Garden and tell your father the good news.'

But before she could leave, Dad came through the door, with good news of his own, waving a postal order for ten pounds.

'It's compensation, for my finger,' he said, as the whole scullery erupted into a scene of jubilation. 'I can't believe it but they have seen us right in the end.'

'Whatever shall we do with it?' said Mum.

'We'll pay off our debts to the rent first,' said Dad, hugging her. Then he looked at his wife. She'd never had so much as a day off work in years. There was still a mark on her cheek from their last fight and the sight of it made him want to die of shame. That wasn't who he wanted to be.

'Let's spend it,' he said. 'We're going to have a little holiday.'

The days in the run-up to their trip to Southend-on-Sea felt like Christmas, only better.

Peggy accompanied her mother to Oxford Street, where they went into the big shops, Marshall and Snelgrove, and

Dickins and Jones, and bought new clothes for everybody.
She felt herself blushing as the shop assistants fussed
around her. Some places, like Selfridges, were full of snooty
women who eyed them with suspicion, until her mother
showed them the colour of her money.

They got a printed cotton dress each for Peggy and
Kathleen, with little flowers and sprigs of green on it, while
Mum had a new blouse and a plaid skirt. Eva had a white
dress with a frill around the bottom, which she was very
pleased with, and the boys got new shorts, shirts and a
little jacket each. To finish the girls' outfits, Mum took ages
choosing hats. Peggy gawped at herself in the full-length
mirrors. She wasn't used to seeing what she looked like
from so many angles. Wealthy people, who could afford to
shop in places like this, must be quite vain, she decided. In
the end, after much discussion with the sales assistant,
Mum chose knitted berets because they were practical as
well as stylish, apparently.

The whole street knew of their going away and there
were a few envious glances and the odd snide comment
about wasting money when others could barely afford to
eat, but Peggy ignored them. It was their good fortune and
why shouldn't they go to the seaside like posh folks, just
for once?

Getting everybody ready and out of the door on time
was like organizing an army. They got up early, so early
that they could hear the costermongers wheeling their
barrows out of the arches around the back of their street,
whistling their way along. Mum smiled more than she had
in ages, even when she noticed that Frankie had a proper

shiner, which he had picked up from fighting again. That worried her mum sick because of his head injury but she knew, as they all did, that they couldn't change him. It just seemed to be in his nature, the rough and tumble of the street. Eva tried to take the blame for it, in case Dad decided to hand out one of his beltings. But today was a happy day, a holiday, so he just shook his head, ruffled Frank's hair and went back to sipping his scalding-hot tea, while the other kids ran pell-mell around the house with the excitement of the trip.

Mum carefully packed up a carpet bag with some fruit and some margarine sandwiches, which she had made the night before and wrapped in brown paper. Peggy watched as her mother peered at herself in Dad's little shaving mirror, smoothing stray strands of hair away from her face, before putting on her new beret. She was enjoying the preparation of it all, the fact that she didn't have to go out and scrub floors for once, Peggy could see that. Peggy had never really thought of her mum as pretty but in that moment, she thought she was properly beautiful.

It was a good day to get out of town because with the warmer days of July well under way, the river was starting to smell: the familiar, cloying stench. As they caught a bus across the water, Peggy watched the boatmen working the rubbish barges, their shirtsleeves rolled up to reveal strong forearms, pulling and yanking at the city's junk with their hooks. That had to be one of the worst jobs in the world, she thought.

Settling down, all seven of them on the bus, Peggy realized that they had rarely, if ever, been out together as a family because one of her parents was always out at work. Frankie and Eva were the most excited and by the time they reached Fenchurch Street Station they were both starving hungry and demanding a bite of the margarine sandwiches. Mum shooed their little fingers out of her carpet bag, telling them to wait until they were on the train.

As they made their way into the station, the noise and hissing of the steam engines was almost deafening. Peggy gave up trying to make herself heard over the din. There was a bit of a crush at the ticket barrier, as half of London seemed to be having a day out like them but they waited their turn and found their way onto the platform. Once Frank saw the steam train, with its shiny, bright-green engine, he forgot all about his hunger pangs.

Dad was spruced up in his best blue serge suit with a little trilby hat, which he carefully placed in the luggage rack above their heads. He and Mum gave each other a little squeeze. It was the most affection that Peggy had ever seen between them and as the train got under way, she watched as her father placed his hand on her mother's lap. She couldn't help but wonder what life would be like if they didn't have money worries. Would there still be fights and arguments? She drove herself half dizzy trying to work that out, as the glum little houses of London gave way to the countryside, whizzing past the window. There were open fields and small farmhouses – so much space compared to their little back-to-backs in London. No wonder everyone liked to go to Kent to go hopping. It was a different world.

Peggy pressed her face to the glass to get a better view, just as Kathleen steamed it up with her breath and drew a little love heart. With a wicked glint in her eye, she wrote 'G loves P' inside it, before Peggy swept her sleeve across it and obliterated it, knocking Kathleen in the process.

'Stop it, you two!' tutted Mum, 'You're worse than Frankie and Eva!' Kathleen poked her tongue out at Peggy, who pretended not to notice but vowed to get even later.

After their sandwiches, there were games of I-spy, but when they got bored of that Frankie gave everyone a fright halfway through the journey by sticking his head out of the window. When Mum pulled him back in, his face was blackened with soot and she spent the rest of the trip wiping his face clean with her handkerchief, much to Eva's amusement.

The smell of salty air was the first thing Peggy noticed when they stepped off the train at Southend, and the cry of the seagulls. It was so refreshing after the choking smog of London, Peggy felt she had been dunked in an ice-cold bath. They joined the crowds thronging towards the sea-front, with everyone dressed up in their best clothes.

'Stay close together,' said Mum. 'And by that, I mean: Frankie and Eva, no running off!'

Peggy walked a few paces behind her parents and her brothers and sisters, indulging a daydream that she was here with George Harwood, and maybe even had a pair of fashionable sunglasses like the little gaggles of ladies she saw bustling along together, sharing jokes. She looked down at her cotton dress and suddenly felt rather childish and unsophisticated, with her hair in bunches rather than waves or curls. On her feet, she wore flat, white sandals. She longed to wear heels like the older women, who seemed to tower over her, although she was not small for her age.

The family made their way down Pier Hill, past the grand facade of the Royal Hotel and a huge statue of Queen Victoria. Jim made everyone hoot with laughter by suggesting that Her Majesty was pointing the way to the public toilets, rather than out to sea. Frankie and Eva couldn't wait to get in the water; they dashed ahead down Marine Parade and were on the beach with their shoes and socks off by the time Peggy and Kathleen had caught up with them. Mum and Dad hired a couple of deckchairs and Jim went off to buy a bucket and spade. Peggy took the two youngest to the seashore. She wasn't afraid of water – she'd learned to swim in the Thames in the hot London summers. There was just one problem – the tide was out and the sea seemed to be a mile away in the distance.

Kathleen looked at the horizon and changed her mind, sensing that walking all that way might be too much for her. She turned and started to trudge back towards Mum and Dad. Peggy called after to her to see that she was all right, and Kathleen smiled and waved her off. The trio set off across the sand and soon found themselves sinking in mud which squidged between their toes. Peggy didn't mind too much and neither did Frankie or Eva. The excitement of getting to the sea kept them going, through little clumps of seaweed with crabs scurrying about, as the wind whipped through their hair and salt dried on their lips. Twenty minutes later, they finally reached the sea and dipped their toes in. It was freezing! But the thrill of seeing such a wide ocean, with the horizon stretching for miles in both directions, made up for it. Frankie and Eva splashed about, shrieking with laughter while Peggy kept a watchful eye and did her best not to get her dress wet. In the distance, she could see Mum waving at her so they set off for the long trudge back to the shore, with the wind blowing a gale behind them all the way, turning their legs blue with cold.

Jim had busied himself building a sandcastle, which Frankie promptly trod on, creating a bit of an argument. Peggy watched her father taking it all in from his deckchair. He smiled a thin smile and seemed too exhausted to intervene and stop the banter between his two sons. Peggy realized, with a guilty pang, that this must be the first real sit-down he had enjoyed in years.

Mum fussed over Kathleen's hair, which had blown every which way, and when the battle with the elements proved too much, she declared it was time for something to eat. Sand had got right in between Peggy's toes and no matter how hard she rubbed, she couldn't get the gritty grains out and her skin felt tight with the salt from the sea as they strolled down to find a pie and mash shop.

A small girl in the most beautiful embroidered dress and a coat with velvet edging and a little cloche hat smiled at Peggy as they wandered past. She had her leg in a caliper and walked with a pronounced limp as she held on to her father's hand. He was a well-dressed gentleman and looked a bit like their doctor. 'Polio,' Peggy's mum whispered in her ear. 'Poor mite. Don't stare, Peg.'

It wasn't the first time Peggy had seen a cripple, of course – she'd seen other kids who were lame – but there was something about that little girl, with her sweet smile, which made Peggy feel lucky, very lucky, to be healthy even if they weren't rich.

She turned to Kathleen, who had colour in her cheeks for the first time in months. 'Are you enjoying yourself, Kath?'

Kathleen nodded. 'I want to see the animals in the zoo after dinner.'

Peggy gave her hand a little squeeze. 'We will.' She forgave her for the silly teasing on the train about George Harwood. Peggy was the big sister, the grown-up, and it was her responsibility to live up to that role, she could see that now.

The nearest place to eat was a shop with black and white tiles on the walls and little tables and chairs with legs made of tubular steel which screeched on the floor when they sat down. It served tinned sausages and mash, which tasted as if the spuds had been boiled in seawater. But the sea air had made them all starving hungry so they wolfed it down. Ordinarily, Peggy would never have dreamed of asking for a pudding but as they were on holiday today and she'd spotted an ice cream shop along the prom, she asked her dad and was rewarded with some coins to go and buy a vanilla cone for everyone. It tasted like heaven, there was no other word for it, and as they held their cones and tried to stop the ice cream melting on to their fingers, they watched a Punch and Judy show in a little theatre right on the beach.

The next stop was the amusement park, the Kursaal, which, as Kathleen had hoped, also had a little zoo. The big attraction was not a live animal but a vast dead blue whale, which even behind its glass case stank of the chemicals the management poured over it to stop it rotting. The boys spent ages looking at that so Peggy took Kathleen outside to see the real animals: sheep, some ostriches, a forlorn-looking bear called Jock, a hyena, and a lion and lioness. Dad wouldn't let them go on the big ride, the Caterpillar, because it made the girls' skirts fly up, which he said wasn't decent, so they decided to go for a walk out along the pier instead. That was quite a walk, nearly a mile out to sea, with the wind buffeting them all. Kathleen was pale by the time they reached the end of the pier and the grey waters washed beneath them, so Mum said they should all get the little electric train back to the promenade.

The town clock struck four by the time they made it back and the boys were hungry again, so they made a final stop at the cockle stall, picking the little lumps of salty seafood out with a pin as they walked back to the station. The juices oozed through the straw bag and on to their fingers and Mum had quite a job mopping everyone with her handkerchief to make them respectable again before they boarded the train back to London.

As the carriage rocked its way along the tracks and sleep filled her eyes, Peggy dreamed of staying in Southend forever, watching the fashionable women parading up and down the seafront and men casting admiring glances. In her heart, she knew she would feel as out of place as one of those caged animals in the zoo. She belonged in the backstreets of Waterloo and her chats with Georgie Harwood were enough, for now.

When she got home, there was a letter waiting on the doormat. It was addressed to her and stamped on the back with the letters GPO.

She tore it open with eager little fingers. Peggy turned to her parents: 'I've got a job!'

9

Kathleen, October 1933

'They need to know their Irish roots, and now you have a bit of money to spare for the train fare, what's wrong with that?' said Nanny Day, wrapping cheese sandwiches as big as doorstops in brown paper. 'It will do us all the world of good.'

Dad knew it was pointless arguing with his mother-in-law. She had waited years to go and visit her brother and his family, and now his own misfortune had provided an opportunity, he couldn't deny her – but he wasn't happy about it. One trip away was enough to set the neighbour-hood gossips ablaze, so Lord only knew what two trips barely a month apart would do. The front door banged shut as he left, signalling his disapproval.

Kathleen skipped downstairs. She was beside herself with excitement. Nanny Day had been promising for ages that she would take her up to Hertfordshire to meet her Irish relatives. The only downside was that Eva and Frankie had to come along too. They could usually both be relied upon to play up but Nanny Day wouldn't stand for any nonsense. Kathleen had already decided that she, at least, would be good as gold. Jim, her twin, wasn't coming because he had a football match for the school. Peggy would normally keep them all in order but she was out at work at her new job.

Mother had put rags in Kathleen's hair last night, as usual. She stuck a finger through one of her curls and played with it a bit. When she was a star in the West End, she'd probably have her own private hairdresser with real curlers, not rags. She'd go everywhere in a big black motor car and have her own driver. For now, she'd have to make do with a trip on the Underground to get to King's Cross Station, which was pretty exciting, as she'd never been there before.

Nanny Day had put on her best clothes for the occasion: a freshly starched and ironed white blouse buttoned to the neck, with a lace collar, and her best hat, made of straw with tiny flowers on it. Kathleen watched as she put on her little fob watch, which hung on a gold chain, reaching almost to her waist. That usually only came out for trips to church on Sundays and when the priest called around for tea. Nanny Day wore the same long black skirt as she always did, which reached right to the floor, so that only the tips of her polished boots were showing. She took ages to do them up, using a little hook with a bone handle to do up the row of buttons which ran the up the sides, grumbling as she did so.

'Let's hope we don't have to walk too far today,' she said. 'Me feet are already killing me.' Nanny Day stuffed their lunch into her carpet bag, fixed her hat with a hatpin and turned to the children. 'Well then, let's go.'

They caught the tram to the Elephant and Castle and

waited while Nanny bought her ticket for threepence before going down into the Underground to catch the Northern Line to King's Cross. The Tube had a funny smell to it – a bit like stale cigarettes – but Kathleen didn't mind that because it was so exciting whizzing along below ground. She was fascinated by the people on the Tube and got told off twice by Nanny Day for staring. She couldn't help it. The women were wearing such nice dresses and cloche hats. They had make-up on too, which was something she had never seen her mother wear. One of them carried a little lap dog in her arms. Kathleen decided she would have one of those too, when she was famous.

Frankie mucked about on the escalator when they got to King's Cross by trying to run down it, much to the annoyance of men in suits and hats trying to make their way up. The next stop was the ticket office, where Nanny Day bought them all return tickets to Hatfield. Eva and Frankie ran along the platform, whooping with delight, especially Frankie, who was thrilled to be going on a steam train again. Kathleen tried to run but when she complained of a pain in her chest Nanny Day told her to slow down. Nanny then herded them all into a carriage, where they proceeded to get up every few seconds to peer out of the window.

'You're like jack-in-the-boxes; sit down, for goodness' sake!' she said, taking out her knitting from the carpet bag.

A man sat beside them just as the train was about to set off and nodded politely to Nanny Day, who nodded back. He lit up a cigarette as they pulled out of the station and started to blow smoke rings in the air. The combination of the cigarette smoke and the rattle of the carriages started to lull Kathleen to sleep. Nanny Day put her arm around her. Eva tucked herself under Nanny's other arm and Frankie rested his head on Eva's lap. After about an hour, Kathleen woke up feeling hungry. Nanny Day unwrapped their sandwiches, and they devoured them as they watched the countryside whizzing by. There were fields with cows in them, which Kathleen had never seen before. They looked so funny, standing there in the middle of such wide open spaces. It was a world away from the grimy bricks of London. Frankie and Eva pressed their noses to the window to get a better look and Frankie then upset Kathleen by pretending to shoot them, just for fun.

'Stop it, Frankie!' cried Kathleen.

'Aw, they're just dumb animals!' he replied with a cheeky grin.

The screeching of the brakes made Eva cover her ears as they pulled into Hatfield Station. They made their way out and through the old town, peering in the shop windows. They couldn't afford to buy anything but window-shopping was fun; in any case, they were keen to get to their relatives' house.

'How much further?' moaned Eva.

'Oh, stop complaining, Eve,' said Kathleen, who was having the time of her life. The sun was high over their heads as they began to walk down a country lane.

'Not too much of a way to go,' said Nanny Day, as the road got narrower and the hedges higher. Kathleen started to skip a bit, taking in lungfuls of fresh air. It felt good to be able to do that and she hummed to herself as she skipped along.

They arrived at a row of tumbledown farm cottages with flowers growing in the front gardens and a creeper covering the front of the houses. Some of the panes of glass in the upstairs windows were broken and others so cobwebby you couldn't see through them, but Kathleen had never seen anything so beautiful. Then one of the front doors opened and a gaggle of children, about the same age as Eva and Frank, spilt out. They had dark hair and brown eyes and their faces were smeared with dirt. Their clothes made Kathleen, Eva and Frank look as if they had stepped out of a shopfront. The girls' pinafores were patched all over and the boys' shorts raggedy and torn.

'Come here and let me look at you!' cried Nanny Day as she gathered them to her skirts. 'You look like the wreck of the *Hesperus*! Have you not a comb in the house between you all?'

A man appeared in the doorway. He had a shock of wild grey hair and a dirty neckerchief at his throat but his eyes were twinkly and he had a kind face. His shirtsleeves were rolled up to reveal forearms as big as hams. Kathleen decided she liked him.

'Are these your grandkids then, Meg?' he said. 'A fine bunch of city dwellers you have here!' He spoke with a stronger accent than Nanny Day.

He ruffled Frankie's hair and patted Eva on the head. 'And you,' he said, giving a little bow, 'must be Miss Kathleen who I have heard so much about. Giving your ma sleepless nights by getting ill, then?'

'Yes,' said Kathleen, blushing.

'I'm your Great-Uncle Joseph and these here are your cousins, Moira, Joseph Junior, William and Eileen. Come on inside. You'll have to take us as you find us but we have fresh raspberries from the garden and cream from the dairy for you.'

A huge bowl of raspberries was set out on the table in the kitchen. Nanny Day hugged a woman with hair as wild as Great-Uncle Joseph's but who looked a lot younger than him. Nanny introduced her as their Aunty Kathy. The two women put a huge kettle on the range to boil some water for tea while the kids grabbed at the raspberries and dunked them in a bowl of cream. Kathleen tried to be lady-like and not scoff too many but she'd never seen so many raspberries and they tasted better than anything she'd had at home. A dog snuffled around by their feet looking for scraps to eat, making Eva laugh.

'Why don't you children go outside and play?' said Nanny Day. Kathleen overheard the start of a conversation about some other cousins – much older ones – working on the railway now, since their mother had passed on.

'May God rest her soul,' said Nanny Day, patting Aunty Kathy on the arm. 'But thankfully Joseph has you now. That is such a mercy, and what beautiful children you have given him.'

The children didn't need to be asked twice to get outside. They couldn't wait to explore. Their cousins took them out through the back door and into a garden which seemed to go on forever. The first part of it was filled with vegetables and there was a big apple tree at the bottom, next to a gate into a field.

'Are we allowed in there?' said Kathleen, as her cousin Moira held her hand.

''Course we are,' she said. 'And all the way to the stream too.'

Kathleen spent the afternoon running around the field, with the grass tickling at her legs, darting in and out of the stream. The boys stripped off and jumped in naked but Kathleen and the other girls just tucked their skirts up into their knickers to avoid getting their clothes wet. They chucked twigs in and raced them like little boats and Frankie and William built a dam.

Before tea, Moira took Kathleen around to the side of the cottage, where a horse stood munching hay in a little stable. She'd only ever seen horses with their blinkers on, working the carts along the roads near home. Moira showed her how to hold her hand out flat and feed him some hay, without getting her fingers bitten. Moira explained how her dad sometimes wasn't at home because he was out on the knocker, selling door-to-door, and could be away weeks at a time. Kathleen said her dad was home every night for his tea, bang on time, which Moira thought was incredible.

As the light faded, Great-Uncle Joseph lit a bonfire in the back garden and Aunty Kathy brought out some sausages, which the children ate with a great wodge of bread. The back porch was lit by an oil lantern and Kathleen watched the moths fluttering around it as she tried to commit everything she had done today to memory, so that she would never forget it. The scent of the yellow bell flowers from the creeper along the back of the house filled the night air.

As they were finishing their tea, Aunty Kathy went back to the house and brought out a funny-looking black case and set it down beside her husband. He opened it and took out a fiddle and began to play.

'Show us your dancing, then,' he said. In an instant, the cousins were on their feet. The boys started to kick up their heels and the girls jigged on the spot, their curls flying. Eva and Frank started to point and giggle until Nanny Day slapped them both over the top of their heads for being rude. Kathleen jumped up in the firelight and copied Moira, holding her arms by her sides as she kicked and bounced up and down in time to the music.

'She's Irish all right,' said Joseph, tapping his foot in approval. Frankie and Eva collapsed in fits of laughter at their sister and were now rolling on the floor clutching their sides. Nanny Day had had enough and yanked them both roughly upwards by their ears, making them yelp. She pulled them into the little kitchen and proceeded to scold them, loudly, for making fun of their family.

'Don't you dare disgrace me by laughing at your cousins and your sister! You are Irish too, remember that!' she said.

Great-Uncle Joseph played on for another tune, by which time Kathleen was quite exhausted. She sat down beside him, to catch her breath. As Aunty Kathy began to sing a sad song about a place called Skibbereen and people leaving because they were starving hungry, Kathleen felt her eyelids growing heavier. She was rudely awoken by a poke in the ribs from Eva. 'It's time to go home, Kath.'

With the fiddle packed away for another night and her cousins sent off to sleep top-to-toe, four to a bed, Nanny Day said her goodbyes and they all set off for the mile-long walk back to the station in the dark. Nanny was still muttering under her breath about how rude Frank and Eva had been. 'To think I brought you all the way out here only to have you make fun of your cousins!' she scolded.

Kathleen wished the day would never end. Great-Uncle Joseph lit the way with an oil lamp and, as she followed close behind down the country lane, with the hedges looming above her, Kathleen saw sparks from the steel studs in his boots striking the road in the darkness. It had sparked something in her, this little trip to see her Irish family. She wasn't a city girl, she was a bit Irish too, a bit wild, her Great-Uncle Joseph had said so. Her love of music made sense. It wasn't just about bashing out tunes in assembly with that stuck-up teacher Miss Price nodding her approval. The music was in her blood; it made her want to dance and sing.

As the darkness enveloped them all, Kathleen vowed never to forget that.

Kathleen loved minding little Billy from down the street. She'd push him up and down in a little crate on wheels which served as his pram, while his mum, Mary, was busy pulling the fur from rabbit skins in the living room of her house. He was learning to walk now, so Kathleen would hold his hand while he took a few steps towards her pal,

Nancy, who might reward him with a lump of sugar from her pocket. He was a skinny little thing, like most of the kids in their street, but he had rosy cheeks and such a sweet smile. Kathleen preferred playing with him to her dolly. She had considered squishing Billy into the cot that Uncle Dennis had made for her and Eva, but Eva told her not to, in case she broke it.

'You'll make a fine little mother one day, Kathleen,' said Mary, emerging from the house, with fluff and blood all over her apron. Kathleen puffed her chest out with pride. Of all the girls in the street, she was the one who was trusted to look after Billy. Kathleen didn't doubt for a minute that she would have a baby one day, but boys were just yuck, so she couldn't imagine kissing one, which was what you had to do to get a baby, Nancy had told her.

When Mary went back to her work, Billy started to cry and so Kathleen wheeled him in his little crate all the way along Belvedere Road, past the wastepaper factory. Kathleen pointed out the big lion on top of the brewery. It was now black with soot because a fire had broken out not so long ago and the brewery had burned down. No one ever found who did it; some said it was just an accident. In any case, the wastepaper company used it for storage now

'There's the Lion of Lambeth, Billy!' she said, smiling at him. 'I wonder if he will jump down and gobble us up?' But Billy didn't laugh at her joke like he was supposed to. He just cried and refused to get out of his crate to have a little walk or play. So she covered him with a blanket and went off to skip with Nancy and the other girls instead. She didn't like him crying – it was noisy and annoying. She even slapped his hand to make him stop but that only made it worse.

'Stop it, Billy,' she scolded. 'I won't play with you unless you stop yelling.'

But Billy didn't stop and so she kept her promise and left him lying there whining while she skipped with the others, to teach him a lesson. He went quiet eventually and when Kathleen wheeled him home, he was fast asleep. Mary picked him out of the crate and the colour drained from her face.

'My God,' she said. 'He's burning up!' Billy's head lolled to one side and Kathleen could see his little cheeks were bright red and his breaths were coming in gasps.

'How long has he been like this?' asked Mary.

'He was fine, really happy all afternoon,' Kathleen lied. She didn't dare tell the truth. What if it was all her fault?

'Oh, Billy, Billy,' Mary sobbed, taking him indoors and laying him on the table. Kathleen watched as she stripped off his clothes and he lay there, not moving at all. Mary turned to her. 'Run and get your mother.'

Mum came running, still wearing the striped overall which she used on laundry days. She put her hand to the baby's forehead and listened to his chest.

'You need to get the doctor,' she said, sponging him down with a damp cloth from the sink on the side.

'No, Margaret. I can't afford a doctor,' wailed Mary. 'I have nothing to pay him with.'

'Don't worry,' said Mum. 'I'll settle it for you. Kathleen, run and get help.'

Kathleen ran harder and faster than she had ever run,

never mind that it hurt her chest and her legs felt leaden
with the guilt of it all. She knew the way to the doctor's
house, with its grand front door and brass knocker.

Kathleen hammered on that for all she was worth and
his wife answered curtly, 'Yes? The doctor is having his
afternoon tea and cannot be disturbed.'

'Please, miss, please, there's a very sick baby in my street
and my mother, Mrs Fraser, has sent me . . .'

In a split second, the doctor had grabbed his coat,
plonked his hat on his head and picked up his big black
leather bag. He marched round to Howley Terrace so
quickly that Kathleen had to trot just to keep up with him.

'How long has he been unresponsive?' asked the doctor,
looking back at her.

'I'm not sure,' said Kathleen, not really understanding
what that word meant. Would she get in trouble if she told
him the truth about Billy being out of sorts all afternoon?
'He was kind of whining a bit this afternoon but then he
went quiet around teatime.'

The doctor must have spotted a look of fear in her eyes,
because he stopped and placed his hand on her shoulder.
'Kathleen, whatever has happened is not your fault, even
if you were looking after him. Babies get ill. They are not
as strong as big children like you or grown-ups. They get
lots of illnesses, but we will try to get him better, you'll see.'

Mary was cradling Billy in her lap by the time the doctor
arrived. He was making a horrible choking noise and
struggling for breath and had gone blue around his lips.
Mum was saying Hail Marys quietly, so quietly that there
was barely any sound, but Kathleen knew from the way

her lips were moving that this is what she was doing. She understood then that Billy was getting worse. The doctor lifted Billy from Mary's arms and lay him back on the table. He took a wooden spatula from his bag and poked it into Billy's mouth, pushing down his tongue and peering inside. Then he listened to his chest with his stethoscope. The horrible rasping sound got louder.

'Mary, have you or anyone in your family had a sore throat these past few days?'

Her eyes were glazing over; she could barely reply. 'Yes. I've had a bit of a tickle but it wasn't anything serious.'

'And has Billy been off his food?'

'He's only wanted condensed milk since yesterday,' she whispered.

'It's diphtheria, Mary, I'm so sorry,' said the doctor, picking the baby back up and placing him, with great care, in his mother's lap. He was fighting back tears as he spoke. 'There is a swelling and a coating at the back of his throat, which is making it impossible for him to breathe. Once the process starts, we can't stop it.'

They were frozen in time, Mum, Kathleen and the doctor, while Mary rocked her baby and hummed to him, stroking his forehead.

The rasping of Billy's breath got louder until a strangled sound came from the baby, his blue eyes flickered open and then closed, forever.

Kathleen watched as her mother started to cry. 'Dear God, no, no.'

The doctor spoke. 'It's too late, there's nothing to be done now. But he is at peace. I'm so sorry for your loss.'

Mary let out the most piercing and terrifying scream. Kathleen thought she might faint from the shock of it. She couldn't move, she was rooted to the spot. The blood-curdling noise brought all the women of the street running. It wasn't a case of knocking or asking to come in: Mrs Davies and Mrs Avens burst through the door.

'Not the baby!' cried Mrs Avens.

'Oh, Lord, you poor angel,' said Mrs Davies, kneeling beside Mary. 'Poor little Billy, never hurt nobody.'

'Why couldn't you have saved him?' said Mrs Avens, her face red with fury. 'We'd have clubbed together to pay for it!'

The doctor shook his head. 'It's diphtheria. With the best will in the world, I could have done very little.'

The women turned to each other. 'It's the Strangler. Dear God, will our children be safe?'

Margaret realized that Kathleen was in great danger, having been exposed to the illness which had last swept the borough ten years previously. She whispered in her ear, 'Go home, Kathleen, go upstairs and don't let the others near you.'

The doctor started to ask questions about how many of the children had been in close contact with Billy since his sore throat. In the end it was decided that Kathleen and Nancy from round the corner should be kept off school for a week and apart from their siblings, to prevent the spread of the illness. Frankie and Eva and Peggy had to go and stay at Nanny Day's.

The doctor turned to Margaret. 'This may seem harsh, at a time of mourning for Billy, but we must do what we can now for the living and prevent any other children getting sick. Diphtheria, or the Strangler as you call it, is a terrible and deadly disease and it can kill very quickly.'

Kathleen wasn't allowed out of her bedroom for five full days, which meant she had to use the jerry they kept under the bed and she hated doing that. Only her mother was allowed in to give her meals and take the dirty dishes away. Mum scrubbed her hands red raw with carbolic to try to stop the spread of any germs. The doctor called every day to peer down her throat and check her temperature. The priest visited and stood in the doorway to the bedroom, saying prayers for her and the departed baby. To everyone's relief, there was no sign of any temperature or the dreaded grey coating in the back of the throat which was the proof that diphtheria, the Strangler, had taken hold.

Frankie and Eva had been allowed to join the procession of mourners who called in to the house to see Mary and her husband Joe, to pay their respects and view the baby's body. People came from all the surrounding streets and as far away as Nanny Day's road.

'He looked like a waxwork,' Frankie told her, through the bedroom door, which made her cry even more.

On the day of the funeral, a bleak November morning, Kathleen watched from the bedroom window as Billy was taken in a tiny wooden coffin covered with flowers to be buried. His father carried it in his arms while Mary, dressed all in black, walked behind him, sobbing, supported by the women from Howley Terrace and Tenison Street. Behind that the children walked in a solemn row. At the top of the street, the brewer stopped his dray, took off his cap and stood with eyes downcast as the funeral procession made its way past.

Kathleen looked on from afar, unable to mourn with everybody else, alone in her grief and isolated by her guilt. The trip to the country with Nanny Day, with the raspberries, the stream and the bonfire, seemed like a distant dream to her now. She couldn't imagine ever feeling happy like that again.

10

Eva, February 1934

The cigarette machine was a big prize. Eva had taken to creeping into the hotel in York Road in the afternoon on the way back from school to look at it, just when the receptionist had gone through half a bottle of gin and was snoring in the back room. Lumps had told her this would be the case, but getting that ciggy machine out of the hotel was going to be too much for her to manage on her own so she'd recruited her little brother Frankie onto her scheme. He was a willing accomplice and was happy to take a small share of the profits – enough to buy a few marbles from the kids in Tenison Street. He was planning to use them as ammo for his catapult.

Mum was still running short every week and Eva had made a promise to get Kathleen a piano. What if she got sick again and died, never having played a note of it? The way little Billy was taken so quickly had scared the living daylights out of her. The last of her dad's compensation money had been spent paying for a headstone for little Billy. The whole neighbourhood had a whip-round to avoid the shame of the baby being buried on the parish. Nobody wanted Mary and Joe to go through that, having lost their only child, but the cost of the headstone on top of the ten pounds for the funeral was too much to ask. Her parents had stepped in because they were the only ones with any savings. Billy got his headstone and was properly remembered but it had left the family in dire straits again.

And then there was Lumps, who had taken to appearing on the street corner near their home, giving Eva a little wave when she was playing outside with Gladys, just to let her know that she knew where she lived. The last thing she wanted was to have to explain to her parents why the local drunk seemed to be her new best mate.

Eva was beginning to regret getting into this game but if she could just get the ciggies for Lumps this once, that would be the end of it and she would go back to nicking a bit of cash from the till when she needed to. She had planned the raid on the hotel as best as she could, agreeing to meet Lumps around the back of Waterloo Station with the loot later that evening. She'd picked up a couple of old sacks lying in the gutter outside the wastepaper factory around the corner to carry it all.

With the receptionist snoring soundly in the back room, Eva and Frankie moved quickly. The machine was situated in the little hallway by the rear, which led up to the bedrooms. Eva knew this because her mother had cleaned here in the past. With Frankie standing guard, she threw a sack over the machine and then signalled for him to come and lift it with her.

She tilted it backwards and he took the bottom end of it. 'It's bleeding heavy, Eve,' he hissed through gritted teeth.

There were indents on the claggy old carpet, where it had stood.

'Come on, Frankie, we can do it,' she said, as they lugged it up the hallway. There was no going back now. It was already getting dark outside, which was a mercy because they did look a very odd sight – two kids struggling to carry something very heavy in an old sack. It would be just the sort of thing to attract the attention of the cozzers. They managed to take it a good fifty yards before they had to stop for a rest.

'I can't take this into Waterloo Station,' said Eva. She really hadn't thought this through.

'You'll have to find a way to get the fags out,' said Frankie. 'I've got an idea.'

They half dragged, half carried it back along York Road and up a side street, to a little health clinic, which was in a mobile hut, on stilts.

'Me and the boys like to hide out under here,' said Frankie conspiratorially. 'But don't tell Jim or he'll want to use it for his mates.'

'I won't,' said Eva, rolling her eyes. As if she was ever likely to want to come here again or tell her big brother! They shuffled themselves underneath the building, pulling the heavy sack with them. Once they were underneath, they pulled the machine out of its sack and Frankie picked up a half brick and started to bash away at it, breaking the glass. Eva followed suit and soon they were able to put their fingers in and grab packet after packet of cigarettes.

'You go home,' Eva ordered. 'I'm going to meet Lumps.'

She gathered her haul into the sack, slung it over her shoulder and marched off towards Waterloo Station.

Lumps was hanging around the steps at the back of the station, with her grimy shawl pulled tightly around her shoulders. She smiled when Eva approached, flashing a row of blackened stumps where her teeth should be.

'Looks like quite a haul,' she said, fishing some coins out of her pocket to give to Eva.

Eva tightened her grip on her loot. 'The price is two quid, there's hundreds of fags in here. I ain't taking a penny less.'

Lumps laughed. 'Show me what you've got first.'

Eva opened the bag and Lumps peered inside. She smelt so bad, Eva wondered if she had ever had a bath in her life. She probably never used the Manor Place Baths like decent folk.

'All right,' she said. 'I reckon I can get the Daleys to take them and sell them on at their stall in the station. Meet me here tomorrow and I will pay you.'

'But . . .' Eva began.

'That's how it works with Old Liz,' said Lumps, as her dirty fingers closed around the bag and took it from Eva's grasp. 'I ain't got that much cash about me but I give you my word that I will get it for you. And as a thank you, come after school tomorrow; there's someone I know who will want to meet you.'

Eva was so nervous she could barely sleep that night and woke up too late to go up to the bakery in Covent Garden before school. She felt such a fool for letting Liz English, the old soak, take away the cigarettes without giving her any money. That was a mistake she wouldn't repeat. She managed to get through the day but got told off twice for napping in class, as her eyelids closed while the teacher droned on. When the other kids ran out of school and home to play, she trudged around to Waterloo Station to meet Lumps and to try to get at least some money for her effort.

Lumps gave her a smile and a wave and produced a ten-shilling note from beneath her shawl and wafted it at her.

'I asked for two quid,' said Eva, with a steely glare.

'Well, this is all you're getting,' said Old Liz, snatching the note away from Eva's grasp. 'But there's half a crown in it if you'll come with me down the Borough and I think you will thank me for it.'

'But that'll take ages and I don't want to go anywhere with you!' cried Eva, who had no intention of going to the Borough with this old drunkard. She probably wanted her to nick a bottle of gin for her.

Lumps looked at her. 'Nah,' she said. 'Maybe you are right. You ain't much of a tea leaf.'

'I'm the best thief around here!' Eva said, before she could stop herself.

'In which case,' said Lumps, 'you will want to meet the Queen of the Forty Thieves, won't you?'

Eva gasped. She'd heard talk of the Forty Thieves, of course she had, with their raids on the big shops over the water up in Oxford Street and their fights with policemen, but she'd only half believed it all. Was Lumps serious or was this just another one of her drunken antics? Eva wanted the rest of her money; she had a piano to pay for.

She set out, walking a few paces behind Lumps, in case any-one she knew spotted her and thought they were friends.

They caught the bus down the Waterloo Road and on to Webber Street, before hopping off and walking down Scovell Road, a side street filled with looming tenement blocks. If Eva's family was poor, the people living here were poorer, with their tiny flats and their laundry hung across from one balcony to another to dry. The screams and shouts of children playing echoed up the walls and bounced back, creating such a din that Eva wanted to stop up her ears.

'In here,' said Lumps, pulling her into a doorway. She clambered up three flights of stairs, her heart beating nine-teen to the dozen as her footsteps echoed up the tiled walls of the dark, dank stairwell.

'I'm not afraid,' Eva kept saying under her breath. In truth, she was terrified. Greying, holey woollen stockings peeked out through the split leather of Lumps's boots as she climbed the stairs in front of Eva, huffing and puffing all the while. At times Lumps grasped the wrought-iron stair-rail for dear life and Eva wondered whether the old drunk had the strength to make it up those stairs. They stopped at a door painted sludge green; it swung open and they were greeted by a tall woman with a broad face and piercing green eyes, with her thick hair piled up on top of her head.

Eva instinctively stuck out her hand and said, 'How do you do?' as her mother had told her to do, when she needed to be polite.

The woman smiled at her. 'Lovely manners!' She didn't look in the least bit scary. 'So, you must be Eva. I'm Alice. Come on in, love. Cup of tea?'

Eva and Lumps entered the tiny flat, peering into the living room, which was stuffed with bags and had a clothes rail full of coats and expensive-looking dresses.

'I bet you'd like to have a good poke around in there, wouldn't you?' said Alice with a laugh. 'Later, maybe, but let's have a chat first.' She took a knitted cosy off the most enormous teapot that Eva had ever seen and poured the brew into a dainty bone-china teacup covered with flowers, with a saucer underneath. Eva's eyes went wide. 'Nice, isn't it? I do have my standards; I like a nice bit of china,' said Alice. 'Why don't you wait outside, Liz? The girls will be back in a minute and I need you to keep look-out.'

It was more of an order than a question and Lumps grumbled under her breath but did as she was told and ambled back down the corridor and out into the draughty stairwell.

'Now,' said Alice, pulling out a chair for Eva and one for herself. 'Sit down, that's right. Old Liz tells me you are making yourself quite handy on the rob, down in Waterloo.'

'S'pose so,' said Eva, with a defiant look in her eye. 'I'm just doing what I can to help my mum make ends meet.'

'That's admirable,' said Alice. 'But you're already attracting attention from the cozzers, from what I hear, which ain't so great.'

'Yes,' said Eva, bowing her head.

'And the thing is, I don't know whether our friend Liz

has put you right on this or not, but I am in charge of all the girl thieves this side of the water.'

'Oh,' said Eva. 'I didn't know that.'

'Well, you do now. You need my protection or the cozzers will come for you and that wouldn't be very nice, would it?'

'No,' said Eva, her heart thumping in her chest. 'So do you mean I have to give you some of what I steal?'

'That's how it works,' said Alice. 'It's like a business. You can't just set up on your own, even if you are only – how old?

'Twelve,' said Eva, swallowing hard. Well, she was nearly.

'But the good news is, I am going to reward you for your work so far,' Alice went on. She reached into the pocket of her cardigan and pulled out half a crown.

She held the coin between her thumb and her forefinger.

'Ever seen one of these before?'

'Yes,' said Eva, 'but not very often.'

'Starting young, then. That's keen. Well, there's one of these a week just for being in my gang,' said Alice. 'And the thing is, I am always on the look-out for clever girls, just like you. I can teach you plenty and show you how to make better money, real money, to make a job out of it. Nicking from the till is a mug's game, ain't it?'

'Yes.' Eva found herself agreeing with Alice; she was scared not to.

'Alice Diamond knows how to look after her girls. Maggie and Ada will tell you as much, won't you, girls?'

Right on cue, two smartly dressed women in long coats and hats appeared in the doorway, laden with bags.

'How did you get on?' said Alice, taking a sip of tea.

'Selfridges have got some new walkers but we managed to give them the slip,' said Maggie, taking off her hat and running her hand through her red hair. She turned to Eva. 'Who have we got here, then?'

'This is Eva, the little magpie from down Waterloo I've been telling you about,' said Alice. 'Why don't you take the weight off and have a cuppa? Are you still carrying?'

Eva's mouth fell open as Maggie opened her coat and lifted her skirt to reveal the most voluminous knickers, stuffed full, with elastic at each knee. She proceeded to pull a fur coat from each leg of her drawers. She unrolled each coat carefully and laid it on the kitchen table, still on its hanger. She then rummaged in one of Alice's cupboards and pulled out a bottle of rum, which she sploshed into her tea.

Ada, meanwhile, took off her hat to reveal a secret pocket inside, in which she had stashed a necklace and some diamond rings. She started to yank silk stockings, knickers and nighties out of pockets sewn into the lining of her coat. Alice's eyes lit up. 'Nice work,' she said. 'I bet you've never seen tom like this, have you, Eva?'

'No,' said Eva. 'I ain't.' Her knowledge of jewellery extended to her mother's thin gold wedding band.

'Well, look,' said Alice, flashing a row of twinkling diamond rings on each of her hands. 'I'm Diamond by name and diamond by nature.'

'But how do you do all that thieving without getting caught?' said Eva incredulously.

'That's what we will teach you, isn't it, Maggie?'

Maggie nodded, in between sips of tea, then she stood up and began to roll the fur coat, nimbly, into a tight little roll. 'You have to do it on the hanger and quickly or the shop assistants will spot you,' she said. 'You can have a go, if you like.'

Eva took the garment and tried to copy Maggie, rolling it, but it ended up look like a fat, furry sausage. Maggie laughed at her effort.

'Don't worry,' said Alice. 'You will get plenty of practice around here with me and the girls before we let you do your own hoisting. But you can come along for a shopping trip to help us in the meantime.'

'Can I?' said Eva. 'When will that be?'

'Soon as you like,' she said. 'In fact, I'm planning a little trip up to Whiteley's in Bayswater tomorrow. Why don't you come with me?'

'I'm supposed to go to school . . .'

'Tell me, what can they teach you in school that is going to be more use than this?' said Alice, crossing her arms and fixing Eva with a steely glare.

'Nothing, I suppose,' said Eva, wondering what her parents would do if they found out.

'I will meet you outside Waterloo Station at nine o'clock. Don't be late. Now, hadn't you better get off home?'

Dad was having tea of bread and dripping when Eva got back. She could tell by the look on her mum's face that something was amiss.

'Where have you been?' he said, brushing a stray crumb from his moustache.

'I was just out with friends and we played around Roupell Street and it got late . . .' she ventured.

'Don't lie to me.'

'I ain't lying,' she said, putting her hands on her hips.

'What have you been doing? And don't you give me any cheek!'

'Nothing,' said Eva, looking at the floor.

'Well, if you can't confess to it, I'm going to beat it out of you.'

Mum started to cry and rushed over from the kitchen sink. 'Please, James, don't . . .' she said, tugging at his sleeve, but he brushed her hands away and slapped her face for good measure.

'Don't interfere, Margaret,' he said. She recoiled from the force of the blow. Then he seized Eva by the arm. 'I have had questions from the police, Goddamn you!' She knew better than to resist. He shook her like a rag doll. 'Why is my child known to the police?'

'I ain't, it's all lies!' she shouted but he was already pulling off his belt.

He seized her by her long black hair and yanked her down, over his lap, pulling up her pinafore.

Mum ran sobbing into the back yard.

Eva's nose was just an inch from the red-tiled floor. She studied it, trying to take her mind off what was to come, as her father folded his belt and grasped it in his right hand. He pulled down her knickers, the cold air of the scullery bringing goose pimples to her naked skin. She resolved not to kick her legs, as she had hidden the half-crown from Alice Diamond in her shoe and didn't want to have to explain where that had come from.

He struck her and she felt the leather bite. 'You will not break the law in my house!' he shouted, bringing the belt down again and again on her backside and her thighs, until she felt hot tears of anger and shame spilling down her nose and sploshing onto the tiles. 'I didn't, I didn't,' she cried. Pain burned her like a fire and with every stroke she hated him more.

'Goddamn you, Eva!' He wielded the belt with such a fury that it cut into her, making her scream.

Just as suddenly as it had started, it was over. He thrust her off his lap in a sobbing heap, onto the scullery floor. Then he stood up without speaking, put his belt back on and left the house, slamming the door behind him.

Through her tears, Eva saw Mum approaching and felt her warm, familiar embrace. 'I'm sorry, love,' was all her mother said. There was nothing else to say, they both knew that. It would never stop. She reached down into her shoe and pulled out the half-crown. She handed it to Mum, who smiled and tucked it into her apron pocket. Eva's mind was made up. Her father was a mug, he went to work and earned a pittance. She was going shopping with the Queen of the Forty Thieves tomorrow.

11

Peggy, July 1934

The General Post Office training school was more exciting than any classroom that Peggy had ever set foot in. For a start, there were little counters for the students, with real stocks and supplies, forms, envelopes and whole books of stamps. It would be months or maybe even years before she was let loose on the public, but for now the thrill of learning to tear those stamps correctly and franking and filling in forms was enough to make her head spin.

She'd already made a friend, a girl called Susan from over the water, in Clerkenwell. Peggy was beginning to wonder whether that was such a good idea because Susan always seemed to be in trouble for talking.

Their supervisor, Miss Oakley, was a tall, cheerless woman whose mouth turned down at the corners; she had eagle eyes as well as a sharp tongue.

'Girls, and Susan in particular,' she said. 'You must remember, you have been selected for training at writing assistant grade because you are the most promising leavers among your year group at school and have come highly recommended. We are not a gossip shop. While we are learning there is to be no chatter. Understood?'

'Yes, miss,' the room of twenty girls chorused but Susan smirked as she did so and poked Peggy in the ribs, making her cough rather loudly.

Every day, Peggy had to be up at the new GPO building at Mount Pleasant to start at 9 a.m. sharp. She was so desperate never to be late that, more often than not, she was awake when her father left the house. The day was divided into lectures and practical training, with a forty-five-minute break for lunch and a fifteen-minute tea break in the afternoon, finishing at 5 p.m. precisely.

Peggy excelled at the written tasks – filling in and col-lating forms. They required quiet concentration, which she relished. There was usually so much noise in her neigh-bourhood, with doors banging and kids screaming, that to be in an environment of enforced peace and quiet and to get paid for it was a luxury. The students had to sit in silence at long wooden counters while Miss Oakley pa-trolled the lines, peering over her horn-rimmed spectacles to check their work and point out any errors. The only sound was the occasional shuffle of papers and the squeak of Miss Oakley's leather shoes on the highly polished floor. Susan struggled to be as neat as Miss Oakley wanted and once even poked her tongue out at her back, which made Peggy laugh – a laugh which she disguised as another coughing fit, much to Miss Oakley's annoyance.

There was great excitement when the girls found out that the class was to be given a tour of the sorting office, which was staffed exclusively by men.

Miss Oakley marshalled her troops. 'Now, girls, this is to be a learning experience. The sorting office will give you an idea of the vast workload of the GPO and its staff. You will not be required to work in the delivery and sorting sections but it is important that you understand how they work.'

Susan whispered in Peggy's ear, 'I think there is a bloke down there who fancies me. He was eyeing me up on the way into work this morning.'

'And Susan, no talking!' said Miss Oakley, knowing by now that she was fighting a losing battle.

They filed down into the sorting and delivery hall, which was a hive of activity, with blokes wearing a kind of apron over their suits, picking out parcels and bundling them into wicker trolleys which were wheeled out to the vans in the yard. Letters were sorted into little pigeon-holes. The men reminded Peggy of worker ants, everyone playing his part. Supervisors patrolled gantries overhead and ran up and down the metal staircases to the manager's office.

'If you think this is busy, you should see the Post Office at Christmas!' said Miss Oakley, beaming with pride. 'That is our busiest time of the year and it really is all hands on deck as the Post Office workers stretch every sinew to maintain the standards we expect and get the post out on time,' said Miss Oakley, with a wave of her hand.

They hadn't got far before Susan started turning heads. Peggy could have sworn she was exaggerating her wiggle more than usual, just for attention's sake. They rounded a corner and were nearly run over by a handsome man wheeling a post trolley, his hair slicked back and cropped high above his ears. He had a toothy grin and gave a little wolf whistle as Susan shimmied past. Miss Oakley tutted at him loudly. 'Come along, girls!' But Susan ignored her and stopped to chat for a minute, earning a firm rebuke from the supervisor. Peggy noticed how she leaned in to him as she chatted, making his eyes light up.

'Who was that?' whispered Peggy, as they made their way back for more form-filling.

'That was him,' said Susan. 'The bloke I was telling you about this morning. He's going to meet me at the bus stop later.'

'Don't do anything daft, will you?' said Peggy, who was beginning to realize that her new friend was about a hundred times more daring than she was.

The next day Susan was desperate for a gossip. Bert apparently was on his own; his wife had died but he still wore a ring out of respect. 'He wants to take me on a date, a proper date,' she gushed. 'Thing is, me dad will kill me. Can I say I'm going with you, and you cover for me if you're asked?'

'Fine,' said Peggy, who was secretly jealous that she wasn't going on a date. Susan had just turned seventeen and was only a year older than Peggy, but seemed so much more grown up, smoking and going out with boys – well, men.

Peggy was eager for the next instalment of the new romance and didn't have to wait for long. The next day, while they were on a break in the loos, Susan lit up a sneaky fag and was blowing the smoke out of the window.

'You ever kissed a boy, Peg?'

'No,' she said, blushing. 'What's it like?'

'Well, it ain't exactly like they show it in the movies. There's a lot of swishing of tongues,' said Susan. 'But it feels nice and leads on to other things, which feel even nicer.'

'You haven't, have you?' said Peggy, her eyes growing wide.

'No, of course not. What do you take me for?' said Susan. 'I'm going to get a ring on my finger before he gets any of that.'

'Are you going to get married, then?'

'Married?' shrieked Susan. 'Don't be daft! We are still at the romantic stage. Bert is very charming. A proper gentleman.'

'But . . . what about your parents, if they find out?' said Peggy, imagining for a moment the beating she would get from her father for even thinking about kissing a boy, let alone anything else.

'Oh, what they don't know can't hurt them,' said Susan, twiddling with her hair. 'Bert will ask me, I'm sure, all in good time. But it ain't wrong to give him a bit of what he fancies. He's a man, not a wet-behind-the-ears boy, Peg. Plus he's grieving for his wife. I know what I'm doing.'

The bell rang, signalling the end of their tea break and the girls filed back into the office for more monotonous sorting and form-checking.

That evening on the way home, Peggy was walking across Waterloo Bridge when she spotted George Harwood. He seemed to have grown taller and his shoulders were broader than she remembered. With his sleeves rolled up, he almost looked quite handsome. She smiled at him.

'Haven't seen you in a while,' he said, falling into step with her. 'How's the job?'

'It's nothing special, but my mum says the Post Office is a good career for a girl like me, so I'm pleased about that,' said Peggy, standing a bit taller. There seemed to be a gulf between them now. She was a working girl, he was still a schoolboy; how could he understand what life in an office entailed?

'I will be leaving school soon, you know,' he said. 'My dad says I should get a job on the buses. It's a growth industry.'

Peggy made a little noise of approval. Working on the buses was a good job, she was sure of that.

'I miss our little chats,' he said, kicking a pebble along.

'Me too,' she said eventually. They turned down by the river and wandered along looking at the barges filled with rubbish and the little tug boats going past.

'I've got a new book for you, if you are still interested?' George said, searching her face.

'Yes, I am, I think,' said Peggy. They had reached the Waterloo Road now. It seemed to be full of drivers forever leaning on the horn and scaring the poor old horses dragging the rag-and-bone cart or the brewer's dray.

'George,' she said, turning to him just as they were about to cross. 'Would you like to come to the pictures with me? I mean, nothing serious, just as friends because that is what we are, isn't it?'

George's mouth fell open. 'I'd love to, Peggy,' he said,

smiling at her. 'And I can bring that book along too, if you like. See you next Thursday? It's half price then. Can I bring my little brother?'

After six months of learning the ropes and nearly another four months' probation, Peggy and Susan were informed that they were to graduate as lower-grade clerks. Some of the girls in their class were not so lucky and were dismissed. Nobody was sure why – possibly they hadn't made the grade in the final exams. For all her chatter, Susan was naturally bright and found it easy to retain rules and regulations. 'I like to break 'em,' she explained with a laugh. 'So I need to know what they are, don't I?'

They had a further fortnight at Mount Pleasant before they were to start their new jobs over at Blythe House in West Kensington, working for the Post Office Savings Bank. They'd heard all about it; it was an austere place, a red and white brick Victorian building, nothing like the modern surroundings of Mount Pleasant, which were so new they weren't even finished yet. The women at Blythe House were kept strictly segregated and even had their own entrance to work, in the south block of the building. Peggy was just relieved to have been kept on. She needed this job and the family needed the money. It was only fifteen shillings a week but that was enough to help her mother and have a bit left over for herself.

Peggy was hoping to save up to buy a new dress. She'd seen one in the window of the dressmaker's up the Cut, in viscose with little rose print and puffed sleeves. Susan had one quite like it and it clung to her and made her look womanly. Peggy felt a bit clumsy next to Susan, if truth be told. She was always presentable but her two white blouses and skirt finishing at mid-calf and flat shoes seemed boring. Susan always had an extra pleat in her skirt or an interesting ruffle on her blouse. Peggy tried to do things with her hair to make it nice; she put a ribbon in it or tried a plait but it just made her look childish. Susan's mother did people's hair in the street and even had a set of curling tongs, which explained why Susan had enviable curls around her neck. In return for lending out those tongs – which were as lethal as a red-hot poker in the wrong hands – she was paid in kind: a dress here, a bit of material. That was how Susan got her fashionable look.

On learning of their imminent departure for West Kensington, Bert was apparently angling for another date with Susan – a proper date, not at the local fleapit like last time, but at one of the big cinemas up in the West End. 'I'll need you to come and meet my folks, if we are going to get away with it,' she said one Friday afternoon, puffing away conspiratorially in the ladies' loos. 'Will you help me, Peg?'

'Of course I will,' said Peggy, who was pleased that Susan had taken her into her confidence like this. She'd always been a bit of a loner at school, with her nose stuck in her books. Now she was working, at least she was on the same wavelength as other girls. Susan said they were best mates.

The following Friday it was all arranged. Instead of going home to Howley Terrace after work, Peggy went home with Susan, picking up a fish-and-chip supper on the way. Susan's house in Clerkenwell was bigger than Peggy's but was divided, so that there was a family upstairs and Susan's lived downstairs. They shared the yard and the lavatory, so the neighbours had to walk through their kitchen when they wanted to go. It all seemed cheerful enough, with the kids running up and down the stairs. There were loads of them – Susan was one of four and there were five upstairs. Her mother was a char lady and her dad worked down the docks. He was balding, smoked a pipe and beamed at his eldest daughter with pride as she stood in the living room, twirling around in her new skirt and blouse. 'Ain't she pretty?' When his wife stuck her head around the living-room door, he added, 'Almost as pretty as you, my angel' which made everyone laugh.

'Back by ten,' he told Susan, pressing some coins into her hand and giving her a peck on the cheek. 'Will you be all right getting home, Peggy?'

'Yes, I'll manage,' she said, hoping the ground wouldn't swallow her up for fibbing about going out with Susan for the night.

'I expect your folks will wait up, won't they?'

'Well, my dad's got to be up but I expect my mother will,' she said, buttoning up her cardigan to disguise her discomfort at telling lies.

They took the bus down into Holborn and hopped off to walk through theatreland at Shaftesbury Avenue. The whole area was alive with surging crowds; women done up to the nines and men all flush with cash, in their best suits and hats, out for a night on the town. The noise and sheer number of people was incredible and Peggy saw more cars nudging their way through the narrow streets in the dark than she had ever seen before in her whole life. It was as if the whole of London had come here to let its hair down on a warm summer's evening. There were street entertainers busking for pennies and raggedy kids offering to go and buy smokes for a penny or shine shoes.

The Odeon cinema loomed large over Leicester Square and Bert was already queuing for tickets, his hands thrust into his pockets, rocking back and forth on his toes as he waited.

He looked askance when he spotted Peggy and jangled some loose change in his pocket. 'You're late and I ain't paying for both of you.' His hair was greased back under his trilby and his jacket was done up to make him look smart. He reminded Peggy of her father.

'It's all right,' said Peggy. 'I've just come this far to keep Susan company. I'm off home now.' She gave Susan a little hug and whispered, 'Have a great night!' in her ear.

Susan gave Peggy's arm a little squeeze. 'Thanks. Will you be all right getting home?' She didn't wait to hear Peggy's reply because the next second she had turned to give Bert her full attention.

Peggy was suddenly alone. She wasn't scared, just out of place. She didn't want to go home too soon because she was supposed to be out with Susan, so she went to a coffee bar and ordered a glass of milk, which she lingered over for an hour. Eventually, she decided to make her way home. As she ambled back over Waterloo Bridge, she couldn't help wondering what her life would have been like if she had been born on the other side of the water. It was a matter of half a mile or so – a mile into Mayfair. She could have been rich and lived in a big house and had servants; instead she lived in a little terrace by the river, overshadowed by the rattle and hum of the railway. The rich people lived in big houses and had drinks parties; she had to make do with a massive advert for Lemon Hart rum on a hoarding overlooking her street from the Waterloo Road.

Peggy couldn't wait for Monday morning to come for once. Sundays had become more important to her now she was working, just to get a bit of a rest and see her family, but she was dying to catch up with Susan and find out all about the exciting date night with Bert. But Susan arrived late at work, sporting a black eye and a bruised lip. She scurried over to her desk and kept her head down all morning. Eventually, Peggy caught up with her in the works canteen at lunchtime.

'Whatever happened to you?' said Peggy.

'Walked into a door, didn't I?' said Susan with a weak laugh.

Peggy nodded. She'd heard that excuse before. 'Was the film good?'

'Not bad,' said Susan. 'Look, can we talk about something else? It's just, I broke up with Bert. I found out he wasn't everything he said he was.' She was talking in a whisper now. 'I can't talk about it at work in case people overhear. Meet me around the back when we get out and I'll explain.'

When the bell rang at 5 p.m. to signal the end of their shift, Susan and Peggy scurried outside and around to the side entrance of the building, where they took shelter from the rain in a little doorway.

Peggy had barely asked her what had really happened before Susan crumpled in her arms, sobbing. 'It was awful, awful.'

The whole sorry saga came flooding out. Bert had only been after one thing and had spent the majority of the film trying to put his hand up her skirt. 'And he was too tight to even buy me any popcorn, the nasty sod,' said Susan. 'I brushed him off but by the time the film was over he said we ought to go for a drink, a proper drink, to relax. Well, I couldn't very well refuse so we went to the pub and he bought me a port and lemon, which my mum drinks so I thought I could handle that. But it was quite strong and then he bought me another . . .' She faltered and started to cry. 'We went outside and he made us go up these little alleyways. I didn't have a clue where I was by then. And then he . . .'

'You don't have to tell me if it's too much,' said Peggy, who felt she had heard enough.

'No, I want to tell you, Peggy. He made me do it and it hurt. We were standing up in the alleyway and I wanted to make him happy, to show him I was not just some young girl but when it came to it, it was scary . . . that thing of his. And it was all this grunting and stuff. It wasn't a bit like the films. Afterwards he sort of said sorry, he couldn't help himself because I was so pretty and he walked me home – well, to the next street from mine. But when I got in, my dad was waiting up for me and that is when it all went wrong.'

'What do you mean?' said Peggy.

'Turns out Bert isn't a widower. He has a wife and kids living in Bermondsey. Someone in the sorting office lives around the corner from my parents and was worried about what Bert was up to so they tipped my dad the wink. Well, of course I never told my dad what happened but he knew I'd lied to him and so he walloped me one and gave me this.'

She touched the bruise around her eye, which was now purple at the edge.

'I feel such a fool,' she said.

'Don't blame yourself,' said Peggy. 'You weren't to know, were you?'

In some ways it was a relief to know that other people's fathers belted them too. She couldn't say that to Susan, of course she couldn't. But for a moment, she was less alone.

'We can always go out to the cinema together, you know. I'm sure your dad won't mind that,' said Peggy.

Susan started to cry again. 'Oh, Peg. You are the best friend I have got in the whole wide world. I don't deserve you, really I don't.'

Peggy hugged her. It was awful of her to think it, but the fact that Susan had broken up with Bert and had such a rough time of it at home made her feel a bit happier inside. She wasn't alone any more.

12

Kathleen, October 1934

Kathleen hadn't sung a note since Billy died last year. Nanny Day did her best to gee her up into a song, tapping her feet around the scullery at Cornwall Road in an enforced show of jollity, humming all the old music hall songs she could think of.

'The Cake Walk' was one of Nanny's favourites, and Old Uncle Dennis got up and joined in as she waved her dishcloth and sang, 'I know a nice walk, just like the cake walk, come along my honey . . .' Uncle Dennis rolled up his trouser legs, thrust his jacket back over his shoulders and swaggered forwards, making Kathleen laugh, but still she wouldn't join in, even when his exertions made him cough and splutter.

'Ooh, cough up, chicken,' said Nanny Day, slapping him on the back. 'Why won't you join in no more, Kathleen? You sing like a little bird.'

'Don't fancy it,' she said, folding her arms and sitting down on Nanny's favourite rocking chair.

'Oi!' said Nanny. 'Sling yer hook! That's my seat.' Even that was done in a jokey way, just to try to make Kathleen laugh, because Nanny didn't really mind one bit if Kathleen sat there while she went about her chores and she never usually spoke in that gorblimey way, like one of the costermongers from down the road.

Kathleen wanted to speak up, to say something about why she wouldn't sing any more, but the words got stuck in her throat. How could she tell them that it was all her fault, Billy dying like that? Sometimes she dreamed about him, lying there in his pram, not wanting to get out and walk. In her dreams, she did things differently; she felt his forehead and rushed straight to get the doctor, who gave him some medicine from a big brown bottle and it made him all better. Except, when she woke with the thin light of the day coming through the curtains, Billy was dead and cold in his grave and she hadn't done enough to save him.

Nobody blamed her, least of all Mary, who asked her to come over and sit with her sometimes, as she pulled the fur from rabbit skins in the scullery. But Kathleen felt, deep down, that Mary would be very angry if she knew the truth. Kathleen had noticed that Mary's belly was getting bigger and she wondered if she had a secret to tell. Maybe that was why she was happier recently. Even that made Kathleen feel bad, because if another baby came along, Billy would just be forgotten about.

Kathleen had thought about trying to buy some flowers and taking those up to the cemetery, to lay them on his grave, but she didn't have any money to do that. So she had made an extra special effort to say prayers for Billy in church, where she said her catechism with real fervour, hoping that Jesus was listening. She'd noticed that her big sister Peggy wasn't so bothered about the church any more. She'd caught her just mouthing the words on more than one occasion. Kathleen thought this was probably what happened when girls left school and went out to work. Her head was probably full of numbers and figures and the like.

Peggy had been extra kind to Kathleen of late. In fact, she was planning to take her to the cinema later, which was a real treat. They were going to go to the Trocadero down at the Elephant. She'd heard all about the Troc, with its carpets so soft you sank into them and its huge Wurlitzer organ, but she couldn't wait to see it for herself. Peggy and George Harwood had a regular thing going, where they'd go half price on a weekday evening, and see a show every couple of weeks. Kathleen couldn't resist teasing Peg about that because she wouldn't admit how much she liked George, who'd left school now and was training to be a mechanic at the bus depot. Dad had murmured his approval: 'Good job for a young lad.' He also didn't mind Peggy going out with George to the cinema, given that George always brought his annoying little brother Harry along with him, so there was no question of any funny business. Kathleen didn't much care for Harry, who was in the year below her at school. She made a mental note to kick him in the shins if he got on her nerves.

Later that afternoon there was a bit of a traffic jam down at the Elephant, as a tram had derailed and a police-man wearing white gloves had to direct all the cars and carts around it. Peggy waited while Kathleen pulled her socks up for the umpteenth time – it was her most annoy-ing habit, according to her older sister – before she took her hand and walked her across the bustling junction to the Trocadero. George was already waiting outside, his hair neatly brushed and parted. He was wearing long trousers with turn-ups, just like his dad. Kathleen was struck by quite how grown-up he looked – and how handsome. She gave him a shy little wave. His brother, Harry, appeared by his side and stuck his tongue out at Kathleen. She'd pay him back for that later. Boys really were just horrid little worms.

Going into the cinema was an experience in itself. Kathleen really did almost sink into the carpets, they were so thick, and there were mirrors everywhere. Harry pulled funny faces at himself but Kathleen was trying to behave as if she came here every week, to keep up appearances, so she didn't copy him. Once they had bought their tickets, they were shown to the stalls by an usherette wearing a neat little uniform with a pill-box hat at a jaunty angle, a black jacket with red piping over her blouse, a tight-fitting skirt and smart heels and lipstick. Once inside, Kathleen gazed at the vast balcony behind her, the curved ceiling with chandeliers and gold eagles everywhere. The last time she had seen anything this fancy was in the Italian church. The drapes were chocolate coloured and the ceiling was painted in a soft rose. The whole place was mouth-watering, good enough to eat.

Kathleen quite forgot to dislike Harry in the excitement of it all and started to chat to him about school until the lights went down and an usherette told her to shush. She obeyed immediately. There was no way she wanted to get chucked out. This was heaven. The main picture was called

The Prince of Arcadia but first they had to sit through a newsreel. Kathleen thought this was about as exciting as watching paint dry but Peggy and George sat with looks of rapt attention etched on their faces. It was mostly to do with Germany. There were soldiers marching everywhere and piles of books on fire.

'Nazis,' whispered George to Kathleen. 'That funny little fella with the moustache is Hitler, their leader. My dad says he looks like Charlie Chaplin but without the laughs.' The usherette shone a light over at George and motioned for him to button his lip.

When the newsreel finished, the curtains came down over the screen and a huge white Wurlitzer organ rose up from just in front of the stage. Kathleen watched as the organist's hands flew up and down the keyboard, the sound filling the whole cinema. He swayed a bit in his seat as he played and when he got to a loud bit, his whole body seemed to quake. When it was finished, he turned and gave an appreciative wave to the audience, who clapped loudly. Kathleen imagined herself playing that organ. Maybe she could, one day, if she practised really hard at school but she'd have to fit it in around her acting job as well. As the Wurlitzer sank beneath the stage, the usherette made another appearance at the foot of the stairs, with a tray around her neck and little cartons of popcorn in it.

George made a great show of pulling some coins out of his pocket to pay for two cartons – one for him and Peggy and one for his brother and Kathleen. Kathleen didn't really want to get too close to Harry while they were eating it. He was known as Nitty for a reason.

The main film had lots of singing in it, which Kathleen liked, and the story was about a prince from a country called Ruritania, who was supposed to marry a wealthy actress but fell in love with someone else instead, even though she was quite poor. While Kathleen agonized over whether he was going to make the right choice, Peggy and George seemed to be more interested in whispering and giggling together. What's more, Kathleen noticed that when the lights went up at the end of the film, George was holding Peggy's hand.

'Shall we stop off for sarsaparilla on the way home?' asked George, casually putting his arm around Peggy's shoulder. Kathleen smirked as she realized that Peggy hadn't brushed it away. Her sister used to tower over George but now he had caught up with her. They did make a nice couple, if only Peggy would admit to it.

They wandered down the Cut in a little gang, past an accordion player with a sign saying 'No Home, No Dole' around his neck. A couple of down-and-outs were sitting on upturned crates selling little bags of tobacco for roll-ups. Everyone knew they had picked it out of the fag butts on street corners but it was all they could do to scrape a living.

'What did you think of the film, George?' said Peggy.

'It was all right, I s'pose,' he said. 'Bit mushy romantic for me. More the sort of thing that you and Kathleen would enjoy, I bet.'

Peggy nudged him in the ribs and Kathleen rolled her eyes at him. She preferred to tag along with Peggy and

George, at the risk of feeling like a gooseberry, because Harry was really such a grubby little oik. He was kicking an empty bottle along in the gutter in front of them, making a bit of a nuisance of himself, as boys do.

They passed a second-hand clothes stall. Women were sifting through old dresses and skirts, holding them up and checking whether it was worth spending their hard-earned cash to remodel them into something more fashionable. Many a summer frock in their house had started life on someone else's back, but their mother always told them, 'Beggars can't be choosers.' Besides, there was nothing wrong with it; once the material had been washed, scrubbed and ironed, it was as good as new.

The man at the sarsaparilla stall was selling it hot, by the pint, mixed with blackcurrant. Kathleen slurped the hot black liquid and felt it warming her from the inside, listening to the sound of the accordion. Harry started tapping his feet.

'Why don't you give us a turn, Kathleen?' said Peggy. Kathleen shook her head. There was so much music, she felt sad not to be joining in like she used to but, as part of her private mourning for little Billy, it had now become a mark of respect to refrain.

When they got back to Howley Terrace there was a big commotion at the top end of the street where there was a patch of waste-ground much loved by the kids for larking about, but which also served as an unofficial boxing ring when scores needed to be settled with fists. The parents didn't like the kids going anywhere near it but of course, if there was a fight on, everyone got to hear about it. The local bookies would meander over from the pub and start taking bets – pennies, really, especially if it was kids. Peggy usually couldn't be persuaded to go down there at all but because George wanted to see, she went along reluctantly. Kathleen and Harry had already pushed their way to the front of the crowd. To the girls' horror there they saw their little brother, Frankie, in the middle, pummelling a huge kid to the ground, while Eva collected pennies for it.

'Frankie! No!' shouted Peggy, but he ignored her and kept punching the other boy in the face until his nose bled. When a big bloke from the wastepaper factory separated them, Frankie had such a fat lip that he couldn't go home but he was still smiling because he had won the fight.

'You'd better get yourself round to Nanny Day's,' said Kathleen, lending him her handkerchief, which he promptly covered in blood from the cut on his lip. 'If Dad sees you, you'll be for it.' Despite meting out beatings to them, their father wouldn't tolerate them being involved in street fights. Eva went off with him, counting their winnings.

As Kathleen, Peggy, George and Harry made their way back down the street, there was another dispute, this time between Mrs Avens and a burly-looking bloke who appeared to be carrying her precious sideboard off to a waiting horse and cart, while she clung on to it for dear life.

'No!' she cried. 'Give me more time. I'll get the money.'

'You've had your chance, missus,' he said, brushing her hands off the furniture, as if he were swatting a fly.

Kathleen turned to her big sister. 'That man is stealing Mrs Avens's family heirloom! We can't let him.'

Peggy held her back. 'No, Kath, don't,' she said. 'I think she must have had it on the never-never.'

Presiding over the whole scene, with a little smile playing on her lips, was Mrs Davies from number 16. So, all the endless stories about Mrs Avens's mother working her fingers to the bone to get that sideboard had been a pack of lies. Mrs Avens had got it on tick from a shop down the Elephant and had fallen into arrears with her repayments, especially now that her son had been laid off again.

Mrs Avens sat down, bereft, on her doorstep and began to cry, at which point several of the other women gave chase to the fella with the horse and cart, shaking their fists at him. It was too late. He was already clip-clopping his way down Belvedere Road and back to the shop, where the sideboard would be sold on, no doubt, to another customer – one who could keep up the repayments.

After the fuss had died down, George escorted Peggy home, while the others tagged along.

'Poor Mrs Avens,' said Peggy.

'The thing is, when you have moneylenders and people having to buy things on the never-never because their wages are so low, that is what you will get,' said George, thrusting his hands into his pockets. 'It's all wrong. The poorest end up the worst off. Something has got to change.'

They wandered along in silence for a bit. Peggy didn't have the answers to that and Kathleen certainly didn't. It was up to the powers-that-be to sort out those kind of things, not kids from Lambeth.

'I've joined a new book club,' he said. 'It's only two

shillings and sixpence a month and I get a new choice for six months on that.'

Kathleen yawned. Peggy's eyes went wide.

'What kinds of books are you getting, then?'

'Just had one on the miners' lockouts,' he said. 'I've got another by Wal Hannington due next month. Do you want to read it after me?'

'Love to,' said Peggy.

'They're having a meeting soon with speakers up in town at the assembly rooms,' he went on. 'Fancy coming along?'

'Ooh, you lovebirds make me sick,' Kathleen butted in. 'Come on, Peg, it's time for tea.' And she grabbed her sister by the arm and yanked her through the doorway before she could answer.

There were no familiar smells of cooking when they came through the door and Mum was nowhere to be seen. Only their father was there, hunched at the kitchen table with a face like thunder, chewing on a crust of bread.

'Kathleen, go on down to the Feathers and get your mother,' he said, barely looking up at them. 'She's been in there far too long, and Peggy, you go and get my shirts from Nanny Day; she hasn't brought them round either.'

'Yes, Dad.'

'Bloody women,' he mumbled to himself.

Kathleen and Peggy exchanged glances before leaving. Mum wasn't like those factory girls who went out for a drink after work. In fact, she'd barely set foot in a pub that they knew of. She'd been working as a cleaner in the Union

Jack Club when she met Dad before the Great War and she'd been mopping and scrubbing ever since.

The noise of the pub hit Kathleen first. You could hear the carousing and the sound of someone playing the piano from the end of the street. They were having a right old knees-up. She went up on tiptoes and peered through the frosted glass. A crowd was gathered around the piano, beer was swilling overhead in raised pint glasses and, to her amazement, she saw Mum smiling and laughing, swaying along in the sing-song with the rest of them. Her old school friend Flo from down in the Borough was by her side. Mum's face was flushed and her eyes sparkled. With a creeping sense of seeing something she wasn't supposed to, Kathleen realized that a tall man with a ready smile had his arm around her waist as they sang and he was gazing down at her in a way that Kathleen had never seen her father do. It was only for a split second because the pianist hammered out a new tune and they broke apart. Some of the women started lifting the hem of their skirts as the kicked their way across the pub and back, drinks flying everywhere: 'My old man said, follow the van, and don't dilly-dally on the waaay!'

Kathleen knew that tune well. It was one of her Nanny Day's favourites. She hummed along to the next verse. 'Off went the van with me home packed in it . . .'

A voice came from over her shoulder.

'Who are you spying on, then?' It was Joe, Mary's husband, from her street.

'No one,' she said, brushing the hair from her face. 'I just need to tell my mum she's wanted indoors.'

'All right then,' he said. Kathleen watched through the window as he pushed his way through the throng and leaned down to whisper in her mother's ear. She glanced over towards the door, a look of panic sweeping across her face. In an instant, she was outside, smoothing her skirt in the evening air.

'Everything all right?' she said, straightening her blouse.

'Dad was waiting, waiting for his tea,' said Kathleen, shuffling her feet. She didn't want to be the one who had to tell her mother that he was in a bad mood.

'That's all right, chicken,' said Mum overly brightly. 'Let's go home!' She was still humming 'My Old Man' as they walked along together.

The house lay silent when they got in; Peggy and the others were already upstairs. Kathleen started to creak her way up to bed but as soon as the door to the scullery had shut, she crept back down to listen at the closed door.

'Thought you weren't coming home,' Dad said quietly.

'Of course I was, just had a bit of fun with Flo, that's all.'

'So much fun you forgot to make my tea and I've been out since six this morning,' came the reply.

'Oh, don't be like that,' she said. 'You know it was only for Flo's birthday.'

'And who else's birthday will it be next week and the one after?'

'You're a fine one to talk!'

'What did you say to me?'

'You heard me,' she said, clattering some plates into the sink.

There was silence and then the sound of a slap and a little cry before her mother shouted, 'Don't hit me no more! I'm warning you!' A plate crashed to the floor and shattered.

'Threatening me, are you?' Her father's voice had such menace in it, it turned Kathleen's stomach.

'I'll scratch your eyes out!'

With her heart in her mouth, Kathleen silently held the door ajar and watched as her parents tussled with each other for a moment before Dad pulled his arm free and swung a blow at Mum's cheek. As it made contact, Mum squealed before collapsing at his feet.

He raised his fists again. Mum was begging him now, 'Please, James, don't.'

Her father spun around. 'Who's there?' But Kathleen had already scarpered up the stairs, two at a time, praying that he wouldn't follow her. She took refuge in the bedroom with Eva and Peggy, who were pretending to be asleep.

Kathleen put her fingers in her ears and started to sing quietly to herself, 'I dillied and dallied, dallied and dillied, lost me way and don't know where to roam, you can't trust a special like the old time copper when you can't find your way home . . .' as the awful cries of her mother's suffering filled the house.

13

Eva, December 1934

The pavement at Holborn Circus was chock-full of people doing their Christmas shopping. Children and their parents formed an orderly queue to see Father Christmas, while customers, weighed down with bags and parcels, bustled in and out of the grand shop entrance. Eva peered into the window of Gamages People's Popular Emporium, which was crammed full of toys for the Christmas bazaar display, and her heart fluttered with the excitement of it all. Then she caught the determined look on Alice Diamond's face. There was little chance of her getting any free time in the toy department. She was here to work.

Percy, their driver, was already parked up in his motor outside and Alice had several other girls from the Forty Thieves working their way through the shop, with its warren of corridors and staircases. Gamages was a hoister's delight: dark corners, nooks and crannies and dozy shop assistants who could be sent off to the backroom to look for something in a particular size or colour while the Forty Thieves pilfered for all they were worth.

Maggie Hughes, the most experienced of Alice's girls – and her unofficial deputy – preferred the West End stores such as Marshall and Snelgrove, and Selfridges, or Derry and Toms over in Kensington for rich pickings, but Alice was counting on the Christmas shopping rush to provide the perfect cover for her gang to clean up. The weather was to play its part too, as a freezing fog hung in the air, already yellowing in the failing light of a London afternoon, thanks to the fumes belched from the factories down by the river. The street lamps would soon be lit and it was not yet three o'clock.

'Right,' said Alice, pulling her mink stole tightly around her. 'It's going to be a pea-souper. Let's get on with it.'

They joined a slow-moving throng edging its way through the ground floor, which seemed to have every square inch of space filled with goods. There were gloves, hats and scarves, books, leather wallets and spectacle cases, alongside binoculars, manicure sets and even a shoe-shine kit. The queue for the till was already three deep and the distracted shop assistant was no match for Alice, who insisted she wanted a pair of gloves in the darkest shade of green, rather than what was on show.

In an instant, as the assistant's back was turned, Maggie was at the display, her vast carpet bag was opened like a hungry mouth, just out of sight beneath the counter, while Eva's little fingers flicked things into it. At one point, Maggie boldly, and with a sweep of her arm, shoved some of the mountain of leather gloves into it. The shop assistant returned and looked quizzically at her half-empty display but Alice kept her talking and made a great fuss of finding the right change for the moss-green gloves, which she paid for at the till. Eva and Maggie, meanwhile, had made their way through the crush of warm bodies bundled up in their winter coats, to one of the many staircases to go up to ladieswear on the next floor.

They started in the undergarments section, which was so quiet it was like a mausoleum, so Maggie said. No fellas would dare set foot in there and the shop assistants were usually snooty old matrons with tape measures slung around their necks and half-moon glasses.

Eva was getting quite an education in underwear: silk stockings, finest slips and corselettes. These things were nothing like the underwear worn by her mother and sisters but Eva knew all about them because she had helped pinch them. They were what posh ladies wore; well, posh ladies and the Forty Thieves, who dressed like film stars around the Elephant, with nice hair and clothes and make-up. Eva was still dressing like a twelve-year-old schoolgirl, because that is what she was and it was part of her cover as a member of the gang, but the moment she was old enough, Alice had promised she could have some really grown-up clothes of her own. Eva couldn't wait.

Maggie held up nightdress after nightdress, humming and hah-ing. She laid each one on the counter. There were so many of them, the shop assistant was getting a little impatient.

'And will madam be buying?'

'Yes,' said Maggie. 'Madam will. I'll have this, please. She picked up the teensiest silk handkerchief and dumped another armload of nighties at the till.

'What about a handkerchief for Granny as well?' said Eva. The assistant turned and pulled out a drawer full of handkerchiefs which she laid reverently on the glass counter top next to the heap of silk clothing. Right on cue, Alice Diamond sidled up and plonked her winter coat on top of the counter. 'Blooming hot in here,' she said, mopping her brow. Her mink stole was slung over one shoulder. 'You are taking ages,' she said to Maggie. 'I'll meet you in the furs department, shall I?' With that, she picked up her coat, taking with it half of the silk nightwear from the top of the counter before walking off briskly. Those clothes were quickly stuffed into her capacious handbag, which she switched with that of another accomplice in the corridor between the underwear and the fur coats section. Eva knew the routine. That girl would make her way down to Percy, the driver, switch the bag and come back with an empty one. The whole procedure would be repeated several times; Alice and her girls had been known to make quite an afternoon of it before leaving any shop.

'No, that's not right,' said Maggie, just as the assistant was about to ring the handkerchief sale through the till. 'She only likes spotty hankies! Silly! We forgot, didn't we?'

The shop assistant scowled. Eva gave her a sweet smile. 'Thanks so much for your help!' And the pair of them walked off, towards the furs department.

This was where Alice hoped to make a few bob. The freezing London winter meant every woman coveted a fur coat or a nice stole or a little fur hat. Eva spied a couple more of Alice's girls trying on the hats and shoving a few in the inside pockets of their voluminous coats. The plan was for Alice and Eva to screen Maggie while she hid a couple of fur coats about her person: down her drawers to be precise. She was wearing her specially made shoplifter's drawers, to the knee, with tight elastic, to prevent stolen goods from tumbling out onto the floor. Maggie specialized in clouting – rolling up the coats and stuffing them down her underwear.

The department was bustling, full of Christmas shoppers, many of pulling coats off the hangers and trying them on, under the beady eye of several shop assistants. Floor space was at a premium, with rail after rail of coats crammed in next to each other, and that was something Alice and her gang liked to exploit because it made it harder for the assistants to see what they were up to. Some stores, such as Selfridges, had started to employ walkers. They were paid by the shop to go around pretending to be shoppers but they were really on the look-out for thieves. Discussions about how many walkers they had evaded that day usually formed a part of the conversation in Alice's Scovell Road scullery, with Maggie chipping in, 'They stick out like a sore thumb, silly cows.'

Alice, Eva and Maggie crowded around some full-length sable coats and in an instant Alice had pulled a coat off and thrown it around her shoulders as she stood behind Maggie. Eva could just see the head of an assistant bobbing closer over the next rail.

'Ooh,' she cried, as Maggie lifted her dress, pulled a coat and a hanger off the rail and rolled it with lightning-quick fingers. 'Ooh, help, I feel a bit faint.'

Maggie had her back turned and was already stuffing the tightly rolled coat into her drawers as Eva half-fell onto the assistant to block her view.

'Are you all right, miss?' said the shocked shop girl, catching Eva in her arms.

'I think I need some fresh air,' said Eva, standing back up. 'It's just so hot in here.'

'Shouldn't you be in school?'

Alice, who by now had appropriated the full-length coat around her shoulders as her own, patted the shop girl on the arm. 'She's been so sick, she's been up the 'ospital and everything. Doctor says it's catching.'

Eva coughed, loudly, and the shop girl withdrew. Maggie, meanwhile, was already waddling her way out of the furs department.

'Watches next,' hissed Alice under her breath. 'Then it's home for tea.'

The Gamages watch department was quieter than the rest of the store, which made getting away with any theft more of a challenge. Eva felt inside her coat pocket. Yes, the watch Alice had given her was there. It was an expensive make, a Rolex, but it was a dud – it had stopped working ages ago – and the plan was to switch it for a similar one, without the assistant noticing.

Maggie and Eva strolled up to the glass-topped counter and smiled at the assistant. He didn't smile back. 'Afternoon,' said Maggie. 'We'd like to have a look at some of your lovely watches, please.'

The man peered at them through a pair of little round glasses, his eyes unblinking. 'What is your budget?'

'I'll tell you that when I have seen what you have got on offer,' said Maggie.

'Very well.' He sighed, as if his entire afternoon had been spent dealing with time-wasters. He produced a velvet-lined tray from under the counter and began to lay a selection of half a dozen watches on it.

Maggie picked one up and passed it to Eva. 'Be careful!' he said. 'These items cost more than a month's wages.'

'Perhaps for some, but not for us, isn't that right?' She gave Eva a conspiratorial little nudge. Eva blushed. That was a silly comment to make and Eva could smell the drink on Maggie's breath. Maggie liked taking risks but Eva wasn't experienced enough to want to do that yet. She just needed to get the watch out of her pocket and swapped with one on that tray.

'I'd like to look at a Rolex, please,' said Eva. 'It's for my mum.'

'Expensive taste,' said the assistant, raising an eyebrow. He pulled out another tray of watches, all of them were Rolexes.

Eva felt the edges of the one in her pocket. She had memorized its shape. It was unusual in that it had eight edges to it and she knew it was gold with a brown leather strap. The exact watch was there on the tray before her, except for one detail: the one from the shop had a black leather strap. Alice drifted past them, smiling. She gave Eva a wink. Eva swallowed hard. She had to find a way to swap it.

Alice stood at the other side of the counter. 'Excuse me!'

The shop assistant ignored her for a few seconds, so she boomed out, 'What does one have to do to get served around here!'

'I'm so sorry, madam.' He grimaced. 'I am just dealing with customers and I will be with you shortly.'

Alice took out a wodge of pound notes and waved them in the air. 'I have got the money to buy, chum, but I haven't got time to waste.'

As he turned and his mouth fell open at the sight of so much ready cash, Eva grabbed the watch from the tray and switched it with the one in her pocket, her heart pounding. He spun back around, his eyes sweeping across the watches on the counter in front of him. The right number were still there.

'Would you ladies excuse me?' he said, sweeping the trays away from Maggie's grasp. 'I have another customer to attend to.'

Eva and Maggie shrugged their shoulders and meandered back through the store. One thing Alice had taught her was to take her time, never to rush, to look as if she was totally comfortable, with nothing to hide. They sauntered through to the toy department, where children were crowded around a miniature boating lake, gazing at the little boats sailing on it. There was a model railway too, with a station and everything. Her brothers would have loved that. Her hands were clammy with nerves. That watch was the most expensive thing she had ever stolen, maybe even the most expensive thing she'd ever seen, and it was burning a hole in her pocket.

She was just following Maggie towards the exit when she heard a voice shout across the shop floor, 'Hey, you! Stop!' She spun around, to see the man from the watch stand, accompanied by another woman, pushing their way through the crowds. Maggie turned briefly and then elbowed a few people out of the way as she headed towards the door. Eva tried to follow, but someone held her back when she was just a few yards from the door, grabbing her arm in a vice-like grip. 'Oi! You are wanted by that man over there.'

In a moment, they were on her, the watch man and the lady assistant. 'Turn out your pockets.'

Eva did as he asked but kept the gold watch in its place, tucked into her pocket.

He reached in, felt inside her coat and pulled it out, with a look of triumph on his face.

'I knew it!' the watch man said. 'You stole this!'

'No, I never,' she said quietly. 'It belongs to my dad.'

'You liar! You switched it with this one.' He dangled the broken watch in front of her nose.

Alice Diamond appeared. 'I think there has been a misunderstanding. My daughter, she's a bit slow.' She tapped the side of her head. 'She's trying to get her father a present, that's all.'

A few people were listening, open-mouthed. Others pretended not to notice and just bustled past to get on with their shopping.

'It's stealing,' said the watch man. 'And you pretended not to know her earlier. You are in on this too!' He turned to the woman beside him. 'Go and get the manager.'

'No need for that, surely?' said Alice. 'She's done wrong and I will make sure she gets punished for it when I get her home.' She delivered a slap to the side of Eva's head, which hurt like hell. 'What have I told you about taking things you like? Haven't I told you it's wrong?'

Eva started to cry, without too much effort, because Alice's backhand was enough to knock someone's block off.

Someone said, 'Oh, leave her be, she's simple, you can see that,' and there were murmurs of approval from the assembled shoppers.

'A likely story,' said the watch man. 'The police will be here—'

But he didn't get to finish his sentence because Alice made a fist, turned suddenly and smacked him right in the mouth with her row of diamond rings. He staggered backwards and as he did so, Alice snatched the working Rolex back from him. Then she yanked her hatpin out and brandished it at the crowd of onlookers. 'Anyone else want some?'

There was now a clear foot of space around them. 'Run!' she said to Eva. Eva didn't hesitate; she made a break for it, tumbling through the door into the street. Alice followed, leaping in through the open door of the motor car, which already had its engine going. It all happened so fast. Eva's legs were carrying her towards the car but the car was already screeching around the corner without her.

The lady shop assistant was through the doors. Their eyes met for an instant. Eva turned on her heel and sprinted, ducking and weaving through the crowds and into the fog, which froze in her lungs as she quickened her pace. She couldn't see more than twenty yards in each direction now but she didn't stop running, her little feet pounding the pavement. A bus was pulling away into the road in front of her, heading towards Tottenham Court Road. She leaped onto it, almost squashing the bus conductor, and took her seat, glancing back over her shoulder. The shop assistant had given up the chase but Eva's heart was still pounding out of her chest with the fear of it all. She hopped off the bus at Holborn Tube Station and lost herself in the maze of backstreets around the Seven Dials in Covent Garden, just to be sure.

From there it was a familiar walk, down Bow Street and back across Waterloo Bridge, where she took the tram down to the Borough, to Alice's tenement. Eva was more than a little bit worried about what Alice would do to her for giving up that watch. At least Alice had grabbed it back but that was not the point. She was supposed to be one of the Forty Thieves and she'd let Alice down.

As she trudged up the three flights of stairs to Alice's flat, she could hear raucous laughter from the women in there. She pushed open the front door and Alice greeted her with open arms. 'And here she is!' she said, ushering her in to the scullery. 'Gawd, we gave them a fright, didn't we?'

'You're not angry with me?' said Eva.

'No, love, of course I'm not! You did a great job of hoisting that watch! If there's anyone at fault, it's Maggie, isn't that right, Mags?'

Maggie looked up from her tot of rum and scowled.

'She should have taken it off you when she had the chance, in case someone checked your pockets,' said Alice. 'Did they chase you far?'

'No, only a little way down the road,' said Eva, brightening. It all seemed such an adventure now she was safely back with the gang in Alice's flat. 'I couldn't get to the car in time.'

'I know,' said Alice, pouring her a reviving cuppa. 'But I knew you'd outrun them. I'd never leave you on a job, you know that, don't you? I always look after my girls.'

Eva held her gaze for a second, wondering if Alice meant that. Would she really have made sure she was all right, or would she have just left her to fend for herself?

Sensing Eva's doubt, Alice came over and patted her on the shoulder. 'In fact, as a reward, I have got a little surprise for you. I know you've been wanting to get that songbird sister of yours a piano, haven't you?'

'Yes,' said Eva. She'd hardly managed to save anything; she'd been giving money to her mum instead.

'Well, a lovely one fell off the back of a lorry down the Elephant the other day. I'll have it sent round at the weekend. Will that be enough time for you and your ma to get it past your dad?'

'I expect so,' said Eva, with a grin. That was brilliant! It was Kathleen's birthday coming up and the piano would make the best present ever.

Alice reached into a shopping bag and pulled out a frock.

'And here's a dress. Your older sister's a skinny thing ain't she? Bit taller than you but not much? This will fit her.'

Peggy would be thrilled! It wasn't exactly like the one

she'd been talking about getting but it was lovely, just the thing for a night out with George Harwood.

'What in the name of God Almighty is that piano doing in this house?'

Her dad was gobsmacked by the arrival of the musical instrument, to say the least, when he got in from a hard day's work to find it taking pride of place in their tiny living room. Kathleen had been bashing out every tune she could think of ever since its arrival this morning and by teatime half the street was crammed into their house, having a good old sing-song.

'I saved some money from the housekeeping and Peggy put a few bob aside, didn't you, Peg?' said Mum airily.

Peggy shot her a look of disbelief, but then nodded in agreement.

'That's all very well but I have been thinking, Maggie, you won't be needing as much housekeeping in the future, will you? Now Peggy is working, I am going to dock your allowance. If you've got enough to buy pianos . . .'

'But it was a special present!' said Eva.

'Don't give me any of your lip,' said Dad. Eva stared at the floor.

The party atmosphere was ruined. People slipped back out into the street. Mum sighed. 'I'll put the kettle on for some tea.' They were just spreading some jam on slices of bread to celebrate Kathleen and Jim's fourteenth birthdays, when Nanny Day came through the front door. She was red in the face from running.

'It's Uncle Dennis. He's had a bad turn with his chest.

Grandad's taken him up the hospital. They are going to see to him but he's on almoner's rates. He's not had a penny to rub together since the four years' war. I will have to go the parish and ask for help,' she said, wringing her hands.

'Don't worry, Ma,' Mum said, looking at Eva, 'it will all be all right, you'll see.'

Eva understood perfectly. Tomorrow she would go shopping again.

14

Peggy, January 1935

The dress was possibly the most beautiful thing that Peggy had ever seen. It was covered in a print of pink roses and had a smart little collar and a belt made of the same material, to pull in at the waist. It would suit her for work and for going out to the cinema with George. She desperately wanted to try it on but she bit her lip and handed it back to Eva.

'I can't take this, Eve,' she said, reading the disappointment in her little sister's eyes.

'Why not?' said Eva. 'Don't you like it?'

'I love it,' said Peggy. 'But that is not the point. I know where it's come from.'

'Well, it's come from a shop, if that is what you mean . . .'

'It's stolen, Eva.'

Eva gazed out of the window. 'How long do you suppose it would take the likes of us to save up to buy a dress like that?'

'A long time,' said Peggy. 'I can't accept it because it is stolen and I don't believe in stealing.'

Eva spun round. 'You think you're better than me, a cut above.'

'No, I don't,' said Peggy, reaching out to give her a hug. 'I know you did it for me with the best will in the world, but I want to work hard to earn what I have. And I believe that if wages for people like us, who work hard, were better we would all stand a better chance in life.'

'Oh, Gawd,' said Eva, 'you're going to give me one of Georgie Harwood's little sermons, aren't you?'

'That's not fair, Eva,' said Peggy, reddening. 'I happen to share a lot of his views about the way workers are not paid enough and the need for us all to stand together. Being part of a gang of thieves—'

'Don't you go saying that in the house where Dad can hear you!' hissed Eva. 'You know he'll give me what for.'

'I won't say anything, of course I won't. I'm your sister, Eva, I want to look out for you. I'm just worried about you, that's all. What if you get caught?'

Eva snatched up the dress and stuffed it under her mattress. 'I won't get caught. Now, off you go, Miss High and Mighty, or you'll be late for work.'

Peggy mulled it over on the way to the office in Kensington. She could have taken the dress; nobody would have known and it would probably have got her a few admiring glances on the tram. But, as she settled down to read her latest book on Communism from George, she soon forgot all about the frock and was too absorbed to notice the way that men were looking at her, in any case. She wasn't as beautiful as Kathleen, who seemed to have inherited their mother's good looks and easy manner, but she was tall and striking, with strong features and dark, wavy hair, which she now wore loose to her shoulders and pinned back above her ears. Her friend Susan had showed her how to style it like the ladies in the magazines.

When she got to work, Edna, who sat opposite her, was already there, working away quietly. She'd been with the company for fifteen years and was still on lower clerical duties, like most of the other women, even though she was as bright as a button and knew the workings of the Post Office Savings Bank inside out. Whenever Peggy had a problem, she'd only to ask Edna. She knew each ledger, each rule, like the back of her hand. She'd adjust her cardigan and shuffle off to the other side of the office and return with whatever Peggy needed, with a ready smile.

Edna lived with her mother over in Acton and only ever talked about her cats. Her hair was grey and wiry and her eyes watered almost constantly behind her glasses. Peggy feared that she was looking into her own future whenever she gazed at Edna. If she wanted to keep working, she could never marry or have children because the Post Office, like all big firms, wouldn't employ married women. The unions wouldn't stand for it either – taking jobs away from men in a time of such high unemployment – and even the Government had been looking into what it called 'the women question', George had told her. He believed that women, married women, should have the right to go out to work if they wanted to. 'And in Russia, they have nurseries paid for by the state to allow women to do just that,' he said. Peggy wasn't sure she would want to work if she ever got married, especially if she had children – not that she had been thinking about that.

Miss Fisher, their supervisor, was one of the few women

who had managed to progress up the career ladder a bit, but she had seen countless blokes promoted past her, even though she could probably have done their jobs with her eyes closed. She was really buttoned up, precise and proper. Peggy couldn't imagine her ever having any fun, or a boyfriend. She'd sacrificed everything for her career and was married to the job. Rumour had it she had even marched with the Suffragettes and campaigned for women's rights but no one had dared to ask her about it. She was such a stickler for protocol, it would seem like an intrusion, talking to the boss like that, but Peggy was secretly intrigued.

Susan arrived ten minutes late that day, looking a bit off-colour. Miss Fisher glared at her and tapped her wristwatch. 'The old dragon's watching me again,' said Susan, shrugging off her jacket and sitting down at the desk next to Peggy.

'Was the bus late?'

'No,' said Susan. 'I wasn't feeling too good and it took my mum ages to persuade me to get out of bed.'

Miss Fisher came over. For once she didn't tell them off. 'Now, girls,' she said. She was including Edna in this, even though Edna was probably older than Miss Fisher. 'Girls, there is a staff-side meeting after work today, in which we will discuss the possibility of some extra work opportunities for women.'

'What kind of opportunities, miss?' said Peggy, whose interest was piqued. Perhaps she had been a friend of the Suffragettes and gone on marches, waving Votes for Women placards, after all, although she couldn't imagine

Miss Fisher breaking the rules. She was just too strait-laced.

'Extra training to work in areas such as a cable room,' said Miss Fisher, with a note of softness in her voice. It was not a tone Peggy had heard from her before. Maybe she wasn't so bad. 'Good opportunities for bright girls such as yourself, Peggy.' She pointedly excluded Susan from that compliment, Peggy noticed. Edna's eyes lit up.

'We're looking for younger girls, Edna,' said Miss Fisher gently, as Edna's shoulders sagged with disappointment. 'But there is no reason that you can't come along and lend your weight to the argument. The point is, the representatives from the union are meeting to discuss the possibility of this and we will hear differing viewpoints . . .'

'You mean, the men don't want us to do this,' said Peggy flatly.

'Well, some men do and some don't, but it is important that as women our voices are heard. I wrote to the union magazine *Red Tape* with some of my own views about it and they just published my letter.' She brandished a copy of the magazine under Peggy's nose. 'In the meantime, the more women we can get along to the meeting, the better. I will put a note up in the women's lounge at lunchtime. Perhaps you can let some of the others know?'

Susan yawned as Miss Fisher walked back to her desk at the other side of the office. 'Sounds dull as dishwater. I won't be going.'

'Oh, don't be like that,' said Peggy. 'Imagine working the cable room!'

'She's turned into a right Mrs Pankhurst; don't you go

joining her!' said Susan. 'Oh, God, I feel sick again. Tell the old bat I'm going to chuck up, if she asks.' And she ran from the room.

The yellowing wallpaper of the men's lounge at the other end of Blythe House was testament to the long hours the workers had spent puffing away in there, on their breaks. Women were normally not allowed anywhere near that side of the building but as it was a union meeting, the bosses had waived the strict segregation rule. This alone had persuaded Susan to join Peggy.

'I can't wait to see what stuff they have got in there. Bet their chairs are more comfy than ours,' she whispered, as Miss Fisher led a delegation of her 'girls' into the men's den.

Susan was rather disappointed to see that their easy chairs, if anything, were less homely than those in the women's lounge. Everything was in shades of brown: the carpet, the table, the seats. There were no cosy touches – no vase of flowers, no pile of magazines to flick through – just overflowing ashtrays and a dartboard.

'Smells like the inside of a bleeding pub,' she grumbled to Peggy. 'All those sweaty blokes.'

The meeting was called to order and the assembled crowd stopped chatting to each other and stared at the gaggle of female interlopers.

'Comrades,' said the union rep.

'And ladies,' interrupted Miss Fisher, who clearly wasn't having any truck with this Moscow nonsense.

He cleared his throat as a ripple of laughter washed

across the room. 'Comrades and *ladies*, thank you for coming along this evening to this very important meeting.

'Management want our views on whether there is scope for some jobs – men's jobs and in the cable room, to be precise – to be made available to our female comrades in the workforce.'

Miss Fisher sighed audibly.

'They'll do our jobs for less pay, and where will that leave us?' said one bearded man, stuffing tobacco into his pipe with vigour.

'And what about the unemployed? There's not enough jobs for the menfolk as it is!' The room became rowdy with an exchange of complaints from the assembled male workers.

'Order!' cried the union rep. 'We want to support our female comrades but the mood of the meeting seems clear—'

'If I may be allowed to speak,' interjected Miss Fisher, as Peggy stood at her side. 'It is not a case of women taking men's jobs. Yes, we are paid less for doing the same tasks, which is something that the union should be talking to the management about in any case, but women are capable of doing more, much more, than they are allowed to do within the Post Office. At busy times, such as Christmas, it would be useful to have women trained and ready to step in and help at the very least in areas such as the cable room.'

'Hear, hear,' said Peggy, before she realized what she was even saying.

Susan nudged her in the ribs. 'Shush! You'll draw attention to yourself.'

Miss Fisher went on, 'We would also ask the union to support the demand for the marriage bar to be lifted, so that if women wed, they should not be forced to resign.'

A loud chorus of jeers erupted. 'Oh, come on, love!', 'Rome wasn't built in a day, you know, we've got enough problems of our own!'

'Who will look after the kids, then?' another man said.

Miss Fisher produced a copy of *Red Tape* from behind her back and waved it in the air. 'If you want a real revolution, let it be a women's revolution. Please feel free to read my letter in the latest edition of the union magazine on equal pay for women and the right for women to have both a fulfilling private life and a professional career.'

The boos were almost deafening but Miss Fisher would not back down that easily and began engaging her detractors, one by one. Peggy was amazed to see her boss calmly taking on the men in this way. It gave her a new respect for Miss Fisher. She was about to ask Susan what she thought of it all but when she turned around, she saw that Susan was no longer by her side. She pushed her way through the double doors and into the corridor, to see her friend running off down the stairs and into the staff canteen.

Peggy followed, quickening her pace, and got into the canteen just as Susan darted into the ladies' lavatories. The sound of retching bounced off the tiled walls.

'Are you all right, Susan?' Peggy whispered, knocking on a cubicle door.

Susan emerged a few moments later, wiping flecks of vomit from around her mouth. Her hands were clutching her stomach. Peggy noticed, for the first time, that it was fuller than usual, and protruding from the tight waistband of her skirt.

Their eyes met, in a moment of recognition and horror.

Susan began to cry. 'I think I'm pregnant, Peg. I'm done for. Me dad will kill me for this.'

Susan disappeared from her work at the Post Office Savings Bank almost overnight, before the shame of her situation became glaringly obvious. Peggy didn't tell her parents about it. She wasn't sure how her mother would react but her father would tell her to cut off all contact with her friend. She desperately wanted to see Susan but was too frightened to go around there in person. Peggy was almost ashamed to admit it but she was scared: scared to face Susan's parents, in case they blamed her. She was supposed to be with her on the night that it all went wrong with Bert, so she felt somehow responsible and now Susan was pregnant, which was the worst thing for an unmarried young woman.

She spoke to the one person she could trust: George. Peggy skirted over the more gruesome details of how Susan came to be in this predicament but she made one thing clear: it wasn't really Susan's fault.

'What do you suppose she'll do?' said George, as they made their way down to the Trocadero to catch another show. They talked in hushed tones, so that Kathleen and his little brother Harry didn't overhear.

'I'm going to write to her and find out,' said Peggy. 'I suppose she'll have to keep it.'

George lowered his voice even further. 'There are other ways . . .'

They both knew that in their neighbourhood there were women who would help girls who had got themselves into trouble. One was rumoured to do it with a knitting needle and the payment was a bag of coal. But there were also horror stories, whispered in the draughty corridors of tenement blocks and passed around in hushed tones at the communal laundry, of things going wrong: of girls left unable to have children or bleeding to death after botched abortions.

Of course, girls did have babies out of wedlock. There was one around the corner in Tenison Street, for a start. But her mother was raising the baby as her own and the daughter just pretended she was her sister and went out to work at the jam factory. Her parents watched their daughter like a hawk, though, and she was never seen on the streets after dark. The whole area knew the child was illegitimate but nobody said anything about it or made fun of the baby, in fact, quite the reverse. It became a sort of neighbourhood secret. Even Mrs Davies from number 16 kept her trap shut on that one, which was a mercy.

'I don't know, I don't know,' said Peggy, wringing her hands. 'I expect she will have to have it but she was worried that her dad was going to beat the living daylights out of her for getting herself in the family way.' Peggy could only hope that people in Susan's neighbourhood would be as nice as her own but she had her doubts.

Back at the office, if Miss Fisher knew the real reason for Susan's absence, she didn't let on to Peggy. Edna didn't have much to say about Susan's departure either, other than a rather barbed comment about her friend having had 'a rather high opinion of herself'. Edna bustled off towards the filing cabinet, singing an old musical hall song: 'Little bits of powder, little bits of paint, make a girl look like what she ain't.' Had Edna guessed what had happened to Susan?

Peggy found it hard to focus and kept glancing out of the window, wondering whether a letter from Susan might be waiting for her on the mat when she got home from work. She'd tried to keep the tone of her letter to her friend jolly, she offered to meet her somewhere for a proper chat and told her she missed her but part of her didn't really expect a reply. Families tended to close ranks when such disasters happened and she wasn't even sure if Susan's father would let her out of his sight to post a letter, in any case.

Just as she was about to go on her tea break, she heard a commotion in the corridor outside. A crowd of clerks were gathered around a notice which had been pinned to the back of the door.

'I saw a fella put it up just now!' said one girl. 'He wasn't even supposed to be over this side and he ran off, sharpish, when he saw me.'

Miss Fisher came storming over from her desk at the other side of the room to see what all the fuss was about.

In bold, black writing, the notice said: 'Miss Fisher is MRS SMITH. We know the truth!'

'What does it mean, miss?' said another girl, as the colour drained from Miss Fisher's face.

The supervisor reached up and tore it down, screwing the paper into a little ball. 'Get back to work!' she whispered.

Peggy tried to put her hand on Miss Fisher's arm, to comfort her in some way, but she brushed her away. 'No, Peggy. Please return to your seat and get on with what you have to do.' Her tone softened. 'Whatever happens, I want you to know that you are a very promising young clerk and I expect the very best from you.'

Then, Miss Fisher turned on her heel and marched twenty yards down the corridor and into the manager's office. Moments later, she left, walking out of the building with her back straight and her head held high. The manager followed her for a few steps, his mouth open in shock.

Nobody ever admitted pinning that notice up about her. Nobody was punished for it but some of the girls insisted it had been the work of the men in the union. Others around the office – including Edna – said she'd let everyone down by lying like that, marrying and still coming to work day after day, to boss them all around.

Peggy just felt sad that Miss Fisher, who had turned out to be a good boss, was no longer working just because she had dared to try to have a life and a career at the same time.

15

Kathleen, May 1935

'It was the gas what got him,' said Grandad.

'What are you on about now?' snapped Nanny Day. 'He had tuberculosis.'

'Yes, but his lungs were never the same after the mustard gas attacks. You ask the butcher.'

'Oh stop wittering on,' said Nanny, who had been ever so grumpy since her brother, Old Uncle Dennis, had died.

Kathleen had been spending more time around in Cornwall Road, with her mother's blessing, to try to cheer Nanny Day up but it didn't seem to be working. Even going up to the Cut to get her a pint of prawns or whelks did little to lift her mood. To make matters worse, Grandad's leg had been playing up and he had to go up to the hospital a lot to see the doctors, which meant he wanted looking after too and Nanny didn't want to be bested in her hour of grief. Kathleen felt she was keeping two squabbling children apart half the time when she was round there. Only the prospect of her new job at the Hartley's jam factory down in Bermondsey seemed to break the deadlock.

'I expect you're excited about going out to the factory,

aren't you?' said Nanny Day, stirring a pot on the range. 'Do you know what section you will be working in?'

'Haven't a clue,' said Kathleen, who was pleased to put her school days behind her, but nervous about entering the world of work.

'She'll be in the clever girls' section because that is what she is,' said Grandad. 'Makes me proud.'

'Of course she's clever! She's my granddaughter!' said Nanny Day, turning to pinch Kathleen's cheeks.

Kathleen smiled. She was bright but she knew she was not as clever as her big sister Peggy, who seemed to have got all the brains in the family. Peggy had helped Kathleen's twin, Jim, to get a job as an errand boy for the General Post Office up at Mount Pleasant, which her parents were really pleased about. Kathleen, meanwhile, was going to be a factory girl, with a few of her friends from school, including Nancy.

Of course, it wasn't her dream job. She hadn't given up hope of going on the stage in the West End but she was realistic enough to know that she had to earn a living. She was young, only fourteen, so there was plenty of time for her to make it to the West End. She had mentioned to her parents about getting some proper dance lessons and maybe trying out as a chorus girl up at one of the shows but the look on her father's face had stopped her pursuing that – for now.

When Dad's back was turned, Mum had whispered, 'We'll talk to Eva about starting a little fund for some lessons. Don't you worry.' And that had made her feel a bit better. She still had plenty of time to make it on stage and some of the big stars from Hollywood started out waiting tables, so there was no shame in it, Nancy said so.

Besides, Mum was cock-a-hoop at Kathleen getting the job because she knew from other people in the neighbourhood that, among the many factories south of the river which kept Britain's larders stocked, Hartley's was one of the most generous firms to work for. There was Peek Frean's for biscuits, Jacob's for cream crackers and Crosse and Blackwell for pickles, but Hartley's gave their workers a share of the profits, a pension, sick pay and a convalescent scheme. There was even a social club and day trips out on a charabanc to Margate – Kathleen couldn't wait to go on one. There'd be bound to be loads of sing-songs for a start, and she relished the chance to show off her singing voice.

'I don't care how boring it is, Kathleen,' her mother told her early on her first morning, as Kathleen sat, bleary-eyed in the scullery. 'You make the most of it, my girl, because it ain't jam tomorrow, it's jam today as far as you are concerned with that factory. You won't find anything better, you mark my words.'

Some of the other girls from Tenison Street had told her how to get to the factory and they had warned her not to be late, so Kathleen got up early on the first day, with butterflies in her stomach which even a chunk of bread and marg couldn't sort out. She met up with Nancy at the tram on Waterloo Road, which took them down to the Elephant, where they hopped on a bus to Rothsay Road. They joined a horde of women and men hurrying towards a vast red-brick building, six storeys high, spreading out in all directions, with a central chimney billowing smoke into the morning sky and the name HARTLEY'S picked out in white lettering on the brickwork. A hooter sounded at eight minutes to eight and there was a stampede towards the wrought-iron gates which guarded the factory entrance. Kathleen and Nancy were swept along with hundreds of people, pushing into a courtyard.

The most delicious sweet smell filled the air. 'Jam,' said Nancy, licking her lips. Kathleen was just happy they didn't have to work at one of the tanneries or the glue factory, which stank to high heaven, but she had a feeling that after a day, she'd be sick of the smell of jam.

Once through the gates, people filed off to different parts of the factory and the girls had to ask where to go. A man in a smart uniform directed them up to the third floor to register for work and get their cards to clock in and out. The thrum of the engines in the basement which kept the vats of hot jam bubbling could be heard and felt as they made their way up the narrow staircase. They walked down a highly polished parquet floor and stopped outside a door with a little sign on it. It said 'MANAGER, MISS KENDRICK'. Knocking quietly, they heard a woman say, 'Come in!'

She was busy with a pile of papers and barely looked up as she said to Kathleen, 'Labelling. Go down to the factory floor and report to the supervisors there. They will fit you out with an apron and hat.'

'Yes, miss,' said Kathleen.

'What about me?' said Nancy, twirling a finger through her hair.

The woman looked over her half-moon glasses. 'You can work on filling. We have a vacancy there. And you'll have to tie that back,' she said, waving a pencil at Nancy's abundant curly hair. 'It's three-quarters of an hour lunch break and if you are late by more than five minutes we will dock you half an hour's pay. Two lavatory breaks per day while you are on shift and you clock on at eight and clock off at six – noon on Saturdays. Clear?'

'Yes, miss,' they chorused. It was as if they had never left school.

'Well, what are you waiting for?' she said, handing them their cards, to clock in and out. 'Run along.'

The factory floor was a bustling centre of activity, with vast vats of red liquid boiling away and the constant chink of ceramic pots. A round woman who was almost as red in the face as the jam liquor came bustling over. She may have looked kindly but her eyes were hard, like little lumps of coal, and she barked at them, 'You're late!'

'Sorry, miss,' said Kathleen. 'We're new.'

The woman threw her hands up in the air. 'I can see that. Talk about statin' the obvious. Come on, come on!' She hustled them over to the supervisor's office, a little white-washed room, with windows overlooking the factory floor, and from a peg behind her door pulled a couple of white overalls which tied at the side, and little caps for their hair.

'These are yours and I expect you to look after them. You will get another set at the end of the week. Take these home and wash them. If you lose them I will dock your pay. Clear?'

'Yes, miss.'

Kathleen wondered if soldiers got bossed about as much as this. She was like a little sergeant major.

'We have quotas to fill on our jam production and you are joining us at our most busy time as the strawberry season is upon us. Everything has to run smoothly. I will give you today to learn the ropes and after that, I expect you to keep up with the others.'

Nancy looked as if she was about to cry.

'Don't worry,' said the woman, patting her on the arm. 'We all had to start somewhere. I was once a new girl, fresh from school, just like you. My name is Miss Bainbridge, by the way. And tie that hair back!'

'Yes, Miss Bainbridge.'

The girls put on their overalls and stuffed their hair into the caps, which made them giggle, as they did look quite silly. They followed Miss Bainbridge out into the factory. 'You, over there.' Miss Bainbridge gestured Nancy towards the filling stations, where ceramic pots were loaded onto a circular turntable.

'Good luck,' Kathleen whispered to her friend, who gave a scared sort of smile in return.

The women at the filling station worked in pairs, scooping little pans full of the hot jam from a sort of metal bath on wheels, before carefully pouring it into each jar. Exactly the same amount had to go in each jar and they wore heavy aprons over their overalls to protect against spills. Now and then, one of the women would go over to one of the big vats in the corner and refill the trolley-bath with boiling hot liquid. The smell of strawberries and sugar was everywhere. The fruit was arriving by the truckload each day from Kent, as the season had begun early, with a warm May, and tons of sugar came each day by barge up the river Thames. The factory looked as if it was full of worker ants.

Kathleen was shown to a workstation at the other end of the factory, where a dozen women were quietly gluing and sticking labels to the Hartley's ceramic jars. She'd seen the jars before in the grocer's shop but she'd rarely bought them, because jam was a luxury they couldn't afford often.

Kathleen was just grateful she didn't have to hull the pesky little strawberries. That was back-breaking work and she'd heard about girls not only nicking their fingers on the sharp knives, but slicing off the tops of thumbs. Besides, once strawberry season was over, it would be back to making marmalade and the last thing she wanted was to have to peel oranges, day in day out.

'I'll leave Beryl to show you the ropes in the finishing section, which is one of the more important areas because how you glue those labels on is the first thing the customer sees when they come to buy our products,' said Miss Bainbridge, before bustling off in the other direction. 'What in God's name are those sacks of sugar doing on the floor?' she yelled at a boy who had just plonked them off his sack barrow in the wrong place. He tipped his cap at Miss Bainbridge and gave Kathleen a wink before loading them back up and wheeling them away.

Beryl was an old hand at the job, having been on labelling for the past five years, since she had left school. Her family lived over in the East End and she was the eldest of six. She spoke in a whisper, so that Miss Bainbridge wouldn't ever catch her talking, but was quite a gossip and she managed to make Kathleen laugh that morning, as she showed her how to position the labels carefully across the middle of the jar and not get too much glue on the brush, or, worse, too little.

'Nice and even, that's right,' she said, as she peered over the divider between her workstation and Kathleen's. She had done ten pots in the time it took Kathleen to do one.

'Don't worry,' she said warmly. 'You'll catch up.'

Kathleen was by nature neat and tidy and by the afternoon she was speeding up but the lettering of those labels seemed to have seared itself into her subconscious: 'W. P. Hartley's Strawberry, Liverpool and London'. And on the bottom, each pot was stamped with 'not genuine unless bearing W. P. Hartley's label'. Miss Bainbridge walked past to inspect her work and gave a little 'hmm' of approval.

When Kathleen clocked off at the end of that first shift, her fingers ached, her eyes were tired too and her legs were killing her from standing up. She couldn't believe she had to get up the next day and do it all over again. At least she was better off than poor Nancy, who had several scald marks up her arms where she had got too close to the vats of boiling jam.

As they joined the surge of women making their way out through the courtyard, Kathleen caught sight of the sugar delivery boy. He was heaving bags of the stuff off the back of a lorry in the yard. Their eyes met for an instant and Nancy smiled at him and gave her curls a little twirl with her finger. 'Stop doing that,' said Kathleen, who felt she was being upstaged.

'I'm not doing anything,' said Nancy, giving her a nudge in the ribs. 'But it looks like someone is interested in you!'

The whole of Howley Terrace was buzzing with excitement for the rest of the week, as a huge tea-party was planned for Saturday afternoon, to mark the King's Silver Jubilee. Being a British summer, there was the risk of rain, but the blue skies overhead looked promising.

Kathleen and the other factory girls were each given a pot of jam by Miss Bainbridge as a present to take home and share with their families. Her new workmate, Beryl, complained that she wasn't likely to taste any of it.

'Once the five others have had their sticky fingers in the jar, there'll be nothing left for me!' she said, departing with a cheery wave.

By the time Kathleen got home, the party was just starting and the street looked breathtakingly beautiful. All the women had organized themselves into an unofficial decorating committee and were now competing to outdo each other because word had got around that a photographer from the *London News* was coming to take pictures of the best-turned-out streets in the borough.

Peggy had found her most prized new possession, a Singer sewing machine, commandeered by Mrs Avens and Mrs Davies from number 16, who had spent every spare moment running up bunting from scraps of material. The strings of colours flags now hung in a magnificent criss-cross, from house to house, the length of the street.

Nanny Day had had a word with some of the flower sellers over in Covent Garden and had managed to get enough flowers for every home to have some around the doorway. The men of the street spent ages nailing little trellises over each door and foliage mysteriously appeared, thanks to the boys, led by her little brother Frankie. Many suspected it had been pinched from the local park but no one asked too many questions, because this was a happy occasion and the whole community was pulling together to make this a celebration to remember. A huge makeshift table was constructed with planks of wood and every home brought out some linen and china. There were jam sandwiches and tarts for the children, as well as bread rolls and currant buns. Every child had a place at the table, with upturned crates pressed into service when they ran out of chairs.

Even Mr Pemberton from the Poor Law had found favour by donating a huge banner, which had God Save the King in gold and silver letters and a little crown underneath, which his wife had spent ages sewing by hand. He had also donated some cash from the Poor Law Authority coffers to provide cakes for the children, as the area was underprivileged.

'He's probably just trying to get his ugly mug in the photograph,' muttered Mrs Avens, who still hadn't quite recovered from the loss of her mahogany sideboard and held Mr Pemberton partly responsible for his failure to give her financial assistance in her hour of need.

Kathleen's piano was lifted outside into the street, where she guarded it with her life from the likes of Eva and her little friend Gladys. The sun shone brightly and for once it seemed that all the cares of the neighbourhood had been forgotten. Women put on their best dresses and hats and men donned their smartest suits. Only Mrs Davies resolutely bustled about in an overall on top of her dress, making sure she was in the thick of the action, serving tea from a giant teapot. Mr Pemberton even gave a little speech about the nation's gratitude to the monarch, until one of the dockers from Tenison Street had enough of it and started hammering out 'Roll Out the Barrel' on the piano, loudly, to drown him out.

The kids had running races with a prize of a penny for the fastest up and down Belvedere Road, while a crowd gathered around the piano to hear Kathleen sing. The fella who normally bashed out tunes down at the Feathers turned up with a crate of beer for the men and soon ousted Kathleen from her spot at the piano stool, much to her annoyance. The piano was her prized possession but she knew that she would have to share it because he was a better player than she was, although she would only admit that reluctantly. He started playing lively tunes, things Kathleen didn't know the words to, but the older women seemed to recognize them and started dancing a kind of funny jig across the pavement and back, as the men lined up on the other side and moved forwards and back in a long line. Even her parents joined in, meeting each other in the middle of the street and twirling around.

At bang on three o'clock, the man and a photographer from the *London News* came and got everyone to wave and smile for a photograph. Some older lads were mucking about on the costermongers' barrows but even they stopped to come and pose. 'Watch the birdie!' the photographer said to the little children, many of whom had never seen a camera before and were too scared to smile. 'Lovely to see the whole street getting into the spirit of it,' the reporter said to Mr Pemberton, who had of course appointed himself spokesman for the neighbourhood. 'Not like that Commie lot down in Red Bermondsey. The mayor's only gone and burned an effigy of His Majesty on the steps of the town hall and there were hundreds cheering him on.'

'Good gracious, no!' said Mr Pemberton. 'Let's sing the National Anthem and show people how London really feels.'

He turned and shouted, 'God Save the King!' and was greeted by cheers as the pianist struck up the tune. The singing and dancing went on into the small hours. Kathleen, Peggy and Eva stayed up late but tiredness got the better of them and they were soon tucked up in bed, peering out of the window at the party still going on outside by the dim glow of the gas lamps. This was their community, their home in 1935, and in that moment Kathleen felt that nothing could ever take that away from her.

16

Eva, January 1936

The woman in the long black coat had a suspicious look about her. Eva had clocked her a few days ago, hanging around on the street corner and she knew then that there was something amiss. Alice Diamond had taught her always to be on her guard in case the cozzers came calling and so she took more notice than most of the comings and goings in the neighbourhood.

Eva had hopped the wag from school to go pinching down East Street Market with Alice earlier on. She took her mate Gladys with her, to start showing her the ropes. Gladys was a year younger but she was game for anything and she looked up to Eva and admired the way she was earning good money hoisting. It was easy stuff, just a few scarves to start with, some tins from the grocer's and a bottle of perfume from the snooty pharmacy, just because Eva didn't like the way that old matron behind the counter looked down her nose at them.

Now she was back home, lurking in the living room and peering out through the net curtains at the activity in the street. It was bloody freezing but she didn't dare light a fire because their coal was running low and then she'd have to explain to Dad why the fire had been lit so early, when he got home from work. He'd probably give her another belting for it. She watched her breath form in little droplets in front of her and took another peek through the net curtains instead.

The woman looked around, as if she was waiting for someone. From the other end of the street, Eva saw Mary bundled up against the cold, and her little daughter, Florrie, toddling along, holding her hand. Everyone had been so happy for Mary when she got pregnant again so quickly after losing Billy to diphtheria. The baby was delivered safely and Florrie looked so much healthier than her late brother. In fact, she was positively chubby and well dressed for the weather in a knitted coat, hat and a fur muff, with stout little boots on her feet. Mary fed her the best cuts of meat and she never went without milk – the real stuff, from the dairy, not evap. In fact, the milkman's horse and cart had become a familiar sight outside Mary and Joe's front door, turning up on a Saturday for payment. But Mary hadn't got a new job or anything like that. She still worked pulling the fur from rabbit skins and was permanently coughing from the fluff which got down her throat and everywhere.

The woman approached Mary, catching her by the sleeve. Mary pulled her daughter close, with a look of panic on her face. This stranger pulled out a notebook and pointed to it. Mary pulled off her wedding ring – a thin silver band – and handed it over. The woman went to stroke the little girl on the cheek but Mary slapped her hand away. 'Don't you dare touch her!' she shouted, loud enough to provoke next-door's dog into a barking fit. The woman shrugged her shoulders and left, turning down Belvedere Road.

Eva pulled on her coat and darted out into the street, falling into step with Mary.

'Was that woman bothering you?' she said, as they walked along, past the corner shop, which had a newspaper hoarding outside with 'THE KING IS DEAD!' written on it in big black lettering. Eva paused for a second to look at it. His Majesty had had a nice life and it wasn't that she didn't care, but the world of rich folk was so far removed from hers that she wouldn't be shedding any tears over his death.

'Don't know what you mean!' said Mary. 'You're imagining things, Eve.'

'No, I ain't,' said Eva. 'How much do you owe her?'

Florrie started tugging at Mary's hand. Mary looked at Eva imploringly, 'You can't tell anyone, least of all Joe because he thinks I'm working sick cover to pay for everything and I did have some shifts over Christmas but they've stopped now. I just borrowed some money to pay for things for Florrie, just until she is big and strong enough to not . . .' She started to cry. 'Well, I went to a moneylender down in the Borough to get a loan, just five pounds, but it's the repayments – they seem to go up every week. You're too young to understand this, Eva . . .'

'I'm only thirteen but I ain't a kid no more!' said Eva. 'I know how to look after myself.'

'Of course you do,' said Mary gently. 'It's just I don't want to burden you with my troubles; they are my own to deal with. I'll have to talk to Joe and we will find the money somehow. It just means Florrie will have to go without . . .'

'What if I help you pay it off?' said Eva, pulling a pound note from her pocket and offering it to Mary, whose mouth fell open.

'Where did you get that?'

'Don't ask no questions and I will tell you no lies,' said Eva. 'I told you I can look after myself. You don't think we got that piano from me dad killing himself looking after the boilers and me mum scrubbing floors, do you? Folks like us shouldn't judge too harshly, Mary, and if I help you, all I ask is that you help me from time to time.'

'What kind of help?'

'I might need to keep a few things in your house, if it's too tricky for me at home.'

Mary knew enough about James Fraser's temper and the black eyes sported by his wife to know that if Eva was bringing home a bit of crooked, she would meet with more than his disapproval.

'All right,' she said. 'But we will have to be careful. I don't want to have to explain a visit from the law to my Joe.'

'It won't ever come to that,' said Eva. 'How much do you still owe to that woman?'

Mary sighed. 'It seems to go up every week. It was a fiver and it doesn't seem to have gone down much, no matter that I must have already paid that back by now. There's no end to it.' She had a haunted look about her as she spoke. 'She keeps telling me how sweet my Florrie is and I'm scared she's going to try to hurt her if I can't keep up the repayments.'

'I will get someone to talk to her about that,' said Eva, smiling to herself. 'Especially if I know I can rely on you to keep mum when I need a bit of help. You help me and I will help you, that's fair, ain't it? Just tell me her name and where she lives . . .'

Maggie Hughes had a fierce temper and when Eva explained that a friend from her street who was prepared to handle stolen goods for the Forty Thieves was being ripped off by a moneylender, she didn't need to be asked twice.

Maggie didn't wait for the cloak of darkness. She loitered on the corner near Long Lane down the Borough and then grabbed her victim by the throat when she walked by. As Eva looked on, Maggie pulled out her hatpin and waved it near the woman's face. 'You keep away from Mary in Howley Terrace. She's a friend of Alice Diamond and the Forty Thieves. Do you get me?'

'Get off me!' the woman shrieked. 'Help me! Somebody!'

People put their heads down and scurried past. Maggie Hughes was well known in the neighbourhood and no one wanted to cross her, or Alice Diamond, for that matter.

'She's paid you enough and if I hear you have been round there again I will slit your little throat,' spat Maggie, with a wild look in her eyes. 'She's one of our own. And don't bother telling the cozzers 'cos we have got them straightened an' all. You moneylenders make me sick.' Maggie released the woman, who ran off shakily.

Maggie smoothed her blouse and stuck her hatpin back into her straw boater. Then she turned to Eva and said, 'Right, that's that. Let's go shopping. Selfridges?'

The January sales were in full swing when they got there, pushing their way through the crush. The death of King George V the previous morning seemed to have done little to dampen the nation's desire to bag a bargain.

'We're going to have to be clever to outwit the walkers 'cos they've got a new lot in, so Alice tells me,' said Maggie. Eva caught the whiff of booze on her breath as she whispered to her. 'Let's keep our wits about us.' Eva was always careful but Maggie on the sauce could be more reckless than daring and Eva's heart fluttered at the memory of her escapade in Gamages a year or so back. There'd been a few close shaves since, but the fright of that first time was enough to keep her wary.

The pair sifted through a pile of leather gloves, Eva acting as a screen for Alice as she stuffed a few pairs into the inside lining of her coat. 'Let's go and find some fur. It's bloody freezing out there and I fancy me a nice mink stole,' said Maggie with a cackle. 'You can clout it. Alice tells me you're getting good at it.'

Eva nodded. She was faster now, much faster, and her fingers seemed to be able to roll things quickly and stuff them down her shoplifter's drawers without the shop assistants noticing. Practice sessions in Alice Diamond's scullery had seen to that. She was barely in school these days. The teacher had bumped into her mother down the Cut and said something about it but Mum, knowing exactly why Eva wasn't in school, covered for her and said Nanny

Day had been so depressed she couldn't work and so they were keeping Eva off to help around the house a bit.

Eva thought about that as she rolled another fur stole, fox this time, complete with a bushy tail, and stuffed it down the other leg of her drawers which Alice had had specially made for her by a little seamstress down in the Borough who was very handy with her needle and thread. Maggie was already nudging her way through the tightly packed rows of coats to go downstairs to jewellery but Eva wasn't done yet. Glancing around, she grabbed another mink stole, rolled it tightly and stuffed it down her other knicker leg. She emerged from behind a rail of coats and bumped straight into a shop assistant, who did a double take at seeing her. Had she been spotted? Eva said loudly, 'Ouch! You should look where you're going! I'm going to tell my mum!' and she ran off to catch up with Maggie.

The jewellery department on the ground floor was a haven of calm compared to the rest of the shop, with smart-suited, bespectacled men heading the sales teams. Beads of sweat formed on Eva's brow from the insulating effect of the furs she was carrying but she didn't dare unbutton her coat, in case anyone noticed. She waddled slightly when she walked. Maggie was already at the counter, asking to look at some rings, which sparkled with emeralds, rubies and diamonds. The shop assistant pulled out a tray which he laid on the counter. Eva grabbed a ring and walked towards the door with it. In an instant, she had been apprehended, roughly, by another shop assistant. 'I just want to see it in the light!' she said. 'I'm not stealing it!'

'Why don't we take it back to the counter, to avoid confusion?' he said in his most paternal tone.

Maggie chided her. 'How many times have I told you? Do not walk off near the doors with expensive things! People might get the wrong idea.' She turned to the shop assistant, who was now acting as an escort to Eva. 'I must apologize for my daughter's behaviour. She just sees beautiful jewellery and wants to look at it in the best light. It is rather dingy in here, don't you agree? And so stiflingly hot. Shall we go now, dear?'

Eva nodded. They made their way towards the entrance and through the doors, out into the freezing cold air of a January afternoon in Oxford Street. 'Worked like a treat!' said Maggie, with a laugh. 'By the time they realize one of their rings is paste, not diamond, we'll be back down the Elephant.' At the Tube station, the newspaper boys were still yelling about the death of the monarch. Eva couldn't say she felt sad about it; he was an old bloke and he had lived a life of luxury, and there would be another king, which probably meant another street party for the coronation – which was something to celebrate, really.

They had bought their tickets and Eva was through the barrier, standing at the top of the escalator, when she heard a voice shout, 'That's her! Hey, you! Stop!'

The shop assistant from Selfridges came running towards them, with a policeman by his side. The cozzer reached out and grabbed Maggie's arm. She started to shout, 'Get off me!', but he held firm. With her free hand, Maggie reached around the back of her hat and pulled out her hatpin. Eva saw it glint momentarily before she plunged it right into the policeman's eye. Blood spurted out and he screamed. Eva saw Maggie disappearing under a hail of blows from bystanders who had turned have-a-go hero after witnessing the dreadful attack. There was nothing else to do; Eva turned, as calmly as she could and walked slowly, very slowly, down the escalator, not looking back, her heart thumping as Maggie yelled like a banshee for her liberty.

'Blood? How much blood was there?' The colour drained from Alice Diamond's face as Eva brought home the news of Maggie's assault on the policeman.

'And you are sure she didn't get away?'

'Certain,' said Eva. 'She had half of Oxford Street sitting on her back, the last I saw of her. I should have helped . . .'

'No,' said Alice. 'You did right, getting away. Makes no sense having both of you in clink. And you are sure you weren't followed?'

'I wasn't,' said Eva. She'd spent an hour wandering around the Elephant to make sure of that before coming to Alice's flat.

Alice stood up and took her teacup to the sink. 'Well, she'd better hope the cozzer doesn't bleed to death because if he does, she'll swing for it, the silly cow.'

Eva blanched. She knew the death penalty was a real threat and the thought of Maggie swinging on the end of a rope made her feel physically sick.

Alice went on: 'And sticking him with her hatpin like that. Well, she's hardly helped herself because I won't be able to nobble the jury, that's for sure. Too many witnesses.

The best I can do now is make life more comfortable for her in Holloway.'

The tentacles of Alice's crime operation seemed to spread below the streets of London, like some giant octopus. Eva found that reassuring and terrifying in equal measure. It meant there was little chance of escape, if she ever wanted to leave. She mulled that thought over as she made her way back home through the freezing fog. The shouts of coster-mongers parking their barrows up for the night under the railway arches echoed up the road as she turned into Howley Terrace.

The savoury smell of liver and onion filled the house as she opened the door. It was just what she needed to put things right. Her mother gave her a weak smile and her father didn't look up from his plate when she came into the scullery.

'How was school?' Mum ventured.

'Just give it up, will you?' said Dad, banging his fist on the table. A splodge of onion gravy landed on the table in front of him. He looked up at her. Eva started to shake. It was as if all the fear of what had happened that afternoon had found its way into her legs, which had turned to jelly. She grasped the back of the little wooden chair in front of her, to steady herself.

'It was a nice day,' she managed to say, before sitting down.

'Liar!' her father said, upending the whole table, sending his plate right into Eva's lap. She yelped and jumped up as the scalding gravy seeped through her dress and onto her bare legs. She cried out in pain and shock.

'Leave her alone!' screamed Mum, running with a dish-cloth to clean her up.

Dad turned to the grate and pulled out the poker. He waved it at Eva.

'You're a liar and a thief. Get out of my house before I give you what you deserve!' he spat. His eyes were bulging out of their sockets and his face was puce with rage. 'I know you're one of those Forty Thieves.'

Thoughts were racing through Eva's mind. Who had betrayed her? Could it have been Peggy? Eva knew she disapproved but she had never thought she'd betray her like that.

'No, James, no!' yelled Mum, 'You'll not throw her out! She is the one who has been putting food on the table all these months. Who do you think keeps us going? It ain't you, that's for sure, with your paltry wages—'

Dad slapped Mum hard, right in the mouth, with the back of his hand, and sat down in his chair. He spoke in a whisper, 'So, I'm to be disobeyed in my own house, am I? You can both get out of my sight.'

Mum put her arm around Eva. 'Don't worry. I'm going. I've had enough of you. And she's coming with me.'

That seemed to take the wind out of his sails. Dad sank down into his chair, with his head in his hands. Mum stormed upstairs, with Eva in hot pursuit. She ran into the girls' bedroom, pulling her few belongings from the chest of drawers they shared. She ripped the sheet from Eva's bed and threw everything in. 'Tie that lot up,' she ordered. Eva watched as her mother reached up on tiptoes and took a carpet bag and a hat box from the top of the wardrobe.

The pair of them hurried back down the little staircase, half expecting Dad to come at them through the scullery door.

Emboldened by the fact that he hadn't stirred, as she slammed the door, Mum shouted, 'And good riddance to bad rubbish!'

The curtains were twitching over at number 16, where Mrs Davies, no doubt, was drinking in the unhappy scene, ready to repeat it to all and sundry. Eva flicked the Vs as she walked past, for good measure, just in case the nosy old bag was watching.

17

Peggy, February 1936

Dearest Peg,

I'm sorry not to have written sooner but there is so much to tell you. The matron in the home is very strict about letting us out of her sight to get to anywhere near a post box, so I had to bribe one of the cleaners with some of the fags my dear old mum sent me to get this letter to you.

I had the baby, Tommy, and he is nearly one now, Peg, and the most beautiful thing ever. He doesn't look anything like Bert to my mind, which is a blessing. We have to do a lot of chores, cleaning, helping, but I don't mind because once you get past the matron, the rest of the staff are quite kind.

And I could do without having to repent for my sins but we have to do that once a week and go to church in a long line, pushing our prams, while the gossips in the neighbourhood stare. I had Tommy baptized as soon as I could because you never met a more innocent little baby and it seemed right.

I came to the unmarried mothers' home up in Hampstead about three weeks before the birth. My dad threw me out long before that and I was with one of my aunts over in the East End for a while, until my bump got so bleeding obvious I looked like the back end of a bus and I couldn't leave the house. Coming here was fine because I was with other girls who had got themselves into trouble, just like me. A lot of them didn't want to keep their babies and they left soon after they had them. Theirs were fostered out but not mine. I'm allowed to stay here until he is one.

My dad still won't speak to me but my mum gets up here as often as she can. She can't afford to take us in, Peg, and in any case my dad won't allow me to set foot in the house again, so that is that.

I am hoping that I might get some help from the Poor Law to keep him, to get a foster grant so I can put him with a foster mother during the day while I work and then have him at night and my days off. If I can do this, I have no idea where I will end up but it seems I will be far from home because my dad won't want me on his doorstep.

How is life at the Post Office? Is that old bat Miss Fisher still ruling with a rod of iron? Write to me soon, Peggy. Just any little bit of news from you will brighten my day.

Take care,
Your friend,
Susan.

Peggy clutched the letter in her hand as she ran to meet George at the Gaumont Cinema in Walworth. Peggy had given up hope of ever hearing from her friend again. The letter came like a bolt from the blue and although it was good to hear her news, Susan had been through so much, all on her own, and Peggy knew that her future was far from certain. At least she saw having the baby as something positive and was enjoying looking after him, but how would she cope on her own, in a world in which being an unmarried mother would make her the talking point of the street? Peggy couldn't help wondering whether Susan might have been better off just giving the baby away at the start, right after she'd had him. As a single girl at least she could have got a job somewhere new and put all of the past behind her.

Peggy wasn't sure what she'd write to tell her. The Post Office Savings Bank hadn't changed much in comparison with what Susan had been through. Edna was in charge now and she seemed to delight in bossing everyone about even more than Miss Fisher had. Who could have guessed that quiet little Edna from Acton would turn into such a martinet? She picked on the weakest and constantly found fault with their work. There was a new girl called Sarah, from north London. Peggy felt sorry for her and tried to show her the ropes, really she did, but Sarah was ever so clumsy and just couldn't get her numbers right. She'd have been better off working somewhere else, maybe in one of the factories.

Peggy knew that having a clerical job meant she was brighter than most, but she also realized that there were hundreds of girls who would give their eye teeth to be able to get such a job, away from the drudgery of packing and filling and labelling, like her little sister Kathleen. Peggy felt very fortunate indeed.

She caught sight of George – tall, blond and handsome – standing around whistling to himself, carrying a single red rose, waiting for her, on their Valentine's Day date. Peggy stuffed Susan's letter into her purse. She didn't want to discuss it with him but she didn't want to leave it at home either, in case her dad found it. He'd been in a terrible depression since Mum walked out. Eva had gone too and wasn't speaking to Peggy any more, which she found so hurtful. Eva seemed to think that Peggy had grassed her up to their dad for stealing, and no amount of talk would persuade her that this was not the case. It was more likely to have been that awful gossip Mrs Davies at number 16. She knew better than to ask her father who had told him about Eva and the Forty Thieves. It was a closed subject.

When Mum left, she went to her friend Flo's down in the Borough at first and after a week she rented a little place, with Eva's help, above a shop on Walworth Road. Throughout it all, Dad sat in a kind of dumb trance at the table in the scullery after work, muttering to himself under his breath. Peggy stayed with her father out of loyalty; she hated to see him like that. She'd always admired him for his strength of character, his understanding of the world and, although she wasn't comfortable with the way he was too handy with his belt, she tried to forgive him for that. Peggy was practical enough to know that he would need help to pay the rent on Howley Terrace, so they wouldn't lose the house. She didn't want them to be turfed out of their family home. Deep down, Peggy was clinging to the hope that her mother would return, although with every passing week, that seemed less likely. Her brother Jim chipped in with some of his wages. He didn't earn much as a post boy but he wanted to stay with his dad. Frankie, now twelve, had gone with Eva and their mother, while Kathleen acted as a sort of go-between, staying over at Nanny Day's and relaying messages between the parents when required.

Peggy suspected, but she didn't know for sure, that Mum might have a fancy man in her life. She'd cut her hair into a fashionable long bob and went to the hairdresser to get a Marcel wave. Mum also took full advantage of the little luxuries Eva brought her – a mink stole, a new hand-bag, some lipstick. She felt she was unencumbered without her brutish hubby and was now a regular on Friday and Saturday nights at the pub. She let it be known that she was out to have fun. Kathleen had told Peggy that Mum had even hosted get-togethers after hours at the flat, with crates of beer and raucous singing until the early hours, until the neighbours complained and the landlord threatened to chuck her out on her ear. It was as if she was making up for lost time, all those years slogging away with the kids and being beaten by their father.

Peggy had told George a little bit about it. He hadn't wanted to pry, he said, and he didn't judge what her father had done harshly – that wasn't his place – but he said that if he was ever lucky enough to marry, he would never lay a finger on his wife in anger. That made Peggy feel quite safe; just seeing him standing there made her feel warm inside. His shoulders were broad and he had a lovely smile. He gave her a little wave and offered her the Valentine's rose. Like the perfect gentleman, he paid for their tickets and slipped his arm around her once the lights went down.

They had kissed a couple of times, just a little peck, really, but tonight when the heroine was embraced by the hero, George took that as his cue. He put his hand on her knee and tried to kiss her full on the mouth. Something inside Peggy froze. She resisted and it ended in a clash of lips and teeth. 'I'm sorry,' she whispered. 'I just can't do that yet.' Her head was swimming with thoughts of Susan and Bert in the alleyways of Soho, of what a man's desire would feel like and how terrified she was of getting pregnant. It all twisted into a big knot in her stomach.

She could sense that George was rather crestfallen, as he whispered back, 'I'm sorry, Peg, I don't know what got hold of me there.'

There was a loud shush from the row in front, and a woman wearing the most ridiculous feathered trilby turned round and said, 'Go and get a bleedin' room. You're spoiling the film for the rest of us!'

'And your hat is spoiling the view!' said George, making Peggy giggle.

When the lights came up, they both scarpered for the exit, like a pair of naughty children, in case she clouted them one with her handbag. Their botched kiss was forgotten as they strolled along, hand in hand.

George was quick to start a conversation and Peggy gratefully joined in, back on the safe ground of politics.

They discussed things they had read in the paper and George seemed to relish Peggy's views, even if they weren't always the same as his own. She loved that too – the fact that they could really discuss things, without falling out with each other.

'I'm going to a meeting next week, Peg; would you like to come with me?' said George as they reached the turning for Belvedere Road. He didn't walk her to her door as she preferred to go up the street alone, in case Mrs Davies or Mrs Avens spotted them and made comments to her father. It was just not worth the grief.

'What kind of meeting?'

'Well, me and some of the lads at the depot have joined the Communist Party . . .' He lowered his voice.

'Some of their ideas are a bit much, aren't they?' said Peggy, who remembered Miss Fisher's scant regard for such left-wing political shenanigans.

'Peggy, there are other views out there which are a lot more worrying: the Fascist lot, for a start. The Blackshirts are holding meetings all over the place, spreading hatred. They've got to be stopped,' said George. 'Their last big meeting in Olympia they beat the living daylights out of anyone who tried to speak against them. Several comrades ended up in hospital.'

'But what can you do? It's not like you have any power over them, working at the depot, is it?'

'Still, we've got to exercise our right to oppose their views. Think about it, Peggy. Extremists like Mosley will be stopped if people are brave enough to speak out. These

Blackshirts have been stirring up the East End against the Jews. People like trade unionists are already being thrown in prison in Germany. We can't let that happen here, can we?'

Peggy thought about it for a moment and felt excitement twisting in the pit of her stomach. Her family had always struggled, worked hard, but they didn't seem to get very far. Eva was busy lining her pockets with stolen goods and Kathleen was bottling jam, while her mother scrubbed floors and her dad was killing himself keeping the boilers going down at the cricket bat factory. They had nothing against people from other countries and places. They were all just as poor as each other. She was stuck in a safe little job as a clerical worker with not much hope of promotion. But George was different. He believed in something, a greater good. This was her chance to make a difference.

'All right,' she said, giving his arm a squeeze. 'Count me in, I'm coming with you.'

Susan's next letter came from a hospital in north London.

Dear Peggy,

Things are pretty bad. They took Tommy away. Matron persuaded me to sign the adoption papers for a couple in Hampstead, but as soon as I had done it, I regretted it.

They are not calling him Tommy any more. They changed his name to Reginald and they wrote me a letter saying how much they love him and will promise him the best of everything because they haven't been

able to have kids of their own. I will get a picture of
him every year on his birthday, they said.

I'm broken in pieces, Peggy. The day after he went,
I slashed my wrists with a kitchen knife. The matron
found me and I got carted off to hospital and now
they are keeping me here, saying I am not right in the
head. They won't let me go until I say I'm happy
about Tommy being with his new family. I don't think
I will ever feel that way.

Write me when you can.
Your friend,
Susan

Peggy was so shocked that she didn't know what to say or
do. It was worse than when the woman in the street had
cancer and everyone knew but no one could say much
about it. She looked at the address of the hospital and
wondered whether she'd be able to go and see her at least.
Susan didn't even say whether she was allowed visitors
and her writing looked scrawled, as if she had written it
in a hurry. Peggy decided she'd write back, just keeping
things light, and say she would come the week after next.

After finishing her note to Susan and tucking it in her
handbag, she had to find a way of sneaking out of work
early to go to the meeting with George. In the end, she
tried to leave ten minutes early while Edna's back was
turned, but her boss caught her putting on her coat.

'Where do you think you're going, Miss Fraser?'

'I was just hoping to leave a bit early, miss. I've an
appointment . . .'

'With whom?' A little smile was playing on Edna's lips. She was enjoying every moment of the power she had over Peggy, at the thought that she might ruin her evening by making her stay late. 'You wouldn't be gadding off to the Chiswick Empire with the other girls later on, by any chance?' Peggy knew that Sarah and some of the others had been planning a trip to see Vesta Tilley and Max Miller – who was meant to be hilarious – but she wasn't going with them.

'It's a political meeting, actually,' said Peggy, reddening with fury that Edna was doing this. All the times Peggy had worked late . . .

'Politics?' said Edna. 'It's best to keep your nose out of politics . . .'

'I'm going to see Oswald Mosley speak.' She had blurted the words out before she could stop herself.

Instantly, Edna's features softened and she came over to Peggy's side. 'My dear,' she said. 'I had no idea. Of course, you must go. It is such an honour to see him. He is so inspiring.' She had a faraway look in her eyes. 'I saw him at Olympia. Such an orator! He held the crowd in the palm of his hand. He has some very interesting ideas. If you ever need to leave work early to go to a meeting again, please don't hesitate. I can let girls go early at my discretion.' She gave Peggy's arm a little pat.

Peggy swallowed hard. She couldn't believe her ears. Edna was a supporter of Oswald Mosley and his Fascist Blackshirts! She could hardly tell her that she was going to disrupt the meeting with George and his friends, could she? It was best to say nothing. Edna smiled beatifically at

Peggy and, as Peggy was leaving, she heard her say, 'No, Sarah, that will not do at all. Go back to your desk and start again. Your work really is disgraceful.'

She caught the bus to Notting Hill Gate and then hopped onto the Tube to Stratford. On the way, she started to have second thoughts. What if there was a riot, like the one years ago in her street, when the mounted police had charged at them? Might she be better off just going to have a laugh at the Empire with the other girls from work? But when she caught sight of George, carrying his copy of the *Daily Worker* tucked under his arm, waiting for her at the Tube station, all her worries melted away. They could fight injustice together, the two of them. It was as if all the years they had chatted about politics as kids had a purpose now.

Crowds were milling about outside the town hall, an imposing white-stone building with a tall, domed tower, and there were mounted police trotting beside a swarm of perhaps fifty policemen on foot. Women in black shirts, berets and long wool skirts strutted past, their waists accentuated by thick leather belts. They were met on the town hall steps by men in black polo necks and trousers, their hair slicked back. They greeted each other by raising their right arms to head height.

'Turns my stomach,' said George, under his breath. 'That's the salute they use in Germany.'

Peggy clasped his arm. Seeing Blackshirts close up brought it all home to her. She was revolted by their extremist views but now these Fascists were all too real and, from what she'd heard from George, they were dangerous and likely to get a bit handy if you crossed them.

'There are about ten of us dotted about the auditorium,' he explained as they were ushered inside. The odds seemed stacked against them: only ten protestors against a crowd of at least four hundred. 'The rest of them are going to try to make a noise outside,' said George, failing to see the colour draining from Peggy's face. She hadn't really thought about what this would mean. They were supposed to pro-test against a hostile crowd and there were so few of them. What would happen to them? Part of her wanted to turn back but George had a determined look on his face and, before she knew it, a man in a black shirt and red armband checked their tickets and gestured for them to take their seats. Peggy smiled nervously at him and noted with a chill the white lightning-strike embroidered into the band. She and George were sitting about ten rows back from the front of the room. In front was a little podium with a table draped with the Union Flag, and men and women dressed all in black sitting directly behind.

'Mosley's most loyal lieutenants,' George muttered.

A hush fell over the hall as Mosley appeared, wearing the same black uniform. Peggy was struck by his com-manding presence; he stood a full head taller than most of the other men in the room and carried with himself a cool self-assuredness. A murmur started up and then Mosley saluted the room, prompting a chant of 'Mosley! Mosley!' which rose to a roar as the audience stomped and clapped. A line of Blackshirts guarded the ends of each row and they stood and returned his salute. Peggy felt George's hand at her elbow; she'd frozen rigid at the sight of Mosley so she hadn't noticed that everyone else was standing and they were starting to look at her oddly.

Mosley cleared his throat and a hush fell over the hall. He looked out over the audience and began to speak. He was mesmerizing, just as Edna had said he would be, but what started as a speech about putting the needs of Britain first, protecting the home economy and bringing higher wages to the masses soon degenerated into hatred for immigrants and Jews in particular. Peggy thought of the lovely Jewish tailor who worked down at the Elephant and Castle and of her father's secret Canadian Indian heritage and felt a chill creep over her. She reached for George's hand and clasped it tight.

Mosley had spoken for no more than ten minutes when a young, bespectacled man stood up and yelled at him, 'Hitler means war, you fool!'

George craned his neck. 'That's Lionel,' he said.

Peggy watched in horror as Lionel was seized by a Blackshirt and pulled from his chair. In a split second, another floored him with a punch. She felt George tense with fury beside her.

'And so,' said Mosley, looking on with a glint in his eye, 'Our detractors discover, one by one, how uncomfortable it is to be on the wrong side of Fascism.' There were cheers and laughter from his supporters as Lionel was dragged to his feet and thrown out through the double doors at the back of the room. His glasses lay broken in the aisle, crushed under a jackboot.

Nonetheless, Lionel's outcry was followed by a young woman and an older man who must have been about the same age as Peggy's father. 'Shame on you and your hatred!' they shouted and disappeared beneath a hail of blows from Mosley's guard, who roughly ejected both of them into the arms of a waiting police officer. Blackshirts patrolled the aisles, looking for troublemakers.

'George, please don't,' whispered Peggy, her eyes growing wide with terror.

But he was already on his feet. 'Fascism means murder! The people do not support you!' shouted George. A Blackshirt grabbed him from the row behind and pulled him back into his seat and a tussle began. Before she knew what she was doing, Peggy hit George's assailant with all her might, in an attempt to make him loosen his grip. Suddenly, a pair of arms was around her waist and in an instant she was being carried, backwards, out of the hall.

Peggy kicked, hard, pushing her heels into the Blackshirt's shins, but he would not let her go. 'Now, miss. Now, stop that!'

George tried to stand again and carry on speaking but was silenced by a punch in the mouth from a Mosley supporter, not in uniform. 'Shut it, mate! I came here to hear him speak.'

Then Peggy was through the doors and dumped at the feet of a waiting police officer, who scolded her, 'What is a nice girl like you doing getting mixed up with that Commie lot? Just think of your parents and how ashamed they'd be. Now, get along home.' He pulled her to her feet, just as George tumbled through the doors, his lip cut and bleeding.

The police officer pulled out his truncheon and raised it

above his head but Peggy threw herself in front of him, 'No, please. He's with me.'

'Off with you both, then!' said the copper, opening the doors to the town hall and shoving them into the fracas unfolding outside. A mob of Communists was engaged in a running battle with the mounted police and the sound of horses' hooves clattering up and down the road was punctuated by the shouts of men trading blows with each other.

George looked at Peggy, who had started to cry. 'Come on,' he said, putting his arm around her shoulder. 'We'd better get out of here.'

They ran along the high street and up a side road, until the shouts of the protestors and the yells of the police grew more distant. They stopped in a doorway, under a gas light, to catch their breath. Peggy pulled out her best handkerchief and started to dab George's lip, which was still bleeding. 'Look at the state of you!' she said.

He pulled her to him. 'It doesn't matter, Peg, we did what was right. We stood up for our beliefs.'

They were both flushed from running so fast. Glancing down, she noticed then that her best work dress was torn; a beautiful blue dress she had saved up for and sewed from a Paton's design with her Singer sewing machine.

George reached out and touched the rip in the material. 'Oh, Peggy, I'm so sorry. Your lovely dress – it's ruined.' He felt the edge of the torn fabric, just touching her skin underneath.

Her heart beat faster, as she felt his arms around her waist. Their eyes met. He leaned forwards, brushing his mouth against hers. She tasted the blood from his cut lip but she didn't care. She just wanted to kiss him and to feel his hands on her body. It was a desire she couldn't stop and she didn't want to, not now, not ever.

18

Kathleen, May 1937

Kathleen never wanted to eat another orange as long as she lived. Crate after crate of those bloody oranges arrived from Spain every day on barges up the Thames and they came tumbling down the chute to the picking lines where she worked alongside dozens of other girls, all of them with hands red raw from the fruit acid. The peeling room was kept chilly to stop the fruit going off and the cold seemed to make her hands worse. Her skin was covered in little keens where it had cracked and the orange juice seemed to find its way into every little cut, stinging like mad.

Nanny Day had been up to the pharmacist and spent good money on some ointment and lint for her, which helped when she dressed her hands overnight but, come the morning, it was back to work in the factory and back to peeling again. At least she was handy with the knife and hadn't cut herself to ribbons like some of the new girls.

Kathleen had been at Hartley's for nearly two years and considered herself quite senior now. Miss Bainbridge, her supervisor, seemed to like her and gave her the responsibility of looking after the new girls, which is how she came

to be on picking. A glut of oranges meant it was all hands
on deck and all the new girls had been put to work there.
Some of them were so dozy, it made Kathleen wonder
whether they were the full shilling or not. One of them,
Nora, seemed to have her mouth open catching flies all the
time and Miss Bainbridge had given Kathleen permission
to chivvy her along a bit.

Nancy had been taken off filling and was put to work
down the line from Kathleen. They'd occasionally catch
each other's eye and make each other laugh. Nancy would
sometimes get a song going, which was fun until Miss
Bainbridge came along and told them all to be quiet.

'Are you coming to the dance on Friday,' she yelled over
to Kathleen, once Miss Bainbridge was safely out of ear-
shot. The council had opened the parks for dancing in the
run-up to the coronation celebrations of King George VI
next month. It had been the talk of the factory for weeks.

'Yes,' said Kathleen, who hadn't told her father she was
going out dancing. 'Don't know what I'm going to wear,
though. How about you?'

In truth, she'd been hoping that Albert, the lad who had
caught her eye on her first day at work, was going to ask
her but she hadn't seen him for days. He'd been flat out
with the barges of oranges, probably. They'd barely traded
two words in as many years but every time Kathleen saw
him something inside her lit up and she could tell from the
smile on his face that he liked her too. At least, Nancy had
said that she was certain of that and they discussed it a lot
on the bus to and from work. But Kathleen hadn't had
time for boys, really. Her father didn't want her getting

involved with anyone and he told her as much. She was living mostly with him in Howley Terrace and sometimes with Nanny Day, just as she had done since Mum left. She loved going round to Nanny, where she got a bit more spoilt than she did at home.

Mum was too busy working and then enjoying herself after work to bother her much. Kathleen didn't begrudge her that. She'd spent years breaking her back bringing them all up. It upset her that her Mum and Dad were living apart, but their fighting when they were together was worse. At least this way, she got to see her mother happy and her father – well, he had made his bed with the way he treated their mother, so he had to lie in it, that's what Nanny Day said.

By the time Friday morning came, Kathleen had hidden her best dress and cardigan at Nanny Day's house and she told her father that she'd plans to go to the pictures with Nancy after work, so he wouldn't catch her out.

He looked up from his breakfast. 'Don't you be back later than ten o'clock, or you'll catch it, my girl.'

'I won't be late, I promise,' she said.

He hadn't hit her in months but she knew that with Eva gone and Peggy grown up, she was the apple of his eye now, and that meant he would knock her back into line if she strayed too far.

The whole factory was buzzing with the excitement of their night out, which soon made Kathleen forget her overbearing father. One of the girls had brought in some lipstick and rouge and they all took a turn with that in the ladies' loos, once they had clocked off. Kathleen had done her hair in rags the night before so it was almost as curly as Nancy's.

As they set out for Leathermarket Gardens, walking arm in arm in a long line, some of the girls started to sing 'I'm Forever Blowing Bubbles' loudly, attracting stares and a few wolf whistles. The Hartley's girls had a reputation for raucous behaviour on an evening out. Behind them, a group of the Hartley's boys walked along, lighting up their smokes and joshing with each other. Kathleen kept glancing back over her shoulder. She saw that Albert was among them and felt her heart flutter.

Dusk was falling by the time they reached the park, which was already filling up. Open-air dancing was becoming quite a thing in the parks these days, with regular events in Wapping and Islington and now Southwark. The band was already tuning up in the little bandstand and a ginger beer stall was doing a brisk trade. Workers from Peek Frean's biscuits mixed with those from Hartley's and Sarson's vinegar. It was as if the pantry of London had come for a big night out.

Kathleen was beside herself with excitement, not least because she couldn't wait to show off her new dance steps. Eva had managed to find a bit of extra cash for her to have some lessons with the little dance school down at the Elephant on Sunday afternoons. She'd kept it secret from her dad, who would have put his foot down to such nonsense, but her teacher, Miss Fawcett, said she was a natural. Over the past few weeks, Kathleen had mastered the foxtrot and the waltz, twirling around the dusty wooden floor at the Labour Social Club where the lessons were held. She'd only ever danced with other girls because the only boy there was Miss Fawcett's spotty fourteen-year-old son and no one wanted to twirl around the dance floor with him! This was different. There was an air of expectancy. So many young people, maybe a thousand or more, gathered in one space but away from the prying eyes of their parents.

The band struck up a tune and before long, girls and boys had paired up and were two-stepping their way, rather awkwardly at first, around the asphalt. A ring of spectators formed at the edge, some girls tapping their feet as a sign that they wanted to be asked to dance. Some unlucky ones never got asked and so they paired up with their friends. Kathleen stood nervously, and then a blond man she recognized from a few roads away shuffled up to her, offering his hand. She barely stood still all night. She'd had three, maybe four, dances before Albert tapped her on the shoulder.

'How about a dance with me, then?'

'I'd love to.' She beamed back at him.

He slipped his arm around her waist and gripped her other hand, quite tightly, actually. She put her hand gently on his shoulder as they broke into a quick foxtrot. It was so free, being in the open air, dancing together. Kathleen's steps didn't falter.

'You move like an angel,' Albert whispered in her ear.

Seeing him close up for the first time, she realized that his green eyes were flecked with gold. His wavy, chestnut hair was slicked back with Brylcreem and in the half-light Kathleen thought he looked rather like Errol Flynn, one of her favourite actors.

'You're a good dancer yourself,' she said, marvelling at how he moved so easily with her. She could feel his muscular torso beneath his shirt and found her fingers gripping his waist a little more tightly.

'It's the boxing. I have to be light on me toes. Maybe you will come and see me. I'm doing a few bouts up at the Manor Place Baths the week after next.'

Was he inviting her out on a date? Kathleen wasn't sure but it sounded like it. She didn't get time to ask him because another chap, who was much taller than Albert and older by five years, tapped him on the shoulder and said, 'Come on, mate, give another fella a chance with the prettiest girl in the park.'

Kathleen blushed. Albert scowled but relinquished her. In an instant, she wished that she had said 'no' because he was clumsy and trod on her toes and they didn't seem to be able to fall into that easy rhythm in the way that she had with Albert. To make matters worse, when the dance had finished he abandoned her for a striking blonde who was almost as tall as he was and Kathleen was left on her own again. She looked around to see if she could spot Nancy to get a drink but she was still whirling around the asphalt with a bloke from one of the barges.

Then she spotted Albert standing over at the ginger beer stand, glowering at her. She made her way over to him and gave him a little wink. 'How about you buy a girl a drink, then?' It was her instinct to try to lighten the situation, to make him laugh a bit. She couldn't help it if she was so pretty that other men wanted to ask her to dance, could she?

Albert grabbed her hand and pulled her to him. 'Let's get one thing clear,' he said. 'I don't like sharing. If you are with me, you are with me. Don't make me look like a fool by going off with other fellas.'

'I didn't mean to do that, don't be daft,' she said. 'He was a right clumsy oaf.' She was shocked by his jealousy but also touched by it because it meant that he liked her, really liked her.

His hands were strong and they gave her little wrists a squeeze. 'I'm not being silly. I want you to be my girl. Come and see me box. You can bring your mate.'

Nancy was hovering over her left shoulder. 'It's gone nine o'clock, Kath, we'd better get a shift on,' she said.

Albert kissed her, full on the lips, and she felt her knees almost buckle.

'I'm sorry, Albert,' she whispered before she knew what she was saying. 'I won't let you down again.'

There was a knock at the door; it was too early for the tallyman to be calling. Kathleen was halfway down the stairs but her father beat her to it.

'And who might you be?' said her father.

Her heart lurched as she heard the reply.

'I'm Albert. I work with your Kathleen down the jam factory.' He was standing with his hands in his pockets. That would be bound to annoy her dad. Kathleen peered down at him. At least his hair was neatly parted and brushed.

'And what do you want?'

'I was hoping to come in and ask your permission to

take Kathleen to see me box today at Manor Place,' said Albert.

'The doorstep will do just fine for this chat,' said her father. He turned around. 'Get back upstairs, Kathleen.'

She trudged back up to her room, leaving the door ajar. Her heart thumped in her chest. Albert had come all the way round to her house to ask permission to go courting. That meant he really liked her! It was like being a heroine in one of those films . . . Except there was no chance her dad would let her ride off into the sunset with her hero.

'Now, Albert, I appreciate you coming round but a boxing match is hardly a place for a young lady, is it?'

'She won't be going alone; she can bring her pal Nancy and I will walk them both home and see they don't get into any trouble.'

There was a pause. 'All right, then. She can go – but only because you had the brass neck to come and ask me in person. But no funny business, see?'

'Yes, sir.'

Kathleen went to the window and watched as Albert walked jauntily back up Howley Terrace, his hands still in his pockets. He turned back and looked up, as if he knew she'd be watching, gave Kathleen a wink and she felt a swooping in her chest.

Her father shut the front door and then called to her, 'Kathleen, get yourself down here. You've got some explaining to do.'

It had been a wet spring but the sun was finally out and the whole street was in the mood for a right royal knees-up at the coronation party for King George VI in May. But Kathleen was a little nervous because it was also the first time that Albert would meet her mother.

The Mason's Arms in Walworth had become her mother's favourite local haunt and as Kathleen walked proudly in, on Albert's arm, she saw that Mum had an admirer too. It was the tall man with a ready smile whom Kathleen had seen singing years before at Flo's birthday party in the Feathers. He had his hand firmly tucked around Mum's waist and gazed at her with adoration as she held court around the piano.

'Well, Kathleen, who is this fine-looking young man?' said her mother, plonking her sherry down on the bar.

'I'm Albert, Kathleen's boyfriend from work,' he said, taking her hand and planting a kiss on it. His green eyes twinkled as he spoke. He just had such a way with women and Kathleen loved that about him.

'Quite the charmer there, Kathleen!' said her mother with a laugh. 'I'm Kathleen's mother, Margaret. Now, you promise me, Albert: you are to look after my little girl because she seems very sweet on you.'

Albert smiled and hugged Kathleen, 'Of course I will. I treat her like a princess, don't I, Kath?'

Kathleen nodded. He really was like a Prince Charming – taking her to the pictures, buying her chocolates and always walking her home on time so she didn't get into trouble with her dad for staying out late.

'Let me introduce someone to you both. This is Patsy, my boyfriend,' said Margaret. There were whoops of delight from the little gang around the piano. Kathleen beamed at her mum. So she was happy at last and had fallen in love with someone new. It seemed right, somehow. If the King could give up his throne for the likes of Mrs Simpson, why shouldn't her mother have a second chance at happiness?

Patsy offered his hand to Albert and then clasped Kathleen's hands in his own. 'I have heard so much about you, Kathleen. You really are every bit as pretty as your mother said. And do you still like playing the piano? I was hoping you could give us a tune.'

'Love to!' said Kathleen. The pianist got up and shuffled off to the bar and Kathleen hammered out the tune guaranteed to get everyone singing along: 'Knees up, Mother Brown! Knees up, Mother Brown!'

The whole pub erupted into an impromptu dance with couples swinging each other around the crowded bar, smacking into people's pints, hooting with laughter. Nobody minded the chaos, it just added to the party atmosphere, although Albert didn't seem to want to join in. He stood at the bar, supping a pint, staring over at a couple of blokes who were leaning on the piano, smiling down at Kathleen as she played.

He only got into the party spirit when Mum shouted at him, 'Come on, Albert, give us a twirl, then!'

Suddenly, the fun Albert, whom Kathleen liked best, returned. Plonking his half-finished pint down on the bar, he slung one arm around Mum's waist and another around Patsy's shoulder as the three of them high-kicked their way across the pub and back, chortling all the while.

There was a lock-in that night and then, when the landlord finally called time, a gang of about ten bought out crates of beer and bottles of sherry and took them back to Mum's flat in Walworth Road to continue the celebrations. Peggy was out at some political meeting or other with George, who had been among the bus workers threatening a strike on the eve of the coronation. It had been called off at the last minute but Peggy and George always seemed to have some cause or other to go off and talk about. Kathleen couldn't be bothered with that; she just wanted to have a day off work and a good time with Albert. Jim had spent the day glued to his wireless set listening to the coronation and was celebrating with his dad, Nanny Day and Grandad and the folks down in Howley Terrace.

One of the Irish fellas from down the road had brought his violin back to Mum's flat and someone else had a mouth organ, and with an upturned crate as a drum, they had quite a party going. The neighbour downstairs banged on the floor with her broomstick to tell them to shut up but they stomped back even louder. 'This is a bleedin' coronation party, for Gawd's sake. Give it a rest, love!'

They danced jigs and reels and when Eva came back from a party down at the Elephant with her mate Gladys, the atmosphere became even more raucous. Kathleen found herself pulled up to dance again and again, with one of the costermongers spinning her around the tiny living room. Albert glowered at her from the corner.

Eventually, he tapped his watch and said, 'Come on, Kathy, it's time to go home now.'

But she was having so much fun. 'Just one more dance, Albert, then we can go,' she said with a laugh. He slunk deeper into a chair in the corner of the room and lit up a smoke, with a face like thunder. Kathleen was quite tipsy and didn't seem to notice his brooding.

It was gone 2 a.m. when they finally staggered downstairs into the cool night air. The whoops and shouts of other parties in the neighbourhood could still be heard. There wouldn't be much sleep in Walworth tonight, that was certain.

Kathleen was just buttoning up her coat when Albert pulled her to him and kissed her, roughly, ramming his tongue into her mouth. She tried to push him off and he grabbed her by the hair. 'Don't pull away from me, Kathy, not when you have been dancing with the other men. You know I don't like that.'

'Albert, please, it was only a bit of fun . . .'

'You want to make me look a fool in front of them, don't you?'

He kissed her again and bit her lip as he did so, drawing blood. Kathleen pushed him off and slapped his face. Albert put his hands around her throat. 'Don't make me hurt you! You know I love you, Kathy, more than anything.' His eyes blazed with anger.

He squeezed; the strength in his fingers was immense, and she gasped for air, pummelling his chest. Then, just as suddenly has he started, he stopped and started to cry. 'I'm sorry, I'm sorry!'

She put her hand to her throat, instinctively, then held out her hand to him. 'Albert, it's all right. Please, don't, it's all right.'

He embraced her, resting his head on her shoulder. 'You

are my world, Kathleen, the most beautiful girl in the world.' She raised her hand, shaking, and hesitantly stroked the nape of his neck, feeling the softness of his skin.

In the flat above them, a curtain moved, throwing a shaft of light onto the pavement. Kathleen glanced up.

It was Eva. She had seen everything.

19

Eva, October 1937

Hoisting just hadn't been as much fun since Maggie got sent to Holloway. The judge gave her two years for blinding the cozzer with her hatpin and Maggie had shrieked her head off when she was sent down to the cells.

Eva had responsibility for her own team now, including her mate Gladys, and they went out to work three days a week. The rest of the time she served up cups of tea in the canteen at the railway station, to keep up appearances. She was determined that none of her girls should get caught and the weight of that responsibility had made her feel older, much older, than her fifteen years. So Eva took her gang to where the pickings were easy: over the water at Derry and Toms in Kensington and at Whiteley's in Bayswater.

Eva always made sure she brought something nice back for her mum. The flat above the shop in Walworth Road was tiny but it suited her and Mum and Frankie. The three of them were happy enough. Mum really wanted her to build some bridges and get over the rift with Peggy. The sisters hadn't spoken since the family split. Peggy was always out saving the world from something or other with George. Kathleen had told Eva that Peggy had even joined some book club where they had speakers talking about the dangers of the Nazis in Germany, the benefits of Communism and God knows what else. In any case, it didn't stop Peggy being a grass to her own sister and Eva could never forgive that.

It wasn't that she missed Peggy much in any case. She was too busy earning money, good money, to support her and her mother and she loved going out and living it up a bit with Gladys in the West End. She didn't generally like to wear the stuff she'd nicked – that was a matter of pride among the hoisters of the Forty Thieves. Alice Diamond would sell it on through her network of fences and Eva would then have enough money to go shopping properly to buy what she wanted. She loved that feeling, of being independent and wealthy enough to walk into Gamages or Selfridges and buy some shoes, a coat, a dress, whatever took her fancy, really. And there was no need to have a fella to pay for it. She'd come a long way since she was a little girl who used to press her nose against the glass at the bakery over the water in Covent Garden as she waited for day-old bread to feed the family.

With her long dark hair and striking looks, Eva had plenty of admirers in the pubs around Walworth Road and the Elephant but she wasn't interested in more than a drink and a laugh. Her mate Gladys couldn't understand it and was forever trying to play Cupid.

Gladys already had a regular boyfriend. 'Why don't you come out with us and we will fix you up with a nice bloke, Eva?'

'Nah, I honestly can't be bothered with it all. I'm better

off on my own. No man will ever be the boss of me,' she said. In truth, seeing how her father had treated her mother had put her right off marriage and everything that went with it. Mum was doing fine now with Patsy, who just doted on her and was so gentle and fussed over her, just as she deserved, but Eva never wanted to risk being the downtrodden one stuck at home with the kids.

And Kathleen, well she was like a little lovebird with Albert but Eva had her suspicions about him, too. She'd seen him grab Kathleen round the throat when they'd both had a bit too much to drink a few months back. When Eva tried to mention it, Kathleen just brushed it off. 'Oh, I was being a bit mouthy, Eve, that's all. Got a bit silly and he'd had a few too many. He doesn't ever treat me like that, in fact he would never lay a finger on me!' Albert might be a boxer but Eva had already made a promise to herself that she would wallop him one if he ever hurt her sister again. She wasn't afraid of anyone and she had Alice Diamond and the girls to back her up.

Some of the other girls in the Forty Thieves liked a good scrap. Fighting wasn't really Eva's thing but there were times when she was expected to provide back-up, just in case, and today was one such occasion. Alice had ordered her and Gladys to meet at a pub down in Long Lane in the Borough on Sunday afternoon, which was usually their day off.

'There's a score I've got to settle and it might interest you,' she'd told her. Eva had been racking her brain all day to think about who might be on the receiving end of Alice Diamond's knuckle-duster but she'd drawn a blank. When she got to the pub, she was amazed to see it rammed to the rafters and had to push her way to the bar to get port and lemon for herself and Gladys. They huddled in a corner, listening in to the conversations around them.

'Place is full of Commies,' said one bloke. 'Hundreds of them have come in from over the East End.'

'Better them than the Fascist lot,' said another. 'All the dockers have come out to give them a hiding.'

Eva recognized Joe from Howley Terrace at the bar, drinking with some workmates, and she realized, with a stab of guilt, that she hadn't seen Mary and little Florrie in ages. She rarely went near Howley Terrace these days, for fear of bumping into her father. She was just about to go over and tell Joe to pass on her best to his wife, when Alice Diamond strode in, with four of the Forty Thieves behind her.

A hush fell over the pub as she made her way to the bar. Then she picked up a pint glass and smashed it. The noise made Joe turn around. In an instant, Alice had stuck the glass in his face. 'Grass!' she said. 'I know you told the cozzers about one of my girls from Howley Terrace a couple of years ago. Got her in trouble with her dad, too. Do yourself a favour, keep it shut from now on.' He staggered backwards, blood spurting from the cut. Nobody tried to stop Alice as she turned briskly and left. Someone offered Joe a handkerchief, which he held to his face, the blood pumping through it and splatting onto the floor. Eva's mouth fell open. So Peggy had been telling the truth all along and hadn't spilt the beans to their father about her hoisting. But Eva would never have wanted Joe to get cut like this, no matter that he had grassed her up. There was no time to say sorry to him because a huge roar went up outside and brick flew through the window, spraying the pub with shards of broken glass.

In an instant, the pub had emptied, men arming themselves with chairs, bottles, anything they could lay their hands on. Eva and Gladys followed to see what the rumpus was all about. At the top of the lane, costermongers had built a barricade with their barrows and a crowd had gathered behind it. They were lobbing rotten fruit over the top at the police and a pack of Blackshirts who were marching to the beat of a drum and singing something in German. They looked so bloody ridiculous with their high-necked shirts, their trousers held up with huge belts and silver buckles, their hair slicked back and their shoes polished so you could see your face in them. 'What a bleeding shower they are,' hissed Eva to Gladys, who was jeering at them, with the rest of the pub.

From the other end of the lane came the sound of the Communists singing 'The Red Flag'. A banner had been hung from a house over the road from the pub, reading 'Bermondsey against Fascism!' The men from the pub broke into an impromptu chorus of 'Land and Hope and Glory' in an attempt to drown out both sides. Eva, still carrying her port and lemon, threw it into the crowd of Blackshirts, just as the mounted police cantered into view, the officers whacking heads here and there with their truncheons.

Despite the efforts of the police to disperse everyone, the crowd kept growing until there were hundreds of people surrounding the Blackshirts, beating them back, booing and shouting. Chamber pots were slung out of open windows onto them, doorknobs and even billiard balls were lobbed into the fray and, in the middle of it all, Eva spotted her sister Peggy, screeching, 'They shall not pass!' at the top of her lungs, linking arms with some old bloke on one side and George Harwood on the other, as she kicked out at a passing policeman.

In that moment, Eva could have almost died of pride: her big sister Peggy, Miss Goody-Two-Shoes, was breaking the law and fighting for what she believed in. Eva ran to her, waving her arms. 'Peggy! Peggy!'

'Eva! What on earth are you doing here?'

'I was trying to have a quiet drink with Gladys but fat chance of that with you Communists about,' she said. 'I need to say sorry, I was wrong about you grassing me up. I know you never did.'

Their conversation was short lived because while George was busy punching a Blackshirt right in the kisser, they found themselves grappled away by two policemen. 'Move along, now, come on! This is no place for a lady.'

Eva looked at her sister and laughed as they were shoved down Long Lane. 'We certainly ain't ladies, are we, Peg?'

Peggy and George came over to Mum's flat in Walworth Road the next day, to show that there was no bad blood between them.

'It makes me so happy to have you two speaking to each other again,' said Mum, putting the kettle on the little gas cooker to make some tea.

Kathleen was moping about by the wireless in the front room. Eventually, Eva tired of it. 'Come on, spit it out, what's up?'

'It's Albert,' she whispered, so that Mum wouldn't overhear.

'What's he done now?' said Eva.

'It's not bad, Eve, quite the opposite. He wants to marry me.'

'Oh my Gawd!' said Eva. 'And what have you told him?'

'I have said yes, of course I will, but the only trouble is Dad . . .'

'You haven't told him, have you?' said Eva, who had visions of her father chasing Albert down Howley Terrace with a poker.

'I have, and he hasn't spoken to me for days,' Kathleen replied. 'You know I can't get married without his permission. If Albert goes round there it will end in a fight but I don't want to lose him, Eva, because half the girls at work fancy him and if I don't say yes, then someone else will, I'm sure.'

Eva thought about it for a minute. Kathleen was would soon be seventeen but she would have to wait until she was twenty-one before she could marry without their father's permission. 'You don't think he will wait for you until you can do it without our dad's say-so?' said Eva. Kathleen shook her head miserably.

'Well, I can't bear seeing you like this, Kath. Leave it with me,' Eva said. She pulled on her coat and caught the bus towards Waterloo Station. She wasn't really sure what she was going to do when she got there, but she found herself walking down Howley Terrace and opening the front door to number 6.

'Is that you, Jim?' came her father's voice, from the scullery.

She walked in. 'No, it's me.'

He was sitting at the table, polishing his boots on an old newspaper, his shirtsleeves rolled up.

'Well, look what the cat has dragged in,' he said.

'I've come about Kathleen,' said Eva, wandering across to the range, where a pan of potatoes was peeled and ready to cook.

'Well, you have got a nerve coming round here, I'll give you that,' he said. 'She ain't getting married and that's that.' He started whistling to himself and went back to polishing his boots. 'Now, unless you have come to cook my tea, you'd better be off.'

Eva picked up the pan and walked over to her father, smiling. She slowly poured the water, potatoes and all, on top of his head. 'That's to pay you back for the gravy you landed on me,' she said as he spluttered. 'I'm sick to death of your bullying ways. We all are! It's Kathleen's life. You have had yours; now you should let her get on with hers.'

Dad wiped the water from his face and pushed the potatoes from his lap. He looked at her for a second. 'I hear you are keeping some pretty tough company these days, with those Forty Thieves, Eva. I saw Joe yesterday—'

'That was nothing to do with me!' Eva spat. 'I would never want Joe hurt.'

Eva knew her dad was only a small old man nowadays, sitting there at the kitchen table, but there was something in his eyes which still made Eva scared as hell of him, though she tried not to show it.

'I tell you what,' he said, after a long pause. 'I will make you a deal. You get yourself a proper job and when Kathleen is nineteen, she can get married.'

'That's two years away!' said Eva.

'If Albert really loves her, he can wait that long. I'll tell him myself. They're too young, Eva. People can make mistakes . . .'

'You are a fine one to talk,' she cut in.

'Don't try my patience, Eve,' he said. 'I've been reasonable. Get yourself a decent job, show me your cards and your pay packet and I will keep my word on Kathleen.'

Eva had no intention of staying too long in the world of work, it was a mug's game as far as she was concerned. But a promise was a promise, and she wanted to help her sister, and so that's how she found herself working in a textile factory down in Southwark. She'd explained it to Alice Diamond, who had agreed she could stop hoisting for a few weeks, just until her father was convinced she was going straight. There was one condition: Eva had to work out a few fiddles on the factory floor while she was there.

It didn't take her long to suss out that her shoplifter's drawers would come in handy. When the foreman's back was turned, she managed to shove a whole bolt of material down her knicker leg and make her way to the ladies' loos. Once there, she stripped off and wound the material round and round herself, until she was wrapped up like a mummy. At the end of her shift, she waddled out of the factory, praying that the material wouldn't slip down and give the game away.

She kept that up for a month, which was long enough for the factory boss to notice that quantities of material were going missing. By then, the whole of Scovell Road had matching curtains and Alice Diamond was very pleased with her haul. Her father had seen enough of her weekly pay packets to believe that she was going straight and Kathleen got engaged to Albert.

The week after that, Eva was laid off. She'd never been happier to lose a job in her life.

20

Peggy, January 1938

As the clock on the mantelpiece struck midnight, Peggy and George gave each other a peck on the cheek, while Kathleen bashed out 'Auld Lang Syne' on the piano in the front room. Peggy had done her best to bring some Christmas cheer into the little house in Howley Terrace, with some paper chains around the door and pinned up along the picture rail, but a few brightly coloured decorations were no match for her father's black mood.

Dad had heard about Mum's new boyfriend on Boxing Day and had been seething ever since. He had refused to go down to the pub with most of the other folk since then, fearing that people were talking about him behind his back. Their neighbour, Mrs Avens, had stuck most of the evening out, bringing round a bottle of sherry, and playing cards with Jim, Albert and Kathleen, but even she had retreated before the New Year arrived.

Kathleen and Albert made their way to the front door and opened it. Peggy and George followed, shouting, 'Happy New Year!' They were greeted by whoops and cheers from other houses in the street, where people also came to their doorways and raised glasses to each other.

Peggy hugged George tightly in the cold night air. She had such a good feeling about 1938. For a start, she would be twenty-one this year and she and George had already secretly planned to get married once she was of age.

With her father safely ensconced in his favourite arm-chair, they seized the chance to have a proper kiss without him seeing. 'I can't wait to be Mrs Harwood,' she whispered.

He nuzzled her neck and whispered back, 'Me too.' She hadn't told Kathleen about her plans – she knew her sister was desperate to marry Albert but had to wait until the end of next year before Dad would allow it. Peggy couldn't tell Kathleen but she had a lot of sympathy with their dad's view; Albert and Kathleen were still very young and she didn't like the way that Albert seemed to have her sister under the thumb. It was as if a little spark in her went out when she was with him. The fact that she was planning to marry George was something she longed to share with her, but telling her would probably only make matters worse. Poor Kathleen seemed to have enough on her plate dealing with Albert's moods as it was.

Peggy looked up at the stars and made a wish. It wasn't for herself – she had so much to be thankful for – but for her old friend Susan. She hadn't been up to the hospital to visit her for a few months but was planning to go at the weekend. She'd just been so tied up with work and meetings of the Left Wing Book Club, where they were raising money to help the Communists in Spain fight the war against the Fascists. Peggy had even met some of the volunteers who had gone off to fight. One of them was a woman artist who had been shot dead weeks after arriving there. Peggy still remembered her owlish face and cheery manner. It seemed shocking that she was killed like that. Peggy had no intention of ever doing anything so brave, or foolish, but she did feel it was her duty to try to raise money where she could and she was happy to rattle tins along the Walworth Road or up in the West End, even if some people did say nasty things to her about collecting for the Commies.

There was so much talk about the possibility of war with Hitler, it kept Peggy awake at night with worry sometimes. The Communist Party had endless meetings and discussions about it, which Peggy attended, listening quietly and occasionally adding her pennyworth. Susan would understand her not visiting so often, she was sure of that.

The hospital in Muswell Hill loomed large over the street, an imposing red-brick Victorian villa with turrets at either end. It had a vast and impressive entrance hall with a highly polished wood floor but, once inside, Peggy noticed there was an all-pervading smell of disinfectant. The little day room where she was to meet Susan was dilapidated, with peeling wallpaper and armchairs which were so ancient that the springs almost poked through as she sat down.

Susan shuffled in, barely recognizable as the bright, funny and daring girl who had started work with Peggy at the Post Office. Her hair was unkempt and she wore an old dressing gown and slippers. Her face, once so pretty, was bloated and she seemed distracted, scratching away at her arms. Peggy saw that one of her wrists was bandaged.

'Well, how are you keeping?' Peggy said brightly, as she handed over a paper bag with some tangerines in it, from the fruit stall up at the Cut. For some reason, she couldn't say why, Peggy had saved up and bought Susan a lipstick from Coty in a lovely shade of pink. It seemed stupid now, out of place, as she handed it over to her friend, who clasped it absent-mindedly for a second, before stuffing it into her dressing gown pocket, along with her old hankies.

A nurse bustled about in the corner of the room, arranging some flowers and straightening a few dog-eared books on a little table.

'They might let me out soon; I'm doing much better,' said Susan, eyeing the nurse's back.

'What happened to your wrist?' said Peggy.

'Accident. Cut myself in the kitchen. It was an accident, that's all.'

Peggy swallowed hard and then nodded. 'Are you feeling better in yourself, then? You look well . . .' Her friend looked so terrible it made Peggy want to cry, but she had to keep going with this, for Susan's sake.

The nurse tapped her watch. 'Just a short visit today, Susan. We don't want you getting upset, now, do we? I'll get you both a nice cup of tea.' She glared at Peggy, then turned on her heel and left.

Peggy didn't know what to say. Was the nurse telling her not to mention the baby? Peggy looked out of the window at the patchy lawn, where a bird was forlornly pecking at the frozen ground. A man was following the bird around and it kept fluttering off to a nearby tree to escape him.

She jumped as Susan suddenly reached forwards, clasped her hand and pleaded with he urgently. 'I've got to get out of here, Peg. They keep putting things in my food to keep me quiet. It all got too much the other day and I slashed my wrists – well, one of them. They caught me with the knife before I could make a proper job of it.' She put her arms around herself and started to rock back and forth.

Peggy put her hand on Susan's knee. 'Oh, Susan, you mustn't do such things to yourself. If you want to get out, you need to tell them what they want. Just pretend you are happy. Can you do that? If you can get out you can start afresh.'

Susan's eyes filled with tears. 'I can't forget my Tommy. My mum says my aunt will have me down in the East End and she can get me work but it's a hard job trying to keep my chin up, Peggy, the hardest job in the world. How can I say I am happy that my baby is with somebody else?'

The nurse returned with two cups of stewed, brown tea in chipped teacups and a little biscuit each, bringing their conversation to an abrupt end. Susan sniffed and looked away, wiping her eyes on the sleeve of her dressing gown. Peggy realized she hadn't managed to have any lunch and was starving. She drank the tea down, almost in one gulp and then regretted it, as it gnawed away at her insides.

The nurse lurked over their shoulders, pretending to flick dust from the window ledge.

'Have you got any news, then?' said Susan.

'Not much,' Peggy lied. How could she tell Susan that she was planning to marry her sweetheart and live happily ever after, to have children and grow old together; to create her own family? 'It's all just the same as it ever was. You'll be back home soon, you'll see. Nothing has changed a bit.'

'Send word to your mother. I need to talk to her.'

Peggy wasn't sure she'd heard Dad right. She turned round from the range, where she was frying a bit of bacon for their tea. 'Pardon?'

There were dark circles under his eyes and his cheekbones were so sharp you could cut yourself on them. He'd not been eating properly since Christmas. He used to like going up the Cut and getting stewed eels or hot pie and mash for a few pennies, but he had stopped doing that of late.

'You heard me, Peg. Tell her we can meet tonight at seven o'clock on Waterloo Bridge. There's something important I need to say.'

She put some bacon aside – she'd have that later – pulled on her coat and hurried up to the Waterloo Road, where she caught a tram down to Walworth to see her mum. Eva was out when she got there, thank God, because Peggy wasn't sure what her views on it would have been but she wanted to try to take the heat out of the situation. Mum had her hair in rollers and was applying some lipstick for a night out up West with Patsy.

'He wanted me to do what?'

'To come and see him on the bridge at seven,' she said. 'And why would I go and talk to him, the bullying bastard?' said Mum. 'Excuse my language, Peggy, but I have done my time with your father.'

'Please, Mum, it seems important to him. I think he might be ill or something.'

'Ill? He can pay to see a doctor like the rest of us, can't he? I'm not his nursemaid!'

'He knows about you and Patsy . . .'

Mum sat down at her little kitchen table with a sigh. 'I knew he would find out eventually. But I ain't done anything wrong. Not after the way he treated me.'

Peggy wished she didn't have to be involved in this but, as the eldest daughter, she could see that it had to fall to her. 'Just hear him out and then you can move on with things; maybe you can both move on.'

'All right,' said Mum, ripping off her apron. 'But if I am seeing him, I am damn well going to look my best. And I am not doing it for him, see. I'm doing it because you asked me to.'

She spent ages getting dressed, so long that Peggy watched the minutes tick by on the clock which Eva had nicked from Gamages, in pride of place on the mantelpiece. It was much posher than the one back in Howley Terrace, Peggy noted with some indignation, because she had worked for theirs.

Eventually, her mother appeared in the doorway, resplendent in a full-length fur coat, matching hat, heels and carrying a smart handbag. A bitter wind blasted down Waterloo Road as they made their way along the pavement towards the bridge in the dark. The river was inky beneath them with the glow of dim gaslight from tug boats making their way home for the night.

Dad stood against a railing, his coat collar turned up and his hat pulled low over his ears.

'Don't you leave me alone with him,' said Mum, clutching Peggy's arm as they drew near. She seemed genuinely afraid.

'Can we just talk for minute, Maggie?' he said, reaching out to her.

'We can chat, but Peggy stays where I can see her,' said Mum, recoiling from his touch.

Dad looked as if he had been punched in the stomach.

Peggy shuffled back a few paces, to give them some privacy. She really didn't want to be here but she had to stay, for her mother's sake. Her father seemed so small and thin standing there, it was as if he was made of newspaper and might just blow away in the night air.

'I have so much to say sorry for, Maggie,' he said, his voice almost a whisper. 'I should never have hit you. Things just got too much. You know, you are the only woman I have ever loved, the only woman I will ever love.'

Mum grew taller with every word he spoke. 'Well, you've a got a funny way of showing your love and I don't need you. I'm doing just fine without you, thanks.'

'Please, Maggie, I want us to be a family again, I want you to come home. I promise you I will look after you . . .' He began to pull something out of his coat pocket.

Peggy gasped as she realized it was money, a whole wad of cash, more money than she had ever seen before in her life.

'I want to give you this, to show you I will never keep you short ever again and I will never treat you badly.'

'And where in the name of God have you got that much cash?' said Mum, her voice rising a semitone. 'Don't tell me you have gone and robbed a bank!'

'No, no,' he said. 'I had an old gold fob watch from my captain in the Merchant Navy. I sold it, Maggie, for you.'

He handed her the money and she leafed through it for a moment.

'All the days and nights I worried about my last farthing and now this,' she said. Her eyes were blazing with anger. 'I always said to myself I would wait until Frankie was thirteen before I could leave you and that is what I did, James. I waited and I was scared every day of my life when I was with you. You have no idea how you made me suffer. You could give me all the tea in China and I wouldn't set foot in the house again. You are thirteen years too late!'

She threw the money back in his face. Then, she turned and walked off the bridge and out of his life.

Peggy's engagement to George brought some much-needed cheer to the little house in Howley Terrace, which seemed to have a permanent black cloud over it after Mum told Dad it was over, forever.

Of course, Peggy knew about George's intentions; they had discussed their future together, much as they had discussed politics, in a calm, sensible manner, when they went out courting. But George had a few surprises up his sleeve, and one balmy May evening, as they were crossing Waterloo Bridge, with the city bathed in a red glow of a beautiful sunset, he suddenly dropped to one knee and produced a ring.

Realizing what was happening, a couple of passers-by cheered and clapped. Peggy blushed as he said, 'Peggy, you are the most beautiful girl in all the world. Would you do me the honour of being my wife?'

'Oh, George, yes!' she cried, as he slipped the engagement ring onto the third finger of her left hand. The ring had belonged to George's granny but was a perfect fit.

'See,' he said, as Peggy admired it. 'It was meant to be. You were always the girl for me, Peggy.'

Peggy couldn't say her dad was delighted by the news but he did at least crack a smile. She was nearly twenty-one now and he wasn't about to stop her having the summer wedding she wanted by making her wait until after her birthday in the autumn; he liked George, that much was clear from the way they spent ages discussing politics in the scullery.

'He's a fine young man, Peggy. I think you could do a lot worse,' he said – which was about as close to giving her his blessing as she was ever going to get.

Being engaged to George filled Peggy's heart with joy and she set about sprucing up the scullery in Howley Terrace, bringing a bunch of flowers home to set on the table once a week and making sure everything on the mantelpiece was nicely dusted. It was as if she was practising to be a homemaker.

They set a date for August and Peggy started to work on the design for her dress. It was the most ambitious thing she had ever made but she was determined to do it and make it the loveliest gown.

Eva had offered to pinch the material for Peggy's dress but Peggy wanted everything about it to be earned, properly earned. She scrimped and saved and bought the fabric from a shop in the East End and then she did the majority of the sewing herself, using the little Singer sewing machine, with a bit of help from the seamstress up the Cut and a few words of advice from Nanny Day.

Once everyone at the Post Office Savings Bank caught sight of her ring, the news of her engagement spread like wildfire. She had every intention of staying on there as long as she could – right up until the day before her wedding, in fact – because she loved that job and they needed the money to start a home life together. Everyone was really kind to her, especially her boss, Edna, who organized a whip-round. Peggy was given a wedding present of ten shillings a week for every year she had worked, which was very generous, and she immediately deposited it into her savings account. Of course, Peggy knew she couldn't stay on at work once she was married – those were the rules – but she did feel a tinge of sadness as she left Blythe House for the last time. Looking round at the office for the last time as she pulled on her coat, she thought about how she'd changed. She'd learned so much, not just about doing her job but about people, and she knew she would miss the camaraderie of working there.

Eva and Kathleen slept over at Howley Terrace that night with Peggy to help her get ready.

It seemed strange, all three of them in that little bedroom again. Their lives had moved on so much; they weren't children any more and Peggy couldn't help feeling that the best was yet to come, for all of them.

Peggy caught Kathleen admiring her wedding dress, feeling the soft white silk between her fingers. The dress had a V-neck and fluttery sleeves and Peggy had made it to skim her trim little waist, before falling in a small puddle train at her feet.

'You will be next, Kathleen,' she said, giving her sister a hug. 'I hope you don't mind me beating you to it up the aisle . . .'

She knew their father was sticking to his word, and wouldn't let her get married until next year.

Kathleen had tears in her eyes as she turned to her sister. 'I don't mind, Peg, of course I don't,' she said. 'It's only right that you get married first. You are my big sister and you make me so proud.'

Suddenly, Kathleen sat down on the bed and started to wring her hands.

'Besides,' she went on, 'I'm worried about having babies, Peg. What if something bad happens, like little Billy from down the road . . .' Her voice trailed away to nothing and she started to sob, covering her face with her hands.

'Oh, Kathleen, no. That will never happen to your baby or any of our babies,' Peggy said, sitting down beside her and hugging her tight. 'Is that what has been worrying you?'

Kathleen nodded. She looked so young then, Peggy felt as if the years had rolled away and they were twelve and ten again. 'What happened to Billy was just a dreadful stroke of bad luck.'

'But I could have done more to help save him. He was ill all that afternoon, you know.'

Peggy held her sister's hand. 'Look, even if you had got him to see a doctor a couple of hours sooner, he would still have died. Diphtheria is incurable. It was never your fault. You shouldn't still be carrying the guilt of it, Kathleen.'

There was a moment's silence and then Peggy ventured, 'I was wondering whether everything was all right between you and Albert?'

'Of course, everything's fine!' said Kathleen, stiffening a little. 'Why shouldn't it be fine between me and Albert? We are every bit as happy as you and George!'

'I didn't mean to upset you,' said Peggy, stroking her sister's shoulder. 'I just meant, if ever there was anything you wanted to talk about, you can trust me. That's what sisters are for.'

Kathleen looked as if she might have been about to say something, but Eva burst into the room, with a bottle of sherry and three glasses.

'Come on!' she said. 'It's like a bleeding funeral in here. You're getting married in the morning. Let's raise a little glass, shall we?'

Peggy barely slept a wink, she was so excited, and as dawn broke, she heard her dad downstairs, whistling to himself in the scullery, and had to pinch herself to make sure she wasn't imagining things. She really was going to get married today.

It was the wedding Peggy had always dreamed of. She walked slowly and gracefully up the aisle on Dad's arm, to find George waiting for her. He was self-assured and handsome, standing there, smiling. Her heart was beating so loudly she could barely get the words out to say her vows and when George slipped his grandmother's wedding ring on her finger, she cried.

Eva and Kathleen were her beautiful bridesmaids, in dresses of matching blue silk, falling just below the knee, with little belts pulled in at the waist and topped with blue pill-box hats. Mum left Patsy at home out of respect for Dad and also so that she wouldn't raise too many eyebrows in church, in front of the priest, who of course knew they were no longer living together, but said nothing. She sat at one end of the pew and he sat at the other and they barely looked at each other but at least they didn't fight. They both wanted Peggy to be happy on this, her big day.

Nanny Day sobbed loudly, possibly because Peggy looked so beautiful but more likely because her beloved grandson Frankie couldn't come to the wedding, having been locked up for breaking into a shop. Peggy didn't judge Frankie too harshly but it wasn't a path she wanted to tread. She felt the same way about Eva, who had risen through the ranks of the Forty Thieves.

When Peggy threw her bouquet, she made sure that Kathleen caught it, glimpsing the look of delight on her face as she did.

It wasn't a fancy affair, in fact it was quite small really, just close family and a few friends and a lovely reception in the back room of the Feathers, with sandwiches and cake for everyone, and a bit of a sing-song afterwards.

Their honeymoon was to be a weekend away in South-end, where she had enjoyed such a wonderful day trip as a child. She couldn't wait to show George the pier and the amusement park. They weren't going away for a couple of weeks, though, because George had to work some over-time at the bus depot to pay for it.

Home, for now, was a room in George's parents in Roupell Street, which Peggy was nervous about but it was just until they had saved up enough to rent a place of their own. They would stay locally; she wanted to be near to her family, particularly because she hoped that she might be lucky enough, soon, to start one of her own. That thought filled her with excitement but she did worry about the world they were going to grow up in. Some people had started talking about the possibility of a war with Germany.

George said that whatever the future brought, they should all get on with their lives, otherwise Hitler and his mob would have defeated everyone through fear, before a shot had even been fired.

'Whatever comes, Peggy, we will face it together,' he said, cuddling her close under the bedclothes. 'With you beside me, I can deal with anything the world cares to throw at me.'

He turned out the light and embraced her. Yes, 1938 was turning out to be more wonderful than she could ever have hoped.

21

Kathleen, April 1939

The imposing white entrance of the Whitehall Theatre seemed to loom over her.

Kathleen fumbled with her dance shoes as she stood on the steps. Was she supposed to go in the front door or around the back somewhere?

Her dance teacher, Miss Fawcett, hadn't explained that bit and now, with her nerves getting the better of her, Kathleen began to wonder whether the audition was a good idea, after all.

And that was before she got on to Albert's reaction to her trying out for a job in the chorus line. She'd thought he'd be happy, encouraging maybe, but he was downright angry about it.

'I don't want my girl wearing next to nothing, kicking her legs up and flashing her knickers for blokes paying ninepence a go!' he shouted. 'You'll be in one of those girlie shows up at the Windmill next, appearing starkers. I won't have it'

'But you know I love dancing, and the Whitehall is a decent theatre. Miss Fawcett only sends girls from her dance academy to good places, Albert,' said Kathleen. 'There has got to be more to life than bottling jam!'

He held her face in his hands and looked deep into her eyes. 'There is more, Kathy, there is more for us, together, when we are married.'

She nodded her agreement and he'd thought that was that. But when Saturday afternoon came around, she made her way to the theatre over the water, driven as if by some unseen force. If she got the job, he'd be happy because it would be the first step up to her becoming famous. Then if she got rich, he'd soon change his tune. All her life, she'd loved performing and this was her big chance, she could feel it, and yet . . . what would Albert say?

As she dithered on the front steps, a door opened and a heavily made-up girl wearing a fur coat emerged. She lit a cigarette and then made her way towards Kathleen.

'You lost, dearie?'

'I'm here for the audition,' Kathleen mumbled, almost apologetically.

'Well, you'd better get inside then because Mr Baker is waiting and he don't like to be kept waiting!' She gesticulated as she spoke and her coat fell open, to reveal a pair of satin shorts which barely covered her modesty, and a sequinned top.

The girl, who couldn't have been much older than Eva, shouted, 'Break a leg!' as Kathleen scampered up the stairs and into the foyer.

She pushed through some heavy doors and into the auditorium, which seemed so modern, all black and silver, compared to the soft, plush, rose and gold of the Trocadero down at the Elephant. The empty hall seemed cavernous, with a balcony extending around the edge upstairs, in a kind of horseshoe shape.

A grand piano stood upon the stage and a pianist, a young, thin bloke with a little pencil moustache was sitting there, picking at his nails.

A voice boomed at her from the stalls, almost making her jump out of her skin. 'You're five minutes late! Get a move on! Time is money.'

She scarpered down the aisle and climbed the steps at the side of the stage. A spotlight fell on her, making her squint.

'What's your name?'

'Kathleen,' she said. Her voice was quavering.

'Well, Kathleen, take off your coat and let's have a look at you.'

The owner of the voice, from what she could see, was a short, squat little fella, sitting in the tenth row, in his shirt-sleeves, brandishing a clipboard.

She took off her coat, folded it and placed it at the side of the stage. And then she stood, just as Miss Fawcett had told her to, with her hands lightly clasped in front of her. She smiled, remembering to breathe deeply.

'Very nice,' said the man. 'Now, lift your skirt up a bit.'

'Pardon?'

'Show me your legs. I haven't got all day!' he commanded.

Kathleen swallowed hard and raised the hem of her skirt an inch or two, until it was just grazing her thighs.

'Lovely pair of pins you've got there!' he boomed. 'Now,

show me some dance steps. Maisie, can you come and help out?'

A girl dressed identically to the one she had seen on the front steps appeared from the wings and took her place a few paces in front of Kathleen. Glancing over to the side of the stage, Kathleen realized that there was someone else standing there watching her, closely. He was a tall man, with slicked-back dark hair and he carried a ventriloquist's dummy, dressed identically, in black slacks and a gaudily striped blazer. She could see the ventriloquist's lips moving as the dummy turned to him and said, 'Ooh, I fancy her!' She felt a blush creep up her collarbone and a horrible sick feeling started in the pit of her stomach.

Before she had time to think, the piano struck up a few chords and the girl in front of her started to dance her way across the stage. Step, step, step, shuffle, change, step, shuffle, tap.

It should have been so easy. Kathleen could do better than that with her eyes closed but her legs felt like lead and her heart was hammering in her chest. She started out – step, step, step – but faltered on the shuffle.

'Try it again. Don't be nervous, Kathleen,' came the voice from the stalls.

The ventriloquist leered at her from the wings, running his tongue over his lips, as the dummy opened and closed its mouth.

The piano started up again and the girl performed her steps perfectly, almost gliding across the stage. Kathleen tried again but all she could think of was the bloke staring at her from the wings with his stupid dummy. She heard

Albert's voice, ringing in her ears: 'You'll be in one of those girlie shows up at the Windmill next . . .' Tears started to well in her eyes. Step, step, step. She tripped over her feet and fell to her knees and started to cry.

'All right, I've seen enough,' came the voice. 'Thank you, Kathleen. Next!'

Her head hanging in shame, she gathered her coat and ran the length of the aisle, out of the theatre, leaving her dream of a career in the West End behind her.

In the months following her failed audition, Kathleen did everything she could to be a perfect homemaker at Howley Terrace, seeing as Peggy was no longer there to rule the roost. And her efforts paid off because that June, Dad finally agreed to let Albert marry her. They would have to wait a while longer, until the autumn, he said, but Kathleen was just over the moon to have his permission at last.

As a special treat, Albert was planning to take her for dinner and dancing up West at the Café de Paris, with Nancy and her boyfriend. She had not one, but two, beautiful dresses to wear and Eva had pinched her a pair of perfect little satin shoes to go dancing in.

The legendary band leader Bert Firman was on. Nancy had seen him perform before, and she said it was the best night of her life, with so many posh people done up to the nines, crowding onto the little dance floor. Kathleen just had to get through the next shift at the jam factory and then it was home to get changed before heading out for the evening.

Dad had been really kind to her lately, paying for her to have the wedding dress she really wanted, using some money he had put by after selling an old gold watch. He had hidden that watch for years under the floorboards in the front room and nobody knew about it. That didn't seem right to Kathleen, after all the times they had struggled for cash, but she was delighted that he had chosen to give it to her to help make her big day as perfect as it could be. She was going down to a special little dress shop in Camberwell Green to have it made up and fitted.

Not one to be bested, Mum had bought her a satin evening gown for dancing, which clung to every curve and had a little bunch of silk flowers on the shoulder. She swished about in it, like a movie star. Her mum was even going to lend her a fur coat tonight, so she wouldn't get cold, and – more importantly – so she would look every bit as good as those women from Mayfair who didn't have to work for a living.

Kathleen only hoped her face wouldn't be too flustered from the heat of the boiling jam. Miss Bainbridge had put her and Nancy in charge of cooking up one of the vats of strawberry jam. The whole factory was packed to bursting with strawberries. It was one of Kathleen's favourite times of year because it marked the start of summer and the warmer weather to come.

'What are you going to wear tonight, then?' she shouted across the factory floor to her friend, knowing full well that Nancy had nothing as good as she did in her wardrobe.

'Haven't decided yet,' said Nancy, with a little pout.

'Maybe that black dress with a fishtail frill on the bottom of it.'

'Didn't you wear that last time you went there, though?' said Kathleen, smiling to herself. She just couldn't resist teasing Nancy a bit.

Nancy muttered, 'Yes, I suppose I did' under her breath. She turned her back on Kathleen and picked up a huge bag of sugar and chucked the contents into the vat.

'Oh, you dozy lump!' shouted Kathleen. 'I already put the sugar in five minutes ago!'

'You should have told me!' wailed Nancy.

They both stared into the boiling pot of red liquid.

'What's going on here?' It was Miss Bainbridge, who had a horrid knack of turning up when she was least wanted.

Kathleen looked at the floor and Nancy shuffled her feet about and said nothing.

'You'd better tell me what is going on,' said Miss Bainbridge, folding her arms and giving them her hardest stare. That look was enough to freeze water.

Kathleen's mind was racing.

'It was my fault, miss,' she said. 'I poured a whole load of sugar into the pot because I didn't realize Nancy had already done it.'

Miss Bainbridge clapped her hand to her forehead. 'Oh, you silly girl! That is all we need. A whole vat wasted. I will have to tell Miss Kendrick about this!' And she marched off to report to management on the third floor.

Nancy clasped her friend's arm. 'What did you go and say that for? You know it was my fault . . .'

Kathleen looked at her friend, who had tears in her eyes. 'It don't matter, Nancy. You know I'm leaving next month anyway. I have got Albert to look after me now. It's just not worth the bother, you getting into trouble.'

At the end of her shift, Kathleen was called into Miss Bainbridge's office and handed her cards. Just like that, after five years of hard graft. She was going to miss out on the works' annual beano to Margate on the charabanc, too, which made it harder to bear.

'I'm sorry to let you go, Kathleen,' said Miss Bainbridge. 'You are a hard worker. I can give you a reference if you like . . .'

Kathleen stuck her nose in the air. 'No need, miss, I'm going to be Mrs Ives soon, so my factory days are behind me now.' And she turned on her heel and left.

The final pay packet would have come in handy to put down as a deposit on a little flat for her and Albert but he was doing well for himself. He had left the jam factory and was working as an electrical fitter: a proper trade, as her father had told her, with some satisfaction. He was probably earning better money than George Harwood now, who had left his job on the buses and was working as a packer in a book printers up Gray's Inn Road. He wanted to be closer to his beloved books, probably, because that was all he talked about these days.

In any case, the last thing Kathleen wanted was to have to go and live at Albert's parents down in Vauxhall. They were nice enough. His dad was retired but his mum and sisters ran a fruit stall and wouldn't have a word said against their Albert. It wasn't that Kathleen ever found fault with him, but it was just the idea that Albert could do no wrong which irked her. She'd been brought up with brothers and she knew blokes could be a pain and there was no harm in saying so, was there? Albert didn't like her teasing him either. She'd try and change that, once they were married. Married! Just mentioning the word gave her butterflies.

Kathleen imagined herself walking down the aisle at St Patrick's Church in Cornwall Road, with the bells ringing out, the sun shining, and Albert, so tall and handsome, with his dark hair swept back and his green eyes looking into hers as they kissed. In reality, they planned to wed in the register office because Albert didn't want the fuss of a church wedding, but she could dream, couldn't she? A honking horn brought her back to reality as she turned in to Howley Terrace. It was the tallyman, in his new van, of which he was very proud.

He stepped out, twiddling with the ends of his little moustache. 'I hear congratulations are in order! Could I interest you in anything for your bottom drawer?'

'Not today,' she said airily. 'I have got everything I need already, so I won't be getting anything on tick, thanks.'

The Café de Paris was every bit as impressive as Kathleen had hoped. She glided down the staircase on Albert's arm, knowing full well that they were the best-looking couple in the place. Nancy followed with Roy, her painter boyfriend, who was always a great laugh. A waitress showed them to their table, right next to the circular dance floor, and they ordered some drinks. A huge chandelier hung above their heads and there were sumptuous drapes and gilt everywhere, which in the candlelight made it seem as if they were on a film set.

The band were already in place, in their tuxedos. As they struck up a tune, Bert Firman, dapper in his tails, looked around the room, which was already filling up, and smiled at Kathleen. 'I think he wants us to dance, Albert.' He didn't need to be asked twice. In a split second, they were on their feet, making their way around the dance floor in a foxtrot, like Ginger Rogers and Fred Astaire. Another couple joined them, then another, and soon the whole place was whirling around the little dance floor.

They barely sat down all evening after that. Roy and Albert paid for all the drinks but Kathleen noticed that for every glass she drank, he had two. At the end of the night, Bert Firman addressed the room. 'Now, I know there's a song you've all been waiting for . . . Shall we do it?'

He turned to the band, who shook their heads, prompting a cheer from the crowd: 'Come on!'

The first few bars had everyone crowding onto the dance floor, elbowing their way in to make space. Kathleen squeezed Albert's hand and giggled, 'Oh, I think they are playing our song!' Everyone from the milkman to the costermongers were whistling and singing it these days and it made Kathleen happy to hear it in this posh club too. Albert smiled at her and threw his jacket back over his shoulders and linked arms with her, as people started to step out in a line behind them, singing along. 'Any time you're Lambeth way, any evening, any day, you'll find us all, doin' the Lambeth walk, Oi!' They all slapped their knees and fell about laughing as the band played on. 'Everything's free and easy, do as you darn well pleasey . . .' They twirled each other around the cramped floor.

A short fella with sticky-out ears leaned over to Kathleen. 'Here, I reckon you're a dead ringer for that Carmen Miranda. I have been dying to tell you all night . . .'

Kathleen laughed nervously as she caught the look in Albert's eye. 'Are you chatting up my girl?' he said.

'No, mate, no,' the man replied. The fool was half-cut, Kathleen could tell that, from the glazed look in his eyes. He didn't get the chance to say much else, because Albert walloped him one, right in the face. He staggered back, falling on top of a dancing couple, who screamed and protested as they were knocked into a table. Kathleen froze with horror as she watched the scene unfold around her. She was powerless to do anything. She hadn't wanted any of this fuss, the whole thing had just got out of hand and it was beyond her control. More pushing and shoving followed and soon the management had put the lights up and some bouncers were wading into the crowd, pulling the little chap with the big ears to his feet and dragging him up the stairs, ignoring his protests, as the band played on.

'Come on, let's go,' said Albert, his jaw set firmly.

The cold night air and abrupt end to her evening sobered Kathleen up instantly. Nancy and Roy didn't seem to mind. They must have seen Albert throw the first punch, but they didn't say anything and seemed more interested in necking each other in a doorway.

'Why did you have to go and do that, Albert?' she whispered.

He turned to her. 'I can't have other blokes messing with my property, Kathleen, you know that. It's only because I love you.' Kathleen thought about that in the cab on the way back across the river. He was so possessive, it was romantic, really.

Trust Hitler to go and spoil her wedding by starting a bloody war. London had changed almost overnight, from a fun place with bright lights, to a blacked-out miserable city of sandbags, with air-raid wardens running around like busybodies, yelling at everyone. Mother had taped up the windows in their Walworth Road flat and Peggy had worked overtime sewing blackout curtains for everyone with her sewing machine.

Kathleen had felt the joy being sucked out of her with every passing day as a deep gloom settled over Lambeth that September. She'd managed to find herself a little job as a football pools clerk, checking the entries collected by the agents at corner shops. It was pin money but at least it gave her something to do and took her mind off her fears about the Nazis invading. She spent her evenings glued to the wireless, listening out in case the announcer said 'Cromwell', which meant that the Germans had landed.

Her brother Jim had received his call-up papers within a few weeks of war being declared and they were all worried sick about him. Frankie, her younger brother, was on the wrong side of the law as a deserter after Mum threw his papers on the fire and said she couldn't bear to lose him and so God only knew where he was. Peggy was on her own, too, because George and his brother Harry had been among the first to sign up in the area, keen to fight Fascism. That was all well and good but George had left Peggy with a bun in the oven. She had been going to be matron of honour at the wedding but she looked like the back end of a bus and was ready to pop at any moment, so she said she'd better not. She didn't mind really. It gave Eva and Nancy a chance to shine.

Kathleen had stayed the night at the flat in Walworth Road so that her mother and Nanny Day could help her get ready on the morning of the wedding. She'd spent so long dreaming about what this day would be like that when she woke up to a grey London sky, Kathleen almost wanted to shout to the world that it wasn't fair, but there was a war on, so she thought better of it. Everyone wanted it to be the perfect day and Albert was her Prince Charming, so she would do her best for him, and for everybody, to be his princess.

As she made her way into the kitchen to get a reviving cuppa, she could hear Nanny Day bustling about, getting Eva into her outfit.

'Always the bridesmaid, never the bride, Eva!' said Nanny Day. 'Maybe you'll be next, my girl.'

'Not if I can help it,' muttered Eva under her breath as Nanny buttoned up her bridesmaid's dress.

Nancy let herself in without bothering to knock – she was as much part of the family as anyone, really. Nanny always said that Nancy could talk the hind legs off a donkey but on this occasion she could barely speak, because she had to squish herself into the bridesmaid's frock that Kathleen had worn for Peggy's wedding. There was no polite way of saying it: she was a bit broader around the beam nowadays.

Kathleen was surprised to find that, as she did her make-up, carefully applying some rouge and lipstick, her hands were shaking. Her mother noticed as she handed her a little posy of flowers. She kissed Kathleen's cheek and told her, 'Just be yourself, Kathleen, because you are beautiful just as you are.'

All her hopes for the future were tied up with this day, the day she would become Mrs Ives. She wasn't just the girl from Howley Terrace who liked to sing and dance and play the piano. She wasn't the girl from the jam factory; in fact, she wasn't a girl any more. She would be a woman, a married woman whom people would tip their hat to as she went shopping down the Cut.

Albert was waiting for her at the register office, his green eyes sparkling, his wavy chestnut hair brushed back to reveal his handsome face. His mother was standing over his shoulder, like a little black cloud on the horizon. Albert beamed with pride as Kathleen walked towards him. Everyone said she looked breath-taking in a full-length white silk dress with lace sleeves and a little puddle train. Once they had said their vows and exchanged rings, they stepped outside into the weak autumn sunshine and Eva and Peggy pelted them with rice for luck, while everyone cheered. Grandad was in a wheelchair now because his leg was troubling him too much too walk but even he cracked a smile.

Just as they were making their way to the pub to enjoy a wedding breakfast of potted salmon sandwiches and a slice of cake, Albert's mother leaned over to Kathleen and whispered in her ear, 'You look lovely today but you'll never be good enough for my Albert, just you remember that.'

22

Eva, November 1939

It was nice to have somewhere new to go shopping. Eva and Gladys got up early to get down to Kingston-upon-Thames before Bentall's threw open its doors to the public, to make the most of their day out. Bentall's was known as England's Wonder Store and, judging by the size of it – a sprawling building which dominated the main shopping street – Eva could see why. She couldn't wait to get inside and go to work.

There was a lot of chit-chat in the queue about the war, of course, with most folks complaining that it was a phoney thing, because there was no sign of Jerry anywhere and now food was being taken off their plates by rationing. That didn't really bother Eva one bit. She was a picky eater at the best of times and had grown up without much food in the house so she barely noticed, and petrol rationing only really affected those rich enough to afford a car. The blackout was a nuisance, she supposed, but it also made moving stolen goods from one place to another a bit easier, at least. She kept her thoughts to herself as she peered at her reflection in the shop window.

Gladys pointed out a lovely blue angora coat on the mannequin in front of them.

'That'd suit you,' she said, smiling conspiratorially.

Eva looked smart with her long black hair pinned back into a neat little bun but the sleeves of her coat were fraying a bit. She could do with a new one. She might buy that blue coat with some of her hoisting money. It was a matter of pride not to wear the stuff she nicked. She enjoyed going shopping for nice things and paying for them, with the money she had earned. Handing out gifts to the family was different but hoisters liked to buy their own clothes.

Alice had given her strict instructions to get as many luxury items as she could in case clothes rationing started. 'It's an ill wind that blows nobody any good,' she had told her. 'Clothing coupons will mean I can put my prices up.' Eva planned to nick a good haul of silk stockings too, as they were so easy to conceal.

The doors opened and Gladys and Eva took their time working their way through the shop, checking out the stairwells and corridors where they could pass goods off to each other. Once they'd checked the place out, they made their way up to the lingerie section. Gladys tried to create a bit of kerfuffle, dropping satin nightgowns all over the place and pulling things off their hangers so that the shop assistants would follow her, rather than Eva, who had sidled up to the hosiery display. She'd already pocketed half a dozen pairs of silk stockings and was going for another lot, when she felt a hand on her shoulder.

'I know you have been stealing,' said the man. He had

such a kind, round face, Eva thought it would be a shame to have to punch it.

'No, I haven't,' she said, putting on her poshest accent. 'You are very much mistaken.'

'But I am not, am I?' he said, pulling open her coat to reveal the stockings, poking out of pockets in the lining of her coat. In an instant, two other blokes were at his side and they seized her.

'We realize the temptation to steal, now there is a war on, but I'm afraid I am going to have to call the police, young lady. Come with me.'

As she was frogmarched off to the manager's office, she spotted Gladys, hurrying away to the exit before she was caught. Realizing she couldn't run or fight her way out in a town she didn't even know, Eva decided to play the innocent, just as Alice Diamond had taught her.

'Most blokes hate it when a woman cries, so be sure to turn on the waterworks if you get caught,' she'd told her. 'It might just persuade them to let you go.'

Eva thought back to when her little brother Frankie got run over by a lorry when he was a kid. That always brought tears to her eyes. She began to sob. 'Please, I'm sorry. It's all been a mistake. I just wanted to help buy some stuff for my family. We're poor, you see . . .'

The kindly faced man didn't look so kind any more. He turned out to be the store manager. 'A likely story. I've met your type before. I can't have thieves pilfering my best stock. There are people out there fighting for King and Country while you are lining your pockets, young lady!'

His mouth set into a thin, hard line. 'I have had enough of it!' He slammed his hand on the desk.

Everything happened in a blur. The police came and Eva tried it on with them, telling them it was her first time, she had just let temptation get the better of her, but they weren't having any of it either.

She was arrested and taken to the police station, where she was charged with theft. As the cell door clanged shut and the lights went out for the night, Eva realized she was alone, more alone than she had ever felt in her whole life. The tears she cried now were real. There was no way out, no Alice to rescue her, no Maggie with her hatpin. She willed herself, in that moment, to be back in Howley Terrace, tucked up in bed with her annoying sister Kathleen, and Peggy on the other side of the room with her nose in a book. Those thoughts kept her going until morning, when the door was pulled open and a policeman told her, 'On your feet. You're up in front of the beak.'

As she made her way up the little wooden stairs into the dock, Eva almost cried again as she spotted her mother, white as a sheet, sitting beside Gladys in the courtroom. There was no doubt that Gladys was here as her friend but Eva knew that everything that she said in the courtroom would be relayed back to Alice and the Forty Thieves. She would be expected to keep silent about her involvement in the gang – or there could be reprisals. There would never be any question of Eva grassing them up; she was the most loyal of all of them, but she needed Alice to know that.

The magistrate looked about a hundred years old if he

was a day, which gave Eva a glimmer of hope. If she turned on the waterworks again, the old sod might not send her down.

As the charges of theft were read out, he peered at her over his half-moon spectacles.

'Well, how do you plead?'

She swallowed, hard. 'Guilty,' she said. Well, she could hardly do otherwise, she'd been caught red-handed. She shed a few crocodile tears, standing there, wringing her hands a bit.

'Pull yourself together,' said the magistrate, who clearly wasn't fooled by this display of contrition. 'You travelled to Kingston from your home in Lambeth, which to my mind brings a degree of premeditation to your actions. What do you have to say about that?'

'No, sir. I mean, I wanted to come and look at the shops, yes, because I had heard that Bentall's was such a wonderful place and girls like me, we never get to see such lovely things where I come from.'

The magistrate nodded. At least he was listening to her.

'And when I got here and saw all the pretty dresses in the shop, I was just overwhelmed by it all. Without realizing what I was doing, I found myself slipping a few things into my coat. It was the sheer temptation of it.'

'Poppycock!' the magistrate shouted across the court. 'You came to Kingston-upon-Thames to strip our finest store of its luxury goods, no doubt to sell on to a network of accomplices back on the grimy streets of Lambeth, I suspect.'

'No, sir, I did not,' said Eva, standing tall and looking

him straight in the eye. 'It was just me, acting on my own, out of sheer stupidity.'

Her mother was crying now, softly, into a handkerchief.

The magistrate sighed. 'Very well, I have heard your mitigation. I have taken into account that this is your first offence but in a time of war these crimes must be dealt with firmly, to send a message to others like you. I sentence you to six months in Aylesbury. I hope you learn your lesson.'

Eva's heart sank. At least in London there was a chance of a cushier time because Alice would have guards paid off and little extra privileges sorted for her girls.

The magistrate waved his hand in the air. 'Take her away.'

Mum stood up to protest, but Gladys yanked her back into her seat. 'I will be all right,' Eva mouthed to her as a policeman led her back down the stairs. She'd heard about prison so many times from the older women in the Forty Thieves, but now it was happening to her it all seemed so unreal. Their stories came back to haunt her in the bumpy ride in the back of the police wagon from Kingston. She was numb. There were no more tears as she realized that she just had to survive the next six months and get back to Lambeth as soon as she could.

Eva was handcuffed to the guard and led through Marylebone Station, with people staring at her, and onto a waiting train. She walked with her head held high. If she was going to survive this, there was no point looking like a victim. Eva thought about how Alice Diamond would carry herself, tall and proud, and tried to do the same. But the hiss of the steam engines and the noise of carriage doors slamming shut crowded in on her and the whole experience made her feel a bit sick. Travelling in their carriage were two other women prisoners – one much older, who reeked of booze and was a dead ringer for Lumps, and another, about her age, who had a livid bruise on her cheek and spent her time staring at the floor. Their guard was a woman who was manlier than many of the fellas around the Elephant. She had shoulders like a docker and wore her uniform buttoned up, right to the top of her thick neck. On her head was a hat like a giant pork pie, the same grey as her jacket. There was no chance of escape. Eva reckoned that if this guard landed on you, it would be like being hit by a falling wardrobe.

As the train made its way out of London, rain started to fall, pattering on the carriage windows. The countryside whizzed past in a blur, rain-soaked and muddy. Aylesbury station, after the grandeur and bustle of Marylebone, was an unremarkable red-brick single-storey building. They were met on the platform by more prison guards and, with passengers staring at them again, were led away in handcuffs to a waiting van.

The prison itself was a foreboding Victorian place. Eva and her two travelling companions were brought before the governor, who couldn't have been much older than Eva's mum. She perched, like a little bird, behind a polished table, with a neat pile of papers in front of her, and watched as all three of them lined up in front of her. There was a bookcase in the corner, stuffed with more books than Eva had ever seen in her life, and an aspidistra, with not a fleck of dust on its leaves.

The governor wore her glasses on a chain around her neck and Eva noticed that a little gold crucifix hung at her throat. Her hair was cut short, showing off high cheekbones, and there seemed to be not an ounce of flesh on her. In a fight, this woman would probably snap in two, but when she spoke, it was with such an air of authority that Eva felt compelled to listen.

Her voice was calm, rather like a schoolteacher's. 'My name is Miss Size but you will address me as ma'am. Is that clear?'

'Yes, ma'am.'

The old drunkard shuffled her feet and slouched but not for long because the guard poked her in the ribs.

'Stand up straight, girls!' said Miss Size, with a sharper tone, which made Eva jump to attention.

'You have all committed crimes, which we need not dwell on here. I want you to listen, to obey the rules but, above all, to learn something from your time in prison, so that you do not have to repeat the experience. Do you understand?'

'Yes, ma'am.'

Eva nodded along with her little speech, to show willing. She had already worked out her game plan – keep her head down, get on with her bird and get home quickly. She wasn't going to be pally with the screws but she wasn't going to cross them if she could help it. Alice had warned her that troublemakers got singled out from the start and had a rougher time. Eva wasn't going to be one of them. The ogre of a prison officer who had transported them in the train was then replaced by a series of grim-faced warders with jangling keys attached to their belts.

Eva was given a uniform – the drabbest, scratchiest cotton button-through dress with barely any semblance of a waist to it. She looked like a sack of spuds in it. God, if Gladys could see her now, she'd kill herself laughing. Once she'd put it on she was shown to the mess hall, where she joined the back of a long queue for meat stew and dumplings. It was then that Eva realized she was starving hungry, having eaten nothing since her prison breakfast of a slice of dry bread and some tea. A lot of the women chatted to each other, they seemed to know each other, but Eva just kept herself to herself.

Once she'd eaten, a warder tapped her shoulder and showed her to her single cell, which was small, maybe six feet across and ten feet long. Eva looked around. She wasn't expecting a holiday camp but the bare walls and tiny window were depressing. There was a little shelf with a Bible on it, a wooden seat and a little table and a proper bed at least, with some nightclothes folded on top of it. She'd heard about women in Holloway sleeping on boards that had to be put away during the day. She tested the mattress; it was thin and lumpy and the pillow was rock hard but she would get used to it. Eva peered under the bed. Yes, there was a chamber pot. Eva had heard all about slopping out in the morning from the Forty Thieves. The keys turned in the lock. A single lightbulb above her head was still on. She didn't have a watch so she had to guess the time. Perhaps it was six, seven o'clock. She took her shoes off and lay on top of the grey prison blanket, willing the hours away. There was so much to take in and, if the truth be told, she was trying not to panic at being unable to leave this place.

After a while the hatch to Eva's door was pulled back and a voice shouted, 'Cocoa!'

An enamel mug was thrust through the opening towards her. She accepted it, gratefully, sipping the hot chocolate which warmed her on the inside and made her feel sleepy. She could hear women chatting to each other through the cell walls, shouting the occasional comment. There was an almighty banging on one of the doors and she heard a warder yell, 'For God's sake, stop that racket or you'll be in solitary again, Mavis!'

Gradually, the prison fell silent. The lights went out. Eva took off her dress and put on the prison-issue nightie and slipped under the covers. 'Day one over,' she said to herself, as sleep enveloped her.

Eva quickly got used to the routine of slopping out and having breakfast in her cell before cleaning the prison all day. She liked mopping floors – it was quiet, she could keep her own counsel, and she could move around the prison and see what was going on. It wasn't that she was un-friendly but she didn't want to get into any of the little gangs of girls who gathered for a gossip at mealtimes. She said good morning to the others, nodded her hellos and then looked forward to keeping her own company in the cell at night. In the afternoons, the 'girls', as Miss Size called them, were expected to take lessons to improve themselves. Eva had taken up needlework and was allowed to do some sewing in her cell before supper but she much preferred being out and about. So after three months, when the chance came for the fittest among them to work in the fields for a local farmer, she jumped at the opportunity.

Half a dozen of them were kitted out in boiler suits and taken out of the prison for the day in the back of an old van accompanied by Brunhilde, the guard from the train. That wasn't her real name – it was Miss Evans – but given her figure, she was given that Jerry moniker behind her back. Even though her new work involved shovelling pig crap and digging the fields until her arms ached, Eva loved the freedom of it, the fresh air and the extra rations from the farmer's wife, who always made sure they had a little cake or biscuit at the end of the day.

Other women had visitors but Eva didn't, even though she missed her mum and her sisters. She had written to her mother, telling her she was doing fine and not to bother coming out because it was a long way to come for just a half-hour chit-chat. Instead, she had letters, lots of letters.

Peggy's latest one was her current favourite:

Dearest Eva,

I am sending you a picture of your little niece, Gloria. Isn't she pretty? I had her at Nanny Day's and she is the most beautiful little thing ever. She keeps me ever so busy looking after her, I don't know how our mum coped with five of us!

I haven't seen much of Kathleen lately. She seems busy with the housework and keeping Albert happy but she says she likes married life very much.

I hope you are keeping your spirits up and let's hope this war will be over soon. George and Harry have both completed their army training and are determined to see action fighting the Fascists but I do worry about them both so much, Eve. I just pray we will all get through this and life will get back to normal.

I miss you,
Peggy x

Eva carefully put the picture of Gloria on the little shelf on the wall, next to her copy of the Bible. The governor encouraged little homely touches; she preferred the idea of imprisoning her girls 'in a park' rather than 'parking them in a prison' because she believed that was how women would change their characters for the better. Eva knew there were old drunks and brasses inside who would never change, no matter what people like Miss Size said or did. Eva had nothing to do with them but had made a couple of mates among her fellow farmworkers – nothing serious, just some girls to pass a bit of banter with. No one actually discussed what they were in for and she preferred it that way.

Eva was five months into her sentence when Miss Size called her into her office. Eva's mouth went dry and she racked her brain for anything she might have done wrong, because since her first day she'd barely seen Miss Size, but in the end there was nothing to worry about. Miss Size just wanted to know if she would volunteer for the Land Army, seeing as she was so good at digging potatoes up and farm work. If she did, Eva would be allowed to leave prison a full month early. Plus, the pay was good – sixteen shillings a week and her board and lodging paid. If she mucked about, she'd be back behind bars for the rest of her sentence, Miss Size made that much clear. 'And I would take it very personally, Eva, if you let me down,' she said. 'As would the guards here.' The veiled threat was clear.

There was no question about it: Eva agreed straight away because she wanted to get out of that prison as soon as she could. There was just time to write a note to her mother telling her she was moving out of prison to help the war effort and would write to her again soon. She was kitted out, along with three other volunteers, in the most ridiculous uniform. Rather than the overalls she had worked the land in, she was given knee-length corduroy breeches, thick walking socks, stout brown lace-up shoes, a little shirt and a green tie, a bright-green woollen jumper with a red and green armband and a massive brown felt hat. Some of the girls started to giggle as they tried their clothes on, until Brunhilde told them off.

'I know there's a war on,' said Eva, struggling to keep a straight face. 'But I look bleeding silly!'

They were herded into the back of an old lorry without a guard. Escape did cross her mind but she remembered Miss Size's words of warning. Absconding could lead to a very tough time indeed back in Aylesbury.

The journey took hours and hours. It was only on a loo stop that Eva found out, to her horror, that they weren't staying anywhere in the Home Counties but were headed 'up north'.

Night had fallen by the time they arrived at a little village near Ribchester, in Lancashire. They were deposited on a farm. The farmer came out to greet them, carrying a gas lantern, and showed them their lodgings, which made Aylesbury Prison look like the Savoy Hotel. Home was a sparse little hut with bunk beds in it. There was no one else in it, so Eva and the others made up their beds and took a few spare blankets to make themselves comfortable because there was no heating, and even though it was spring it was bloody freezing. It was a bit like a prison in its sparseness but Eva felt relieved as she settled down under the covers for the night that there was no locked door and no prison guard waiting outside in the corridor.

Just as she was nodding off, she was rudely awakened by a sharp poke in the ribs and someone shining a torch in her face. She squinted into the light and lashed out with her hands. 'Oi! I'll knock your bleedin' block off!'

'Oh, we've got a right live wire here, lasses,' said the bearer of the torch. 'You've nicked me blankets, Cockney! I'll be havin' 'em back, if you don't mind.'

Eva sat bolt upright and came face-to-face with a sturdy, squat young woman with curly hair and a ruddy, round face. She was backed up by a gang of five others, who were little more than shapes, looming out of the darkness.

Eva's three other prison comrades were cowering in their bunks at the other end of the dorm. Seeing she was going to have to handle this herself, Eva leaped out of bed and put her fists up, ready to fight, her heart pounding.

'All right, all right,' said the sturdy young woman, taking a step back. 'This isn't a boxing match. Our only enemy is Hitler. We're Land Army, just like you. I'm afraid you've missed out on the pub with us lasses tonight. We can patch things up in the morning, but I will need a blanket or I will freeze to death in this hut.'

She offered Eva her hand. 'I'm Dot. And you'd better get back to bed or you'll catch your death by the looks of it!'

Eva realized she was shaking from the cold – or maybe it was fright – or possibly both. The flannelette nightie she'd been issued with by the prison was three sizes too small and barely covered her knees and goosebumps were prickling up her legs.

'I'm Eva,' she said, shaking Dot by the hand. 'And where I come from, it ain't polite to go sneaking up on folks in the dark but, like you say, our only enemy is that Hitler fella, so I will let it go this time.' She was determined not to show too much weakness, just like she'd learned from watching her little brother Frankie in fights.

There was an uneasy truce that bedtime but by the morning, once the farmer's wife called them all over for breakfast, they had made friends.

Eva quickly got into the routine of mucking out the farmer's horse in the morning, helping to feed the pigs and even milking the cows. She had to learn how to groom and tack up the horse too, to fix him to the cart, just like the ones back home in London when she was a little girl. She liked that but the horse was a sly old devil who would aim a kick or bite when he could, just for the hell of it. Animals were fine; in the end, it was the digging which got to her, an entire field of it, endlessly, day after day. The other girls started talking excitedly about the harvest in the summer and the big dance in the village but Eva began to long for noise and traffic and London.

She waited until she had fulfilled her month at the farm and then one morning, rather than going out to work with the others, she pretended to feel ill and went back to bed after breakfast. They were a nice enough bunch and she knew that they'd try to persuade her to stay. Dot was really committed to the farm work; she saw it as her duty to dig for victory to beat the Nazis. Eva liked her best of all and she didn't want Dot to think she was unpatriotic, so leaving without making any fuss was the best way. Eva packed up her belongings in a little rucksack and set off down the country lanes, towards civilization.

On the first main road Eva came to, she hitched a lift. The lorry was headed towards Blackpool and so that was exactly where she said she wanted to go. As the lorry trundled along, the hills became more distant and she started to think about what Blackpool would be like. Dot had been on holidays there with her family, before the war, and still raved about the promenades and the piers and the Blackpool Tower. She had made it sound like the promised land and had even told her about the best guest house to stay in. Well, after those muddy fields, it would be a relief to get back to proper roads and pavements.

Eva had money to last her a few days but she wanted to earn enough to get her train fare back to London and to have some left over to treat her mother to something nice. She found the little guest house Dot had talked about but the landlady sucked in her cheeks when Eva asked if there was a room to spare. 'I'm supposed to keep a few free rooms in case the military need them, love,' she said, shaking her head. Eva showed her some money and she agreed to let her stay, on the understanding that if an airman was billeted on her at short notice, Eva would have to sleep on the floor in the lounge. As a mark of goodwill, the landlady cooked Eva some spam fritters because she hadn't eaten all day. She wolfed them down but then regretted having done so, because the food seemed to sit like a lead weight in her stomach.

Eva headed along the promenade to see if she could pick up a little job and found herself wandering by the North Pier. A bloke was pinning up a sign: 'NEW! Under the Sea. Exotic Entertainments to Delight and Entertain.'

Eva took a deep breath and approached him. 'Got any jobs going? I'm exotic, see.' She loosened her long dark hair, which hung almost to her waist. 'In fact,' she said. 'I'm half-gypsy and I can tell your fortune.' With her Canadian Indian heritage from on her father's side, she could easily pass herself off as a Romany, she thought.

'That sounds great, love,' he said. 'But I need someone to lie in this fish tank and lure the punters in.' He gesticulated to a large glass aquarium beside the sign.

'And what am I supposed to wear?' asked Eva.

She followed him along the pier and into a little shed. He pulled a costume out of a box and threw it at her. It had a very small top – a bit like a bra – and a very large fishtail, covered in sequins. He looked at her with his eyebrows raised in anticipation.

'All right,' said Eva. 'But you are going to need to pay me up front, because, even though there's no water in it,

I'm likely to freeze to death.' She could feel the spam fritters repeating on her something terrible as he left the shed
while she got herself changed. The mermaid tail had little
holes where you could poke your feet through to walk and
Eva waddled back along to the glass fish tank, attracting a
few wolf whistles from passing soldiers. Her new boss put
up a little step to help her into the tank and she clambered
in and settled herself down as he put a wooden lid with
holes in on the top so she didn't steam up the glass. She
propped herself up on one elbow and smiled and waved at
people as they strolled past. It was all going well until her
insides started churning. She had gone a bit of a funny
colour – several people had remarked on that as they
gawked at her.

Eva went hot, then cold, and her face started to sweat.
Before she knew what was happening, she had thrown up
all over herself and right up the glass of the tank.

'Oh, for God's sake,' she cried, wriggling herself out of
the tank. 'I've had enough of this for one day.'

Her boss was quite cross but he agreed to give her
another chance, this time reading palms in a tent at the end
of the pier. She got to wear a scarf over her head and
around her shoulders, which she was grateful for because
it was bloody freezing in Blackpool. Mostly it was young
girls coming to see her. She told them that they would find
love, or if they had a wedding ring on, that their loved one
had gone on a long journey overseas but would be coming
home soon.

One woman was less than impressed. 'Well, I dunno

about overseas but he is square bashing with the Army in Kent, so I suppose that counts as a long journey.'

Eva did her best to bring them some comfort, but she was glad to have saved up enough for her train fare back to London after a fortnight. Would things have changed much? She wondered whether Gladys and the other hoisters would treat her differently, now she had been inside. She tried not to let that thought worry her. Most of all, she couldn't wait to see her sisters, just to get back to normal and to hold Peggy's little Gloria. If Eva had ever doubted it, she knew now, more than ever, that she was a London girl, a Lambeth girl, and she didn't ever want to stray too far from home.

The bustle of London hit her as she stepped off the train. She took her time, strolling down the street, enjoying her liberty. In the sky above her were barrage balloons, loads of them, but there was still no sign of the enemy. She made her way to Walworth Road, spotting a few familiar faces and then she knocked on the front door and said the words she had been longing to say, all those nights in prison and in the Land Army: 'Mum, it's me, Eva. I'm home!'

23

Peggy, May 1940

With George away with the Army and Grandad's leg playing up, Peggy moved back to Cornwall Road to be with Nanny Day. Nanny doted on baby Gloria and Peggy didn't mind wheeling Grandad up to the hospital to see the doctors. His old injury from the Boer War had got infected and the nurses were just lovely, doing all they could to make him more comfortable, but as the days went by he didn't show any sign of improvement and the pain made him irritable.

Peggy lived for the letters she got from George, who was away with his regiment in France. They'd been posted near the Maginot Line to keep the Germans out, and although the letters had to pass through the official censor, she got the impression that he was kicking his heels a bit, waiting for action.

Albert had made some unkind jokes about all the soldiers he knew having a whale of a time out there with the pretty French girls in the villages. Peggy ignored him as best as she could, but in her heart of hearts, she worried about it. She couldn't wait for Albert to get his call-up papers, come to think of it. She didn't talk to Eva or her mum about it but she feared that behind closed doors, things between him and Kathleen were not as they should be. Her sister was looking thin, too thin, and she seemed to jump like a frightened little rabbit every time Albert raised his voice, which was quite often.

Jim, was in France, too, with the Royal Fusiliers, and Mum was beside herself with worry about him, although he wrote as often as he could. Only her little brother Frankie was safe for certain, but that was because he was behind bars, for thieving this time. Mum didn't seem to mind as long as it kept him out of the war. She could face having one son at risk but two would kill her, she said.

The first cherry blossom was appearing on the trees in the park, bringing with it the promise of a lovely hot summer, which would be Gloria's first. If only George were here to share it with her. She read the newspaper avidly for any crumbs of comfort. Most of the stories last week had been all good news about Belgium, with the British troops marching into towns and being welcomed like heroes, but only a couple of days ago she had read a report about the Germans breaking through into France in one area. The politicians said this had happened before in the Great War but they were calling for a national day of prayer for the troops at the end of the month.

Peggy turned on the wireless that evening to hear the first address by their new prime minister, Winston Churchill. Nanny Day bustled about in the background, making comments under her breath about all politicians being the same. Grandad agreed: 'When you have lived as long as I have, Peg, you come to see that the boys are just cannon fodder.'

Nanny shot him a filthy glance. 'Except George and Jim,' he added hastily. 'They will be just fine, you'll see.'

Churchill's words were stirring but they also warned of a fight for Britain which would bring the war to their doorstep, sending a shiver up Peggy's spine. 'There will come the battle for our islands, for all that Britain is and all that Britain means.'

Within a week, Peggy's worst fears were confirmed, as news of fighting in the Channel ports broke. British forces were trapped in and around Dunkirk as they retreated from an advancing German Army. The only solace was the devastating losses inflicted on the German air force by British fighter pilots. She barely slept, sitting instead in Nanny Day's rocking chair, covered by a blanket, waiting for the latest reports from the BBC announcers. Her dreams were fitful, of George and his brother Harry, fighting in the woods in France, pursued by Germans in their jackboots and grey uniforms. She wanted to switch off her imagination but she couldn't. Every time she held Gloria, she saw George's clear blue eyes looking back at her.

Finally, on 31 May, the BBC announcer revealed that France had fallen to German hands and a massive evacuation of troops at Dunkirk had been underway for several days. The billboards screamed the good news: 'SAVED!' and 'RESCUED FROM THE JAWS OF DEATH' as they reported that thousands of troops had been brought back to British shores, with the help of every seaworthy vessel that Britain could muster. All that day, Peggy sat in the living room staring into space.

'Come to bed now, Peg. You must rest,' said Nanny Day, putting her hand on Peggy's shoulder. 'He will come home safe, you'll see.'

'I won't rest until I know it for sure,' said Peggy. 'And I need to go and visit George's mother to see if she's heard anything.' George's mum, Lizzie, was on her own these days, after his dad passed away, and she lived for her sons, Peggy knew that.

The next morning, Peggy made her way down to East Street and when she knocked on the door, there was no reply, so she let herself in. She found Lizzie sitting in the living room, weeping, with a crumpled letter in her hand. They looked up at each other.

Peggy rushed in and grabbed it. It was from the War Office: 'I regret to inform you that your son, Pte Harold Harwood, of the Black Watch, 1st Battalion, is missing in action following active service in Europe. Any communication you receive from your son should be passed to the office at the above address without delay.'

'Oh, God, no,' she said. 'Poor, poor Harry.' They clung to each other, crying. 'We have to look on the bright side. It only says missing and all the reports I have heard say that there is so much chaos, with people getting separated from their regiment and getting onto boats, he will be bound to turn up.' They both knew that this was not likely.

'What about George?' said Lizzie, rubbing her eyes, which were red with crying.

Peggy swallowed hard. 'I'm sure he's fine and he will be

round here having a cup of tea before you know it.' She sat with her mother-in-law all day, leaving only when the neighbours promised to keep an eye on her.

Dusk was falling as she made her way back to Cornwall Road. She was just settling the baby for the night when there was a knock on the door. Nanny Day answered it and came down the hallway, her hands shaking, holding a telegram.

Peggy snatched it from her and ripped open the envelope: 'Safely back in Blighty. Home soon on leave. Love. George.'

If she had ever doubted the existence of God, she didn't in that moment, because her prayers had been answered.

It was a few weeks before he could make it home, but the moment she heard George knock three times on the door one Saturday afternoon, she knew it was him.

He stood on the doorstep, his uniform cap in his hand, looking thinner than she remembered, but twice as handsome.

There were no words as they embraced. People in the houses over the road came out into the street and started to cheer and clap. There were a few wolf whistles from the neighbours, all of whom knew that George had had a close scrape getting back from Dunkirk. Many of them had family and friends who had not been so lucky.

Nanny Day afforded them a few moments' privacy before she came bustling up the hallway with baby Gloria in her arms. 'Daddy's here to see you!'

Gloria held her hands out to him and smiled and Peggy felt that everything in her world was complete once more.

George wouldn't talk about what had happened at Dunkirk other than to say that there was a lot of hand-to-hand fighting in the woods and he had seen things he never wanted to tell her. During his escape, he had spent hours in the freezing water of the Channel before he was picked up and hauled over the side of one of the small ships. When he had finally got back to barracks, he had slept for twenty-four hours straight and taken about half a dozen hot baths before he wanted to put clean clothes on again. He considered himself lucky to have got out alive.

'I just thank God that I'm here with you all now,' he said.

As the blackout enveloped them all that night and she lay next to George, listening to him breathing, she feared that her happiness could be taken away from her again, at any moment.

The council had issued homes with either an Anderson shelter for the back garden, or a Morrison shelter, which was like a giant reinforced metal cage. Nanny Day viewed the Morrison shelter with suspicion. She put her best tablecloth on it, to make it less ugly, but it squatted in the living room, like some unwanted guest.

Grandad muttered, 'There is no way on God's green earth I am hiding in that thing at my stage in life. If a bomb or a bullet has my name on it, that's that.' Peggy didn't share that view. She had every intention of surviving this war and had already worked out a plan to grab the baby and get her in the shelter. Mum and Eva's landlord had dug out the garden to put in the Anderson shelter for them down in Walworth Road. It was damp and when it rained the ground water rose to ankle level. Eva wasn't looking forward to spending the night in there, that was for sure.

George was billeted back with his regiment in Dorset and came up to visit when he could. When Peggy told him of her fears about him going off with Land Army girls at the village dances, he just laughed and kissed her. 'Why would I bother about them, when I've got you waiting for me here at home?' That made her feel better. He was such a fine-looking man and every time he had to go back to his regiment it broke her heart, but with his brother missing and presumed to be a German prisoner of war, he was more determined than ever to do his bit.

Some of the local newspapers had got pictures of lads who had been captured at Dunkirk in work camps back in Germany and Peggy had scoured those to see if any looked like Harry but to no avail. Just to know that Harry was alive, even if he was a prisoner, would be some comfort to his poor mother, who was taking his absence horribly. Peggy didn't tell George what she was doing because she wanted his time on leave to be as happy as it could be, playing with the baby.

Sometimes Peggy would catch him sitting alone at the kitchen table, fighting back tears, and she knew in those moments he was thinking of Harry and what had become of him. He couldn't talk about it but he would clasp her hand in his and they would sit in silence until he felt able to get on with things again. He was a proud man and she had never seen him cry or break down about it; that wasn't his way.

The summer of 1940 was every bit as hot as Peggy had thought it would be. Right in the middle of July, poor Grandad took a turn for the worse and was taken into hospital. He became more and more confused and, in the end, he fell asleep, with Nanny Day by his side, and never woke up. All the family came to his funeral and it was sad, as funerals are, but Peggy couldn't help feeling that it was sadder still for those who had already lost their sons and brothers fighting the enemy, at such a young age. Grandad would have agreed; he had had a good innings.

As September came around, it seemed the summer would never end; the hot days continued, one after the other, and the kids played out in the street until bedtime. Peggy had some good news, at least, from her old friend Susan, who had been released from the mental hospital and was now living back with her aunt in the East End. She wrote that she'd got herself a little job in the sugar factory and sounded positive for the first time in months. Peggy made plans to go over there and visit her in a few weeks, to see how she was getting on.

Some boys were out playing kick the can in Cornwall Road as Peggy wheeled the baby back from a little stroll up to the post box. A kid was messing about with a toy aeroplane on his doorstep, recreating the dogfights he'd seen high in the sky while he was hop-picking in Kent with his family, mimicking the drone of their engines. He was just defeating the enemy when the air-raid sirens sounded and he froze.

The war had been going on for a year and no bombs

had fallen on the capital so far but the threat was now very real. 'Get in your shelter, now!' Peggy shouted.

Children ran pell-mell down the street and Peggy followed them, pushing the pram like a woman possessed. Grabbing the baby, she flung open the front door and found Nanny Day, open-mouthed, standing at the window. Nanny pointed skywards. There was the ack-ack of anti-aircraft guns but they seemed to do little to stop the Luftwaffe, which was gathered en masse in the skies over London.

'Quick, take the baby!' said Peggy, shoving the now-wailing infant into her grandmother's arms as she yanked the pram over the threshold. They ran into the living room, crawled into the little Morrison shelter with the tablecloth still on it and waited. The sound of bombs exploding in the distance reverberated through the late afternoon air and, even more frighteningly, they heard the tap-tap of shrapnel from anti-aircraft shells ricocheting off the roof tiles. Peggy lay shielding the baby, in case a shell, or worse, a bomb, landed on the house. Her heart pounded in her chest. Minutes became hours. How had it come to this? Being attacked in their own homes? Nanny Day said Hail Marys and every prayer she could think of.

Eventually, the all-clear sounded and Peggy ran out into the street, where the neighbours were already congregating. Air-raid wardens were doing the rounds, checking everyone was all right.

She followed a little gaggle of people making their way to end of the road. The sky on the other side of the river glowed orange from the fires burning in warehouses and factories. It would have been breath-taking if it wasn't so horrific.

An auxiliary fireman hurried past. They'd always been a bit of a joke until now. Some kids even liked to taunt them, yelling 'Army dodgers!' but Peggy was relieved to have them close now, more than ever.

'Where's been hit?' she asked.

'Jerry's gone and bombed the docks and the gas works but Bermondsey has taken a pounding and the East End is well alight. Think yourself lucky to be in Lambeth tonight.'

'What about Walworth?' she shouted. But he had already scurried off.

News started to filter through of people trapped in their homes as fires raged through the dockers' homes in Bermondsey, and whole streets had come down in the East End. Peggy thought of all the trade unionists she and George knew, and prayed, against hope, that they were safe. She worried about Eva and her mum and Kathleen. She needed to know they were safe but couldn't go out and check because the sirens sounded again and everyone charged back into their houses, with the wardens checking for any chinks of light through the blackout curtains. With baby Gloria safely asleep in her arms as the next wave of bombers flew overhead, Peggy resolved to get up at first light to go down the Walworth Road to find her mum and Eva and then on to Vauxhall to see Kathleen. Nothing mattered more to her now. They were her family.

As dawn broke, she took Uncle Dennis's old bike, a proper boneshaker, and set off. There was an eerie silence as she pedalled along towards the Elephant. She realized then that the trains weren't running and the trams weren't either. As she passed Manor Place, the acrid stench of smoke caught in her nose. The fire service were still there, battling to control the blazes in one of the tenement blocks, which looked to have taken a direct hit because the walls had crumbled like plaster of Paris to reveal the inside of people's homes, their lives reduced to a pile of rubble. It was a terrible sight. Rescuers dug with their bare hands, pulling at bits of masonry to see if there were any survivors. Peggy felt sick rising in the back of her throat and clasped a handkerchief to her mouth, willing herself not to vomit. She had to be stronger than this. She thought of George, Harry and Jim and everything they had witnessed and were going through and pulled herself together.

She got back on the bike and pedalled on, as quickly as she could, down Walworth Road, She was relieved to see that her mother's flat was still standing – unlike some of the houses in the road around the corner, which had collapsed like a pack of cards.

Eva answered the front door, with her hair in curlers. She was in a very bad mood indeed, having spent most of the night in the Anderson shelter. Kathleen was already there – she had dashed over as soon as she woke up, to check on everyone and try to make sense of it all.

'Well, thank God that is over,' said Eva, putting the kettle on. 'I will swing for that Adolf for ruining my hair, having to spend the night in that bloody shelter, and that is before I get on to sharing bunk beds with the woman from downstairs, who snores like a bleeding train rattling along.'

Kathleen managed to raise a smile. Peggy didn't say anything but she had a horrible feeling that as far as the bombing was concerned, it was just the beginning.

24

Kathleen, November, 1940

The queues for the Little Ritz cinema in Leicester Square were round the block, despite the blackout and the threat of air raids. Kathleen and Nancy waited patiently for their tickets to see *Gone with the Wind*, carrying their gas masks over their shoulders in little cardboard boxes on string. Nancy had stuffed a couple of extra hankies in hers because she'd heard the film was a real weepy and Kathleen had managed to find a few boiled sweets to keep them going throughout the show. She had hoped that Albert would come with her but he had refused to sit through hours of 'romantic claptrap' and had gone for a few pints with his mates instead.

The girls who worked with Nancy at the jam factory were sick with jealousy that she was going to see it and had made her promise to tell them all about the film in great detail, which would be their lunch breaks sorted for the next week or so. Nancy was doing well at the factory but Kathleen didn't mind that she didn't work there any more – she couldn't say she missed all that fruit peeling and labelling.

Albert had stopped her going out to work for the football

pools, saying she was better off at home or helping his mum with the fruit and veg stall. Kathleen hated having to do that because she felt sure her mother-in-law was keeping a close eye on her. She tutted every time Kathleen chatted to customers and even told her off for giving people the wrong change, when she never did. At least seeing the film would give her some escape from reality for an afternoon.

They settled in the dark of the cinema and Kathleen lost herself in the world of Scarlett O'Hara and Rhett Butler. When he swept her up in his arms and carried her upstairs to ravish her, despite her protests, she thought of Albert, forcing her some nights when she was too tired. She couldn't talk to anyone about it, what would she say? She was a married woman now and it was expected that she would give him what he wanted, wasn't it? Besides, he wanted to start a family and was cross with her that she hadn't fallen pregnant. Nancy wasn't married yet, although she had an engagement ring on her finger, but Kathleen didn't want to tell her what married life was really like, in case it put her off.

Yes, Albert was passionate and powerful, just like Rhett, and she was small and helpless, like Scarlett. He gave her a slap now and then, to keep her in line. It wasn't anything like what her father had done to her mother, she was sure of that, but he didn't seem to think that being physical with her was wrong and his mother just pretended not to notice. Once he had slapped her at the kitchen table for some silly comment she had made and her mother-in-law just smiled quietly to herself as she cleared the plates away.

It was almost as if she had enjoyed seeing Kathleen humiliated like that.

The cloak of darkness in the cinema seemed to allow her thoughts free rein, away from the claustrophobic little terraced house, with its china ducks flying up the wall and going nowhere fast. When Rhett walked out on Scarlett, with a 'Frankly, my dear, I don't give a damn!' Kathleen found herself sobbing uncontrollably and Nancy had to give her a hankie. She loved Albert, of course she did, but why did being in love with him make her so unhappy?

On the way back home, the girls chatted about some of the scariest nights they had endured so far in the Blitz, swapping horror stories about people who didn't make it to the air-raid shelter and were found by the ARP, or the Air Raid Precautions wardens, sitting up in bed, dead as a doornail. Of course, no one knew these people's names; they were always a friend of Mrs Davies at number 16 or someone who knew someone down in Bermondsey.

There had been some really dreadful losses up in town: a bomb flattened the John Lewis store in Oxford Street; thankfully Eva hadn't been in there at the time. Every morning after an air raid, there were houses reduced to rubble, buildings burned out and the landscape of the local area was changed forever. The old Canterbury Music Hall down in Westminster Bridge Road had taken a direct hit too, which she felt really sad about, because Nanny had taken her there when she was very little, to see the singing and dancing acts, which she loved so much. One of the worst disasters was when a huge landmine drifted onto Queen's Buildings, Scovell Road, home of Alice Diamond and many of her girls. More than forty people died that night and countless more were injured. Alice was lucky to have escaped with her life. Some said she had the luck of the devil himself.

Kathleen had a growing sense that she should be doing something for the war effort, to make a difference. She discussed it with Albert, who told her not to be daft, that the country needed men like him, not women like her. He was expecting his call-up papers any day now. Albert wasn't afraid of going off to war, in fact he relished the chance to put on a uniform, but his mother had begged him not to join up before he was called on, because she couldn't bear to be parted from him.

When Albert's papers came a week later, his mother was inconsolable. Kathleen cried on the doorstep as she kissed him goodbye. But somewhere deep inside, there was a little flicker of something else, a sort of excitement at the prospect of having a bit more time to do what she wanted, without him breathing down her neck all the time. She'd have to get past her mother-in-law, though, who seemed to delight in treating her like a skivvy.

Mum dropped a bombshell of her own late one afternoon, after she had gathered all the girls together at her flat.

'Me and Patsy are getting married tomorrow!'

There was stunned silence, before Kathleen said, 'But Mum, you aren't even divorced, are you?'

'There is a war on,' said her mother, turning her back and busying herself at the kitchen sink. 'If I don't marry Patsy he could well get called up and I can't bear to lose him, not with Jim overseas and Frankie God-knows-where. If we get wed, he can join the Auxiliary Fire Service and serve his country right here in Walworth.'

The Auxiliary Fire Service was doing vital work at home in the Blitz, but married men were given priority as volunteers.

'But won't you get into trouble?' said Peggy, sitting up straight in her chair. The prospect of her mother turning into a law-breaker was too much to bear.

'Only if someone grasses me up, and who is going to do that?' said her mother, turning round and casting her beady eye over them all. 'We'll do it tomorrow; no time to lose.'

'Well, congratulations are in order, then,' said Eva, pulling on her coat. You could have sliced through the atmosphere with a knife at that point and Eva had such a way of defusing the situation. 'I think we need to celebrate, don't you?'

Peggy relaxed over a glass of port, which the landlord brought out from under the counter, especially for them. Kathleen was genuinely delighted for Mum and Patsy, because they made such a good couple. He was loyal and kind. Her one worry was what her father would do if he found out and so the girls made a pact, there and then, to keep it a secret.

The next morning, they accompanied their mother to the register office, where Patsy was waiting for her, looking pleased as punch. She signed the register in her maiden name and, before she knew it, she was Mrs Patsy Duhig and off to the pub for another knees-up.

Patsy soon went on to sport a fireman's uniform and tackled blazes in the Blitz with the best of them. He told Kathleen that there was a need for smart girls like her, who could work in the control centres and help coordinate the teams going from fire to fire. 'I reckon I can get you in there, if you fancy.'

Kathleen twiddled her hair and thought about it. Albert was due back from training for the weekend and she didn't want to have to confront him about it. 'I'll come along on Monday morning,' she told him.

Once Albert had gone back to barracks, she made her way to the headquarters of the Fire Service by Lambeth Bridge and joined a queue of young women her age. Many had skills as telephone operators already and Kathleen felt sure she would be refused as she had only ever bottled jam and collected forms for the football pools but she was greeted warmly and kitted out with a smart uniform before she knew it. It came with a little peaked cap, a fitted jacket with military detailing and brass buttons and a knee-length skirt. She wore it home, rather proudly.

'What in the name of God have you got on?' said her mother-in-law, her jaw agape.

'It's a uniform for the Auxiliary Fire Service,' she said, giving her a little twirl; she just couldn't resist it.

'What on earth will Albert say?'

'He can say what he likes because he's down in Dorset and the country needs girls like me; that's what the man at the Fire Service said. In fact, if I don't join up now, the likelihood is I will end up in the countryside digging up spuds with the Land Army because they are bound to make it compulsory soon for all women to do war work. And Albert wants me close to home, doesn't he?'

'All women will have to do war work?' Her mother-in-law was horror-struck at the prospect.

'Well, I think you'll be safe,' said Kathleen, making her way up the stairs, smiling to herself. 'Because you are the wrong side of forty, aren't you?'

Dad beamed at her with pride when she showed him new uniform and her silver badge with 'AFS' in red lettering. Albert was less pleased when he found out by letter that she had volunteered and left his mother to it.

'It isn't on, Kathy, really you are taking a liberty,' he wrote. 'With me away fighting for King and Country you should be helping to look after me dear old mum.'

She wrote back:

Dear Albert,

Please don't be angry but seeing what is happening here with the bombs dropping all over, I knew I had to do something.

I will make it up to you when you come home on leave. And I promise I will still look after your mum.

Love,

Your Kathy

By the time Albert returned for Christmas, she had already completed her training at the Fire HQ and had been posted to the school in Fount Street, where she joined two other girls running three volunteer watches – red, white and blue. She worked a forty-eight-hour shift on with twenty-four hours off to recover. She had to parade in the mornings and man the telephones and run a book recording all the fires, casualties and responses. Albert didn't want to hear about any of it and he made that perfectly plain, egged on by his mother, who tutted every time she mentioned her work.

Christmas that year passed off in a haze of sherry and Albert's mother's mock 'goose' of lentils and carrots, which was so inedible that Albert suggested sending it to Berlin to force the Germans to surrender. He earned a clip around the ear from his mother for that comment.

Kathleen waited until mid-afternoon before slipping away to Nanny Day's to get some proper food. The butcher had somehow managed to put aside a small chicken out of respect for the memory of his old Army mate Uncle Dennis. Nanny had saved Kathleen a leg and a wing, which she devoured with gusto, washing the lot down with a large glass of Guinness, which Nanny treated as a health drink because of the iron in it.

The Blitz had claimed so many lives and made so many homeless that it should have taken the shine off Christmas but it seemed to have the opposite effect. The pubs were full to overflowing; everyone drank too much. There seemed to be a 'live for today' attitude and everyone wanted to stick two fingers up to the Nazis who had hoped to bring London to its knees. Just seeing familiar faces on the street was a comfort because it meant that they had survived another night of bombing and Kathleen felt the closeness of Lambeth more than ever.

It wasn't peaceful for long, though, and the night of the

27th brought a new terror – incendiary bombs, which lit the way for the Luftwaffe to find their targets. The nightmare sound of them swishing down brought people running from their homes to extinguish the flames if the volunteer fire crews weren't immediately on hand with their stirrup-pumps.

Albert had barely been gone a day when Kathleen packed up her things in a little suitcase. She couldn't explain what made her do it. Perhaps it was the knowledge that every day they were living could be their last. She bloody well did not want to die next to Albert's miserable mother-in-law, that much was certain.

As Kathleen was lifting the latch on the front door, she appeared at the foot of the stairs in her flowery housecoat, her arms folded across her chest. 'And where do you think you're going?'

'Home to my dad's,' said Kathleen, turning on her heel. 'I'm married to Albert, not you.'

Her mother-in-law was such a funny sight in that moment, her mouth opening and closing like some goldfish scooped out of its bowl by the kids at the fair. That thought made Kathleen laugh more than she had in ages, as she made her way back to Howley Terrace.

The house was poky and gloomier than ever in the blackout, and her father barely had enough money for coal. But she didn't care. It was home.

The first week of January started quietly enough but Kathleen and the other Auxiliary Fire Service girls had a feeling it couldn't last.

On the night of 8 January, reports came through of a major incident at the Hartley's jam factory off Tower Bridge Road. Kathleen's blood ran cold as the phone started ringing off the hook, calling for back-up because a bomb had fallen between the factory's shelter and one of the blocks, blasting a massive hole in both.

It was B Block, where the bottling took place, and Kathleen knew it well. She also knew that the supervisors allowed people to bring their families into the factory overnight, sleeping on bags of sugar, and Nancy was one of them. People preferred the factory floor and the factory's shelter to the Anderson or the little Morrison shelters at home. Many felt they would be safer there.

It was hours before Patsy and his watch reappeared; the horror of what they had seen was etched on their faces. Four people had been killed outright but nearly two dozen more were seriously injured, many by flying glass and the shards from broken jam jars; the firemen had had to tunnel through wreckage to get to them. There were stories of the rescuers building a makeshift shaft from timber to tunnel their way through the debris as bombs rained down and of victims suffering terrible burns from marmalade, which turned to a lethal boiling liquid in the heat of the blast.

'What about Nancy?' she said. 'Did you see her?'

'I'm sorry, love, I can't say,' said Patsy. 'The burns were terrible, people were covered in dust and jam and you just couldn't tell one from the other. They were all moaning and screaming. The survivors were carted off to hospital . . .'

Kathleen couldn't leave the Fire HQ until the morning, but as soon as she was able to, she headed straight down to the hospital, where a nurse showed her to a ward filled with people wrapped in bandages. 'These are the ones who are likely to survive but they are very poorly, so, unless you are certain that you know them, please don't disturb them too much,' she said, giving Kathleen a little pat on the arm. 'We are giving morphia for the pain, it's all we can do at the moment.'

Kathleen worked her way down the rows of beds, looking for any sign of Nancy or her mother. She saw her hair first. From one side of her head, Kathleen recognized Nancy's beautiful curls. The other side of her friend's face was completely obscured by bandages. Her arms were wrapped up too and her lips were swollen and her cheeks covered in scratches. She was lying with her eyes open, awake, but not moving. She saw Kathleen approaching and tried to smile but then cried out in pain. A solitary tear rolled down her cheek.

'Nancy, oh, Nancy, you are alive, thank God,' said Kathleen, falling to her knees at her bedside.

'Kathy . . .' Her voice was just a whisper. 'I can't move. The pain . . .'

'It's all right, don't speak, I will get the nurse to give you something more for it.'

'My mum, she's down the end, her leg got broken.' Nancy pointed a finger to the far end of the ward.

'I will go there next and check on her,' said Kathleen. 'I'll come every day to see you and you will get better, you'll see.'

The nurse arrived, brandishing a syringe. 'Just a sharp scratch.'

Nancy's eyes closed, as she fell into a deep sleep.

Kathleen made a point of going to visit Nancy and her mum every day, just as she had promised to. She got a couple of hours off in the afternoons when she was on shift and she sat with Nancy for the full hour of visiting time. Sometimes Nancy didn't know she was there – she was knocked out cold with the morphia – but Kathleen chatted to her anyway.

As the weeks passed, Nancy's burns started to heal but the scars they left on her face were terrible and the nurses had removed the mirror in the bathroom, so that she couldn't see herself. The skin on one side of her face looked as if it had melted, with livid, raised patches and lumps where the skin had thickened.

Somehow, though, Nancy did catch sight of her reflection because one day, when she was sitting up in bed and Kathleen had brought her a copy of the *People's Friend* to flick through, Nancy started sobbing. 'Who will want me now! I look hideous!'

'You don't,' said Kathleen. 'You look beautiful; you are still you.' How could she reassure her friend, who was once so pretty? 'These things take time to heal. And Roy loves you just the same.'

Nancy's fiancé Roy had been a total rock, bringing flowers, coming up to visit every time he was home on leave. He had made it clear: he had every intention of sticking to his word and marrying her.

'I just thank God you are still alive,' he told her. 'And I don't want to put off the wedding a day any longer. As soon as you are out of here, let's get married!'

The bombings were relentless throughout that spring. Despite the hard work and the danger, Kathleen felt more alive than she had done in ages. Once Nancy was well enough, they would meet up in the afternoons at a little tea dance down at the hall above Burton's at the Elephant. The dance floor was filled with people in uniform, making the most of their leave or their break, never knowing what peril the evening might bring.

The music sustained Kathleen, she barely had time to sit down because she was always being asked to dance. People weren't as quick to ask Nancy, but she learned to make a talking point of her scars, if anyone should stare. 'I got this fighting, Hitler, mate. Now, are you going to ask me to dance or not?'

Kathleen never took anything any further. She was wearing Albert's ring, for a start, but even that did little to dampen the ardour of some of the men, who were proper waist-huggers when it came to the waltz. One bloke even suggested meeting up in town later that night and going to the Café de Paris, which was more popular than ever because it was twenty feet below ground and the manager boasted it was the safest club in London.

'No, I can't. I'm married, see?' she said, tapping her wedding ring. 'And I have got to get back. I'm on shift tonight, sorry.' A lot of married girls still went out dancing when their fellas were away. She wouldn't have gone, even if she were free. The Café de Paris was a place Albert liked to take her, so that would have felt like a betrayal.

She'd only been on watch at Fount Street with the other volunteer Fire Service girls for a few hours when the dreadful news came that a bomb had plummeted right through the ceiling and exploded on the dance floor of the Café de Paris, instantly killing dozens of diners and dancers. Kathleen left her post for a moment, went to the loos and threw up at the thought of her dance partner being blown to smithereens, just because he was in the wrong place at the wrong time. It could have been her.

Early the next morning when she got off shift, she made her way back to her dad's house. When she walked in, she found Albert sitting at the kitchen table, sipping some tea. Her dad was beside him, chewing on a crust of bread. Dad didn't even look up at her. It was as if he knew he could not interfere, not between a man and his wife.

'Pack your bags,' said Albert. 'I've come to take you home.'

25

Eva, March 1942

'I am not leaving this bed again for Adolf bleeding Hitler!' cried Eva, pulling the bedclothes over her head and turning over.

Mum tugged at the sleeve of her nightdress. 'Come on, Eve! We can't stay here, it's dangerous. The siren has gone again.'

A dog was barking its head off in the street and their neighbour downstairs shouted up to them, 'Are you two coming or not?' They'd already spent half the night in the Anderson shelter while Jerry dropped his bombs all the over the borough.

'Honestly, Mum, I'll be fine. It's probably a false alarm. It's getting light out there now,' said Eva, whose head was killing her. She had made a bit of a night of it with Gladys down the pub. 'You go, I'll come in a minute.'

Her mother sighed and Eva heard the front door click shut. She'd just about had enough of the Blitz.

The next night, she and Gladys wandered over to the snooker hall after the pubs had chucked out, taking a pillow and a quilt each from the flat. It would be better than that dank hell-hole at the bottom of the garden, at least.

A bunch of blokes at the bar turned round and there were a few wolf whistles. Eva ignored them, laying out her bed beneath the snooker table. Then she made her way to the bar.

'I'll have half a Guinness, please,' she said to the bartender.

'Can I get that for you?'

She turned and came face-to-face with a tall bloke with sandy-blond hair and sparkly eyes. It was Jimmy, a friend of her brother Frankies. She'd met him once before when he came to the flat with a message for her mother. She had liked him straight away but didn't want to let him know that. It troubled her a bit and she didn't want to turn into one of those soppy girls who thought that men walked on water.

'I'll get it myself, thanks,' she said.

'Suit yourself,' he said. 'Just let me know if you need anything. Me and the lads will take care of you girls.'

Gladys was standing there with her tongue practically hanging out. Eva nudged her in the ribs. Jimmy was quite gorgeous but he probably knew it and there was no need to make it obvious that she fancied him, was there?

'Well, we can take care of ourselves, can't we, Gladys?'

Gladys nodded shyly. 'We might need some help.'

Eva rolled her eyes and went over to the pool table.

A bit later on, just before the air-raid warning sounded, Jimmy came over to her again. 'I hope I didn't offend you by asking to buy that drink. I realize you can take care of yourself, Eva.'

'Been looking after myself my whole life,' she said, looking him straight in the eye.

'I meant to tell you, I run a fruit and veg stall down East Street, so if you are ever passing and need anything . . .'

Eva smiled at him. He was all right really. Perhaps he didn't fancy himself after all. 'That's very kind of you, Jimmy. I'll bear that in mind.'

She was just settling down under the table when there was the most almighty explosion from the other side of the street. The force of the blast blew the windows out in the snooker hall, sending glass flying everywhere.

'Oh my God!' screamed Eva. 'Mum!'

She crawled out from the table and scrambled to the window, cutting her feet on broken glass in the process. The house over the road – her house – was missing half the roof and the exposed timbers were well alight, with flames leaping into the night air. Her bedroom had been reduced to rubble, collapsing onto the flat of the lady downstairs.

'Jesus Christ!' said Eva, running down the stairs from the hall, leaving a trail of blood behind her.

The firemen were there in minutes, training their hoses on the blaze. Outside in the street was a scene of absolute pandemonium, as people came out of the surrounding houses. Rescuers were already inside, wading through the rubble, shifting bits of masonry. Children were crying and the firemen were trying to keep people away. She ran forwards. An air-raid warden shouted at Eva, 'Get back!'

She started to tussle with him and he took hold of her by the shoulders and yelled into her face, 'Is there anyone inside?'

She had lost her voice. She tried to speak but she was shaking too much. She looked down at her feet and saw they were cut and bleeding.

Out of nowhere, she felt an arm around her shoulder, steadying her, and a voice said, 'I think her mother might be in there. Is that right, Eva?' It was Jimmy.

'The shelter, there is a shelter in the back garden,' she spluttered.

'All right, all right, keep back now,' said the other man from the ARP; they always worked in pairs. 'I'll go and see.'

He legged it round a side street and over a garden wall. About ten minutes later, he emerged with Mum, wearing her best fur coat and mink stole – there was no way she was leaving that behind for the Germans to bomb – and the woman from downstairs, with her little yappy dog.

'All accounted for here: they were safe in the shelter,' said the ARP to the fireman. 'There's no one inside, thank God.'

'Will you be OK?' asked Jimmy, giving Eva a little squeeze. He produced her shoes from behind his back. 'Well, there you go,' he said. He had brought them down from the snooker hall for her.

She brushed her hair out of her face and looked up at him. 'Yes, I think so, thanks all the same.' Being bombed out was such a common occurrence. Some people fell apart but Eva wasn't going to be one of them.

'You know where I am if you need to find me, Eva. Perhaps I'll see you back at the snooker hall tomorrow night?'

She nodded. He was very nice but she didn't want to

give him any funny ideas. It wasn't as if she was desperate or anything, even if she had just lost her home. Eva linked arms with her mum and they made their way to a rest centre run by the Women's Voluntary Service in the school round the corner, where they were given a bed for the night and a cup of hot, sweet tea and a biscuit.

Mum drank up and then allowed herself a few tears. 'We've lost everything, Eve,' she sobbed. 'I told you staying in that bedroom was bleeding dangerous.'

'I know, I know,' Eva soothed. 'You were right and I was wrong. But we have got each other and whatever you want, I will go and hoist it for you, I promise.'

As she fell into an uneasy sleep on the world's most uncomfortable camp bed, Eva could only think about one thing: Jimmy, with the sparkly blue eyes.

The next morning brought a visit from a familiar face: Mr Pemberton, from the Poor Law.

'Oh bloody hell,' said Eva under her breath. 'That is all we need.'

'Good morning, Mrs Fraser and Eva,' he said, with a tight little smile. He looked older and thinner than Eva remembered. Trust him to turn up like a bad smell when disaster had struck.

'I suppose the Poor Law will tell us we are not deserving enough, even though we don't have a roof over our heads,' muttered Eva, loudly enough for him to hear. She also wasn't about to point out that her mother was no longer called Fraser, in case he went back and blabbed to her dad about it.

He looked hurt. 'No, no, it's not like that,' he said. 'We are all in this together. We're called the Assistance Board now. You'll be rehoused. In fact, I've found a flat down in Tabard Street in the Borough which might suit and we can give you a grant for some basic furniture. I realize it cannot replace things you have lost . . .'

'You have no idea,' said Eva, thinking of all the best bits of Gamages she had pinched and displayed on the mantelpiece.

'But it will go some way at least towards making your new home comfortable.' He sat down next to her mum. 'Mrs Fraser, I'm only telling you this because we have known each other a long while now, but I have some china and things I no longer really need because, well, my wife died at the start of the war and I am on my own these days.'

'Oh, goodness, Mr Pemberton, I'm so sorry,' said Mum, clasping his hand in hers. 'I hope she didn't suffer . . .'

'No, it was a stroke: sudden and unexpected.' He was welling up. 'Although I'm sorry to say it, I'm almost glad she has not had to live through the things we're seeing today. You'll have to spend a few more nights here in the rest centre and then we can get you moved into Tabard Street.'

He lowered his voice, so that the family sitting at the next table wouldn't overhear. 'The clothes and household goods I can give you are far superior to anything you can get from the WVS and I would really like you to have them. It just seems the least I can do now.' Mum nodded, as he wiped tears from his eyes. 'Good, well, that's settled then. There's a mobile washing service in a van around the corner, which can take in any laundry you may have, and packs of essential personal items such as combs and toothbrushes from the Red Cross. It's not much but we are trying to make things as comfortable as we can for you.'

'Thank you, Mr Pemberton, that's very kind,' said Eva, who could hardly believe she was saying those words. Times had certainly changed in Lambeth.

Kathleen came over that afternoon with as many things as she could spare, but she didn't have much herself as she tended to live in her AFS uniform these days. She had confided to Eva, though, that her days in the Fire Service might be numbered because she'd skipped two periods now. Albert was thrilled about it but mainly because Kathleen would be back at home all day, she told Eva with a little shrug. Kathleen seemed excited about the baby but not as much as Eva had expected.

'Come on, Kathleen, what's up?' said Eva, offering her a sip of WVS tea. It always fell to Eva to get the truth out of Kathleen, who could be a bit of a dark horse about her feelings.

'I'm scared, if the truth be told, about what having a baby will be like. Not just the pain of the birth and all that, but they are so tiny and delicate, aren't they? What if the baby gets sick, or really ill, like little Billy from down the road?'

'Oh, Kathleen, I reckon every mother feels worried about their baby but poor old Joe and Mary never had two brass farthings to rub together, so no wonder their little Billy got so poorly. You will have me, Peggy and Mum and

Nanny Day to help look after you. The whole family will
chip in. Your baby will never go without and I will always
be there for you, I promise, sister to sister.'

Eva held her hand and they hugged for a moment. She
only had the clothes she was standing up in but she knew,
if it came to it, she would take them off her back and give
them to her sisters, in their hour of need.

Kathleen smiled at last, reassured that Eva would be
there for her. She reached into her pocket and pulled out
some clothing coupons.

'I've heard that Colliers down the Elephant has some
stockings in – fancy popping along there later?'

They queued up for some stockings, along with half the
neighbourhood, but in the end it was just one pair each.

Eva thought about getting some stuff from the tallyman
but when she saw him, he was hawking a few bits of old
tat on a barrow. His precious van had been burned to a
cinder by an incendiary bomb, along with all his best
stock. There was nothing else for it: she would have to go
to work up in town. She had barely pinched anything since
her prison sentence. It had upset her, being away from
home like that and, because of the war, the authorities
took law-breaking so much more seriously, even for petty
offences like shoplifting.

She felt bad that she hadn't been to see Alice Diamond
since she got out but now she'd been bombed out, she had
bigger fish to fry, Alice would understand that. Eva decided
she'd hoist a few nice things which the Forty Thieves could
sell on, as a kind of peace offering for her absence these
past few months.

Later that day she set off for Selfridges with a sense of trepidation in the pit of her stomach and Gladys's spare shoplifter's drawers under her dress. Gone were Selfridges' beautiful shop window displays of furs and glamorous evening gowns. In their place were mannequins sporting the latest in government-approved Utility wear – hard-wearing, practical and, in Eva's opinion, not very stylish. She'd even seen some pictures in a magazine of women wearing coats made out of a bedspread. As if she'd ever go out looking like a bleeding bed!

Eva longed for the days when the rails were full to bursting and the shop was rammed to the rafters with punters, elbowing their way through to get to stuff; not least because it made her job easier. Now it was like a waste-land: a few sad rails of drab dresses and coats, stockings guarded by a fierce-looking woman and walkers every-where, keeping an eye out for people pilfering. These were desperate times and amateurs fancied they could turn a quick profit by nicking stuff and selling it on the black market but, as Alice always pointed out, it took years of practice to be a good hoister.

After rifling through a few pinafores, she decided that the thing she and her mother needed most were shoes – not a popular choice for the hoister because they were actually quite difficult to nick; they were bulky, for a start. Eva started the usual process of asking for one pair of shoes, then another and not quite making up her mind about what to buy. Once she had a good half-dozen pairs out on the floor in front of her, she kicked a pair under her seat and when the shop assistant went to the store cupboard to get something in a different colour, she nudged them into her open shopping bag.

When the shop girl returned, she said, 'Oh, I forgot to bring my coupons! Silly me!' and got up and left her to clear up the mess.

She was just about to get into the lift when she felt a hand on her shoulder and her heart sank.

'Show me what you have in that bag, please, miss.'

Three months; three miserable bloody months in Holloway and all for nicking one measly pair of shoes. The beak saw she had previous and said he needed to make an example of people like her, who were making a living on the black market. Well, that wasn't true. She wasn't making a living on it, she had lost all her stuff to a German bomb and was just trying to find something decent to put on her feet.

HMP Holloway would have to provide that for the time being. Eva had to get used to the Victorian jail, with its echoing wings radiating from the centre and the constant clanging of iron doors. The floor of that centre was kept so highly polished you could see your face in it and you weren't allowed to cross it directly. Only the governor could do that. The inmates had to walk around it or be put on report. The cocoa was the same, though, which she liked. Her family wrote letters, but the ones she liked most came from Jimmy. He just told her what was going on around Walworth and tried to make her laugh a lot. She tried not to think about it but the more he wrote, the more she missed him. Her mum came to visit, which she was grateful for, although she didn't like her mother seeing her dressed in the drab prison dress, or the way the screws kept such a close watch over them. They weren't allowed to hug or touch and she told Mum not to bother coming again because she missed her even more afterwards.

The prison was buzzing with news that the Fascist leader Oswald Mosley and his wife were inside, living in a little house in the grounds. One of the girls she got to know said she had seen him sunbathing with his shirt off. Eva couldn't get excited about that. She remembered him and his idiot followers stomping around in Bermondsey and getting a proper clipping. If he'd had his way, they'd all be talking German now.

By the end of her sentence, she'd met Diana Mosley a couple of times because the governor decided she was a suitable candidate to go over and help clean the cottage for the Mosleys. Diana was polite enough. Eva just got on with her work and was grateful not to have to talk about politics because she felt sure she would have told Lady Mosley she didn't care for her Fascist views.

It was a beautiful summer day when she was released, a proper swelterer. She'd ticked the days off in her head, one by one, and when the warder opened her cell door and called her name that morning, she knew she was going home.

With other inmates wishing her luck, she made her way across the landing and down to the little office, where all her personal effects were held.

A grim-faced screw handed her back her belongings in

a cardboard box and she went through them all and signed for them, before taking off her hated prison uniform and changing into her own clothes. She'd got used to wearing flat, regulation pumps and it felt strange putting her high heels on again. Stepping out of the prison gates, she glanced back over her shoulder and muttered, 'Goodbye, good riddance, I won't be back soon.'

She went home to her mum in the Borough and then straight round to East Street Market. Jimmy was standing there, looking as handsome as ever, selling strawberries from his fruit and veg stall.

'Well, hello Eva, it's good to see you again,' he said, giving her a smile which could light up the blackout.

She sauntered over to him, as casually as she could. Her heart was beating faster and she could feel herself colouring up. It was silly, really; she was only chatting to Jimmy, for God's sake. Eva helped him out on the stall a bit, and when it was time to call it a day, he pushed his barrow around the back alley and parked it up for the night and then got his bicycle.

'Want a lift up to the snooker hall?'

She nodded and he motioned for her to sit side-saddle on the crossbar, just as she did with Frankie when they were kids – only back then, Frankie had probably nicked the bike they were riding on.

As they set off down Walworth Road, Jimmy began to whistle the tune to 'Daisy, Daisy' and then he started to sing, 'Eva, Eva, give me your answer do . . .'

She turned round and grinned at him. 'Oh, leave it out, Jimmy!'

But he continued: 'I'm half crazy, all for the love of you . . .' She felt herself blushing again.

When they reached the snooker hall Gladys and some of the others were already outside, having a smoke.

Eva hopped off the bike and, as Jimmy was parking it up against the wall, he looked into her eyes and said, 'Well, will you, Eva? Will you give me your answer? I want you to be my girl.'

She glanced down at the floor and then back up at him.

'OK,' she said. 'But don't make a big thing of it and go telling everybody, all right?'

He smiled quietly to himself and nodded. 'That's fine by me, Eva. You can kid yourself, but we both know it's serious.'

When everyone had tired of cards, snooker and beer, Jimmy laid his coat down under the snooker table for them to lie on.

In the darkness, he turned and kissed her. She kissed him back.

26

Peggy, September 1943

'You don't have to volunteer, you know. You're married.'
Nanny Day's needles clicked furiously as she knitted a
jumper and bootees for Eva's new little one, Beverley. The
whole family had fallen head over heels for Eva's Jimmy,
who had proved himself to be a hard worker and a real
provider, which Nanny Day was delighted about. She practically clucked with pride every time Eva brought the baby
round and had reminded Eva, on more than one occasion
that she'd always said the right man would persuade her
to settle down.

Nanny Day chuntered away into her knitting, 'Eva and
Kathleen are perfectly happy at home with their babies but
that's not enough for you, for some reason!'

Peggy sighed. 'I already have experience working for the
Post Office and I need to do something.'

She didn't want to say that being at home every day and
worrying about what danger George was putting himself
in was making her feel depressed. Nanny's generation just
got on with it when the men went to war. They saw the
home as the right place for a woman to be. Peggy had
loved going out to work and now there was the chance for

her to retrain as an operator in the Central Telephone Office up in town, she wanted to take it.

'But it's dangerous, going out to work over the water,' said Nanny, pursing her lips. 'The Germans have already dropped a bloody great bomb on the telephone exchange.'

'Keeping the phone lines running is vital war work,' said Peggy. 'You know that. I'm not afraid to do it. I just think about how brave Jim is fighting in North Africa and God knows where else, and the same goes for George. I should be able to do my bit. And you know Gloria loves being with you. Some of what I do will be nights, anyway . . .'

'Oh, that is just the living end!' said Nanny Day, throwing her knitting aside and going over to fill the kettle. 'You are going to be stuck in the middle of all the air raids! You'll need more than a tin hat and a gas mask, my girl!'

She clattered about in the sink, muttering to herself as she did so, 'It's good enough for them but not good enough for you, for some reason. I just don't understand it.'

Peggy sighed. They both knew her mind was made up. The war had been going for four years now and it showed no sign of stopping. The air raids were just part of everyday life and people had got used to sleeping in the Tube stations night after night. Spirits were high, with regular sing-songs down there and everyone sharing what they had to make life that bit more comfortable, but it wasn't enough for her to hide away from the enemy like some rat in a sewer. She wanted to make a difference.

The victory against Rommel at El Alamein had been a real morale boost and her brother Jim had fought bravely and was mentioned in dispatches. George had volunteered for a new battalion of paratroopers when he was out in Egypt. The training appeared to involve the men hurling themselves out of an aircraft in the desert and anyone who didn't suffer broken limbs got their red beret and their wings. George landed safely, thank God, and he had seen action in Italy already. Peggy understood why he wanted to do it; they had known for over a year that his brother Harry was a prisoner of war in German hands after Dunkirk and George wanted to bring him safely home to their mother.

George was a Bren gunner in the 10th Parachute Battalion and was so fastidious about cleaning his gun that his comrades in the unit had nicknamed him 'Rags', which he didn't mind. It was just in his nature: if he was going to do something, he would do it well. The regiment was biding its time in Sussex for the time being but she knew that couldn't last and he would have to see action again soon. She hadn't told him about volunteering for the Post Office but once she had got the job for sure, she would. He wasn't the sort of man who would try to stop her, Peggy knew that much. That was one of the reasons she loved him.

Peggy carried George's most recent letter with her as she crossed the bridge and walked up into King Edward's Buildings in the City towards the exchange. She remembered his wistful words off by heart: 'Kiss Gloria every night for me and remember that everything I am doing is for you and her, Peggy.'

She was used to the systems of the General Post Office, of supervisors and refresher courses, of steady learning on the job. Only this time, the emergencies would be real and the margin for error very slim. One crossed wire and some-one could die, that much was made clear. A large poster on the wall was of a telephone dressed as a soldier in a tin hat at a jaunty angle, declaring: 'I'm on war work! If you must use me, be brief!'

The exchange itself was a mind-boggling array of wires and sockets, with a row of girls sitting in front, connecting parties to each other. A supervisor kept close watch and, if it was an emergency, listened in. Once or twice, Peggy overheard the supervisor say, 'Shall I scramble?' and she realized that she wasn't talking about eggs.

During her first day's training, she found herself sitting next to Edna, her old boss from Acton, who had also volunteered. There was little time for chit-chat but Peggy noticed that Edna blanched when she saw her. At tea break, Edna sidled up to her and took her to one side, over in the little kitchenette.

'Peggy, I just need to say something to you,' she said. 'You know, I have always found you a very sensible young woman, much more so than your silly friend, Susan, who went and got herself pregnant—'

Peggy cut in. 'Susan is dead. She died in an air raid a year ago, over in the East End.' Edna's lips pursed into an 'O'. 'So don't you dare speak ill of her, Edna. She wasn't silly, she was braver than you will ever know.'

Peggy had tried to make sense of her friend's sudden death but she couldn't, so she'd just buried it and got on with her life. Now it was as if the floodgates had opened and there was no stopping her. 'Susan went through hell. They locked her up in the mad house after they took her baby away but she pulled herself together and she'd got herself a nice little job and was doing just fine until the Germans landed a bomb on her aunt's house.'

'I am so sorry,' said Edna, putting her hand on Peggy's arm.

Peggy snatched her arm away. 'No, no, you are not sorry in the least. I know you were in favour of the Fascists, of Mosley and his lot, and that is what you are worried about, isn't it?'

Edna lowered her voice to a whisper, 'Peggy, I don't understand. I thought we were singing from the same hymn sheet. I was simply going to warn you that we need to be careful now, more than ever, about expressing any views which may be interpreted in the wrong way in the current climate.'

'You disgust me!' Peggy spat, her mouth twisting into a sneer of disdain. 'I was never in favour of Mosley. I should have told you back then but I was too scared because you were the boss. Well, the war has made us all equal now, hasn't it? I was going to the Mosley meeting to protest. If I had been as gutsy as Susan I would have done it, I'm sure, but it took me a while to get the courage up, Edna. I did it in the end; I joined the other Communists and we kicked Mosley and his followers right out of Bermondsey when they came on one of their stupid marches.'

Edna looked as if she was about to faint.

Peggy went on, 'I won't cover for you, you filthy Fascist. So I would get yourself out of here, before I reveal your true colours to the whole of the telephone exchange, if I were you.'

The last she saw of Edna, she was grabbing her hat and coat, and heading for the door.

Over the months which followed, Peggy worked her way up to being one of the most trusted operators at the exchange, always showing up for her shifts and volunteering to work overtime when other girls couldn't make it. Her supervisors also noted her selflessness. Whenever the air-raid siren sounded, the younger girls were ushered down into the shelter in the cellar, but Peggy donned her tin hat and stayed on to run the telephone exchange with the men. As she was married, people treated her differently from the single girls and allowed her to make her own choice about taking shelter or working. Peggy relished the chance to do something useful. She wasn't scared, not a bit. Rather than politely asking, 'Which number, please?' callers were greeted with, 'Is this call of national importance?'

On more than one occasion during an air raid, Peggy caught some posh woman trying to be put through to her grocer to complain about her weekly order and disconnected the call. The men she worked with still laughed about cutting off some lord or other who was trying to ring his tailor as the bombs dropped all around them.

George had gone away on an important mission in Europe. He couldn't say more, but Peggy now scoured the newspapers daily for any information. On 18 September she bought all the papers she could carry because of reports about a great 'sky army' which had landed in Holland. She knew George was among them, and imagined him floating silently downwards with his parachute, landing behind enemy lines. The days after that seemed to blur into one. She had no memory of getting up and going to work, but she knew she must have done. She lived for the drip-drip of news about the airborne invasion.

The first reports were encouraging, about how a massed army of men in gliders and parachutes had taken the Germans completely by surprise, but as the days turned into a week, the reports got shorter and then bad news started to leak out. She cut out all the stories and pored over them after she'd put Gloria to bed. Nanny begged her to leave it alone, to stop reading, but she couldn't.

'You're torturing yourself, Peg, please stop,' she said, as Peggy read the story from the front page of *The Times* over and over. The headlines said it all: TANK BATTLE 5 MILES FROM ARNHEM, AIRBORNE FORCES FACE GRIM FIGHT. There were reports of reinforcements and supplies being flown in, but the paratroopers were effectively cut off. The thought of George being killed was too much. Peggy thought that she would know instinctively if he was. It was like Dunkirk; she had sensed then that he was in terrible danger but had never given up hope or feared him dead. People in the neighbourhood had strange superstitions about things like that. Mrs Avens back in Howley Terrace still talked about how a black cat sat on her doorstep and refused to budge on the day her son Johnny was killed on the beach at Dunkirk. Mrs Avens knew then that Johnny had died, she said so. Peggy played out the scene in her mind, imagining George hiding in the woods or by a river, trapped and trying to cross to safety, with his trusty Bren gun still by his side.

Three days later, reports from the front line were carried in the newspapers, bringing news of the most tragic and glorious battle of the war being over. The survivors of the British airborne force had been ordered to break out of the forest near Arnhem and get back across the Rhine to join up with the Second Army on the south bank. Peggy spent the next two nights in the rocking chair, listening to the BBC World Service, waiting for any news. At first light, Nanny got up and made her a cup of tea. There was a knock on the door. Peggy couldn't move. She sank her head in her hands and began to cry.

'I'll get it,' said Nanny overly brightly, bustling down the hallway. She came back carrying an official-looking letter, her face as white as the envelope in her hands. Peggy was shaking as she opened it; it was from the War Office. She was blinded by tears at first, so she couldn't take it all in but it gave the incident date as 18 September – the day George had parachuted in to Holland. Just seeing his name, rank and number there in black and white didn't make it real at all. Could they have got it wrong? She was hoping against hope. There was today's date. He was confirmed as a prisoner of war, in German hands, location unknown.

Eva and Kathleen came to comfort Peggy, bringing their daughters, Beverley and Della, to play with little Gloria. Eva had bought Gloria a set of peg dolls which Nanny Day had dressed up to be a whole family and Gloria carried the daddy one with her everywhere, which almost broke Peggy's heart. Just having her sisters close at hand eased the pain of being parted from George and she leaned on them now, more than she ever had done when they were growing up. At least he was alive, they told her. And George being George, he would do everything he could to survive the war.

Eva even tried to make her smile. 'He's probably converting the blooming Nazis to Communism!'

Peggy had always been the eldest, the clever one, the one who had all the answers – but she didn't have the answers to work this out. When she cried, they picked her up and forced her to carry on, for Gloria's sake. She still went out to work – that, at least, gave her a focus other than the worry of what George might be going through in a prison camp.

A new terror had arrived in the past weeks, in the form of lethal rockets, which Londoners nicknamed 'doodlebugs' because of the horrible whine they made as they flew overhead. More terrifying still was the silence as the engine cut out and they plummeted to the ground. Nanny Day was with Peggy and Gloria in the back yard at Cornwall Road when one appeared, sailing high over the rooftops, and there was no time to get to the shelter. Peggy prayed out loud: 'Please God, don't fall here!' even though it meant the bomb would land on some other poor souls a few streets away. The engine whined on, across towards Bermondsey, and then cut out and fell from the sky. They all felt the shudder of the explosion. Peggy cried with relief that they were safe and in anguish for the victims a few streets away. Nothing about this war was fair, she felt that now, more than ever.

*

It was a clear, crisp October day when Peggy finally received word from George. She recognized his neat, copperplate writing, in pencil. She traced each stroke with her finger, over and over, seeking some connection with him. The words were not the words he would have chosen, she realized that. He had probably been told to copy it down, sitting in a room with his fellow captives. But the very fact that he had written to her, managed to send word that he was alive, meant the world. The letter read: 'I have been taken prisoner of war in Germany. I am in good health. Please do not worry. I will be transferred from this camp in a number of days so please do not write until I send word. George.'

Peggy knew she would have to hand it in to the War Office, because the authorities had told her that if she heard anything from him, she must do so without delay. But she held that note close for the rest of the day and put it under her pillow that night, just to have his words beside her for a moment longer.

Peggy blew out the candle and drifted into a dream about a chatty blue-eyed boy and a tall girl with dark hair, carrying a book under her arm, making their way down a cobbled street by the Thames. They wandered in a time between the wars, when children played without bombs falling from the sky and everyone knew their neighbours, even if they were all as poor as church mice and didn't always get along.

27

The Lambeth Girls, May 1945

For once, the paperboy was shouting good news and the billboards screamed victory. Peggy hurried back across Waterloo Bridge, clutching her sheaf of newspapers, her heart pounding in her chest. Hope had been building for days, with the Nazi armies falling like dominos and the Allies gaining ground, despite so many years of defeat. George would be free soon, she could feel it in her bones, but she wouldn't be truly happy until he was back home.

People were already celebrating, beeping their car horns and Peggy saw two vans piled full of teenagers, with some hanging off the doors and others crammed into the cab, laughing, smoking, drinking and waving flags, heading up into Trafalgar Square to join the crowds dancing in the fountains. Celebrations had already kicked off up there last night but today the whole of London was going to have a massive knees-up for VE Day.

The excitement was palpable. After more than five years of blackouts, bombings and misery, the war was over. The city had been blasted to bits in places but its spirit was not broken and with two days to celebrate Victory in Europe, Churchill intended to show that to the world.

Peggy made her way down to her mum's flat in the Borough and found Kathleen and Eva already there, with a bottle of sherry open on the table.

'George will be home soon, don't you worry no more,' said Mum, embracing her. 'We can put all this behind us and get back to normal again, you'll see.' Peggy reluctantly took a sip of the drink that had been poured for her.

'You have to come and celebrate with everyone, Peg. I won't have it any other way,' her mother added. She was right. The war was over and Peggy needed to trust that things would be all right. They couldn't go back to how they used to be; so much had changed, not just for her, but for everyone. Now was not the time to say that, Peggy understood. Eva and Kathleen were already chucking back the sauce and plotting a great evening.

Street parties for the children were hastily organized and Nanny Day clubbed together with Mrs Avens and Mrs Davies from number 16 Howley Terrace to do a big celebration. It was decided that the kids would all go along to join in. It was fitting, somehow, for the family to gather there, rather than down in the Borough. It was where they belonged, they all felt that.

Mrs Davies had kept a load of old bunting from the King's Jubilee Party back in 1935 and that was strung from house to house, while the women pooled their resources to bake some fairy cakes and scones. There was no shortage of booze: rum, whisky and sherry were pulled from the back of cupboards and from under floorboards, where they had been stashed and held back for the moment it was all over. Tables and chairs were arranged in time-honoured fashion, in the middle of the road, with best tablecloths and china carefully laid out and endless cups of tea poured.

The kids from Tenison Street were there, bashing on up-turned pots and pans with wooden spoons, making such a racket, as everyone sang 'We'll Meet Again' and the 'White Cliffs of Dover'. It was a case of the louder, the better. Punters brought their pints from the pub around the corner to join in and in the middle of it all, Mrs Avens sat down on her doorstep and sobbed her eyes out because her Johnny wasn't there to see any of it. Mum and Mrs Davies gathered her up, dried her eyes and poured a stiff shot of brandy down her throat.

'That's the spirit!' said Mum, as Mrs Avens managed a weak smile. 'We cannot cry now, for the children's sake. We have to put on our best face and show them the way forward. We've won and we can't give in, for Johnny, for all of them.'

Patsy gave Mum a hug, just as Dad sauntered out of the house. He looked at them both, spat on the ground in disgust and walked off to the pub, where he spent the rest of the day. He could never accept his Margaret being with another man, but she'd made her mind up, he knew that, and there was no changing it.

A huge bonfire was lit on the waste-ground at the end of the street and the smell of burning wood filled the evening air. People were doing the same all over the borough, lighting fires like little beacons to end the blackout. Children looked on in wonder, many of them having been born in a time when night only meant pitch black and fire was the consequence of bombs dropped on innocent families.

As darkness fell, gangs of good-natured revellers, rowdy men and women in uniforms, came across the bridge into Lambeth, looking for more parties. No one wanted the celebrations to end. Someone had an accordion out and a fiddle and Kathleen's old piano was pulled from its place in the front room to provide music. Kathleen wasn't playing – she was too busy dancing, twirling around, as Albert watched her from the side-lines, leaning on a walking stick. His leg had been badly shot up in Italy and he'd been shipped home a few weeks ago to convalesce. Kathleen didn't talk about it but Eva and Peggy both feared it hadn't done his temper any good. Eva caught the look in his eye as an American GI swept Kathleen up and down the street in a foxtrot, while everyone clapped and whooped them on. Albert would have started another war there and then, if his leg had been up to it, Eva felt sure of that.

Peggy was woken by the most almighty hammering on the door the next morning. She wasn't one for drinking but she'd definitely had a few too many and she could have done without the early-morning wake-up call.

'All right!' she yelled, pulling on her dressing gown. 'I'm coming.'

She pulled open the door to find Kathleen's mother-in-law, her hair still in curlers, standing there with Della in her arms. The baby was crying as she was thrust towards Peggy.

'It's Kathleen,' she said. 'There was an accident last night. She's in the hospital. I can't look after the baby, I've got Albert to care for, you see, with his leg and all. You'll have to take her.'

'What happened?' said Peggy, stroking Della's hair to calm her down.

Albert's mother couldn't look her in the eye. 'She slipped and fell downstairs and hurt herself, silly girl.'

Peggy and Eva sat at Kathleen's bedside, holding her hand as she slept.

She had two black eyes, a swollen lip and her head was swathed in bandages. Her beautiful curls were all matted with blood and her face so pale she looked like a broken doll lying there, rather than their sister.

The nurse came over to them. 'She will sleep for a good while now. The doctors say rest is the best cure. Her skull is fractured but although they are confident that there is no bleeding to worry about we need to keep a close eye on things. You can come back later in the day, at visiting time. We'll take care of her, I promise.'

Eva was shaking as she stood up.

'We'd better tell Mum,' said Peggy eventually.

'You go,' said Eva, her hands closing into fists, 'I'm going to find Albert.'

Eva had never been one to judge people by where they lived; she'd grown up poorer than most.

But this grimy little street in Vauxhall really was a disgrace. It had houses with dirty windows and grubby net curtains and the front steps hadn't been swept in an age, judging by the state of them.

She arrived at Albert's door. A pint of milk was still on the front step, so she picked it up before banging loud enough to raise the dead. She noticed, with a self-satisfied smile, that a few curtains were twitching.

His mother answered, hair in curlers, still wearing a housecoat and slippers. She folded her arms. 'What do you want, then?'

'I need to talk to Albert,' said Eva. 'I have got a message from Kathleen.'

'Who is it?' Eva heard his voice from the scullery and he hobbled out with his stick as his mother retreated down the hallway.

'Well, what's up?' he asked, leaning on the doorframe, as if he hadn't a care in the world.

'You'd better step outside,' said Eva. 'I can't tell you this in front of your mum.'

He was easing himself down the front step and into the street, when she raised the milk bottle high in the air and smashed it down, hard, on the top of his head.

Albert screamed, from the shock of it and the pain, as splinters of glass embedded in his scalp. Milk coursed down his face, mixing with blood from the cuts on his forehead, and his walking stick fell to the ground.

'You stupid bitch!' he cried, putting his hands to his head and sweeping shards of broken milk bottle to the ground. 'What did you do that for?'

Eva held the broken bottle by the neck and jabbed it

towards Albert's face. 'That is from me and Peggy and Kathleen.

'If you hurt her, you hurt all of us. We're sisters. Blood is thicker than water and don't you forget it.'

Epilogue

1949

The little terraced houses which had nestled by the river since the last century were seen as insanitary now. Hitler hadn't managed to flatten them in the Blitz but London County Council had bulldozed them into the ground. People wanted gas and electric, in neat little prefabs, with bathrooms inside the house and not just a lavatory and a tap in the back yard. Peggy, Kathleen and Eva stopped off at the seafood stall in the Cut to pick up a pint of prawns and some whelks for the kids before taking a trip down memory lane. Peggy and Kathleen had moved down to Brixton, which was quite posh compared to the back-streets of Waterloo, and Eva had a nice flat down in the Borough.

The war seemed so long ago. Everything was about rebuilding, making things better, from the new National Health Service to the welfare state. People who had lost so much didn't want to look back, only forwards.

George had returned from the prisoner-of-war camp in Poland so thin and dishevelled that when Peggy asked, 'Where's Daddy?' little Gloria ran to get her peg doll because she hadn't recognized him at first. The war had not broken him – far from it. He was promoted and stayed on with the Army and was now in Singapore. Peggy and Gloria would be joining him out there any day now, which was the beginning of a whole new adventure.

And Kathleen, well, she was divorcing Albert and was writing to a GI she had met at the end of the war who wanted her to move over to the United States, to be with him, and start afresh with Della.

Only Eva planned to stay put in London. Jimmy was making a good living running betting shops and a toy shop too, down the Elephant. They were happily married, with two little girls to think of: Beverley and her little sister, Shirley. Jimmy provided more than enough for all of them and although Eva had always earned her own money, she was content at last to give up hoisting and let him look after her.

Their father, James, had moved out to a tenement block down in Southwark and was as satisfied as he was ever likely to be. He was still working down at the cricket bat factory, although he was already into his sixties. Kathleen's twin, Jim, had married a lovely local girl, Hannah, and they were proud parents to a little boy.

Mother and Patsy were as happy as larks down in the Borough, where she now had a telephone installed in the flat – the first in her neighbourhood – thanks to Frankie, who bought her everything she could wish for. It was best not to ask how he paid for it all.

As the girls rounded the corner, Howley Terrace and Tenison Street lay in ruins before them. A few walls were still standing, here and there, but even they'd be gone soon.

Weeds were growing where tidy little homes had once stood and women had fussed over the state of their front steps.

Della, Gloria and Beverley skipped along the cobbles, holding hands, dressed in their best clothes, singing nursery rhymes as they went, their feet covering the ground which had been the scene of everything from street fights to street parties.

Eva, Peggy and Kathleen linked arms and paused for a moment. It was strange to see it all reduced to a wasteland. 'They call this progress,' said Peggy. She held a flyer for the Festival of Britain, which was opening down the road, a massive exhibition, showcasing everything new the country had to offer. 'Shall we go and have a look?'

They turned and walked back, passing the gate of the Lion Brewery, which was all that was left of it. The whole building had been razed to the ground too, in the slum clearance. The Lion of Lambeth, the statue which had presided over the comings and goings on Belvedere Road, had been scrubbed clean of soot and now had pride of place along the way, outside County Hall on Westminster Bridge. That lion used to scare the living daylights out of Eva when she was little, and Nanny Day hadn't helped, joking that he'd jump down and gobble her up if she misbehaved. Nanny Day was dead and gone; her heart had given out in the winter of 1947, so she couldn't say what needed to be said.

Eva turned to her sisters, with a twinkle in her eye. 'Come on,' she whispered. 'We're going on a lion hunt.'

Acknowledgements

I would like to thank Evelyn Wolff and her mum, Beverley, for all their assistance and their memories of the Fraser family, and especially to Evelyn (Bub) for continuing with her genealogical research.

Thanks to Ingrid Connell of Pan Macmillan for seeing the potential in the life stories of three sisters from Lambeth and her expert guidance, which ignited the spark for this book. My agent Tim Bates at Peters, Fraser and Dunlop was a brilliant support during the writing process, and it was a pleasure working with editor Zennor Compton and desk editor Natalie McCourt and all the team at Pan Macmillan.

I am grateful to Sophie Buhler, my unofficial first reader, and to my husband Reuben, my boys Idris and Bryn, and my friends Mark, Jo and Sally for their enthusiasm for the project throughout.

The research for this book was wide-ranging, taking me from sources as varied as Hansard, Pathé News and the photographs of Edith Tudor Hart, to personal blogs about war-time memories and local history groups on Facebook. Recreating the world of the 1930s and the 1940s was rather daunting at first and I am very grateful to the wide range of personal memories shared with me, including some from my own family, who were Londoners at the time of the Blitz. Some characters from Howley Terrace are composites of local people and their names have been changed to protect their real identities. Thank you to Professor Helen Glew for sharing her knowledge of women working in the Post Office between the Wars, and to Jon Baker, curator of the Imperial War Museum at Duxford, for help in tracking down military records.

The following books were invaluable to me during my research:

Branson, N. and Heinemann, M., *Britain in the Nineteen Thirties*, Herts, Panther Books Ltd, 1973.

Pember Reeve, M., *Round About a Pound a Week*, London, Persephone Books, 2008.

Madge, C. and Harrison, T. *Mass Observation Britain*, London, Faber and Faber, 2009.

Tebbutt, M. *Women's Talk: A Social History of Gossip in Working Class Neighbourhoods, 1880–1960*, Hants, Scolar Press, 2005.

Glew, H., *Gender Rhetoric and Regulation: Women's Work In The Civil Service And The London County Council 1900–1955*, Manchester, Manchester University Press, 2016.

Howell, G., *Wartime Fashion: From Haute Couture to Home Made, 1935–1945*, London, Bloomsbury, 2013.

Spring Rice, M., *Working-Class Wives*, London, Virago, 1981.

Collins, M., *The Likes of Us: A Biography of the White Working Class*, London, Granta, 2004.

Levine, J., *Forgotten Voices of the Blitz and the Battle for Britain*, London, Ebury, 2006.

Camp, J., *Holloway Prison: The Place and the People*, London, David and Charles, 1974.

Bright, N., *Southwark in the Blitz*, Stroud, Amberley Publishing, 2016.

I also viewed archive material, films and images from:
Pathé News
East Anglia Film Archive
British Newspaper Archives
Getty Images
The photographs of Edith Tudor Hart
Hansard

I also am grateful to the following online resources and blogs:
A London Inheritance: A Private History of a Public City blog – www.alondoninheritance.com – for images and descriptions of Howley Terrace and the surrounding area.
Lydia Syson's blog, about the Battle of Bermondsey in 1937 – www.lydiasyson.com
Bombsight – www.bombsight.org
Hertfordshire Memories blog – www.hertsmemories.org.uk
The West End at War blog – www.westendatwar.org.uk
The War Time Memories Project – www.wartimememories.co.uk
'Now and Then Walworth' Facebook group – www.facebook.com/groups/69569490746/
www.paradata.co.uk
www.forces-war-records.co.uk